T0258713

points of viewing
children's thinking

points of viewing
children's thinking

A Digital Ethnographer's Journey
http://www.pointsofviewing.com

Ricki Goldman-Segall

Ψ Psychology Press
Taylor & Francis Group
NEW YORK AND LONDON

First published 1998 by Lawrence Erlbaum Associates, Inc.

Published 2014 by Psychology Press
711 Third Avenue, New York, NY, 10017

and by Psychology Press
27 Church Road, Hove, East Sussex, BN3 2FA

*Psychology Press is an imprint of the Taylor & Francis Group,
an informa business*

Library of Congress Cataloging-in-Publication Data

Goldman-Segall, Ricki.
     Points of viewing children's thinking : a digital ethnographer's
journey / Ricki Goldman-Segall.
          p.   cm.
     Includes bibliographical references (p.   ) and index.
     ISBN 0-8058-2431-6 (c   ). -- ISBN 0-8058-2432-4 (p)

     ISBN 978-0-805-82432-2 (pbk)
     1. Video recording in ethnology. 2. Education, Elementary-
-Massachusetts--Jamaica Plains--Computer-assisted instruction.
3. Education, Elementary--British Columbia--Vancouver Island-
-Computer-assisted instruction. 4. Child development-
-Massachusetts--Jamaica Plains. 5. Child development--British
Columbia--Vancouver Island.   I. Title.
GN347.G65 1997
305.8--dc21   97-17260
                                                              CIP

to
baba sarah
and her daughter, auntie phyllis,

rest in peace.

Using this Book with the Accompanying Website

The video screen shots, which you will find at the bottom of the pages in Part III of this book, correspond to digital movies located at the *Points of Viewing Children's Thinking* website. To explore the online information and discussions, enter the main website address <http://www.pointsofviewing.com> into your web browser. Once at the website, you may add your views after registering as a participant. To view a specific movie, enter the website address followed by the page number on which the video screen shots are located (e.g., http://www.pointsofviewing.com/177). For quick reference, you can find each movie's address below the corresponding series of screen shots.

Credits

Design by MERLin
Multimedia Ethnographic Research Lab
University of British Columbia
http://www.merlin.ubc.ca

Design Director	Ricki Goldman-Segall
Page Design and Layout	Lawrence Halff
Website	Lawrence Halff
Cover	Elaine Ayres
Cover photographs	David Beers
Chapter photographs	Ricki Goldman-Segall

contents

reface and acknowledgments

Experience is outside and inside, and the skills that are required
to know it are as diverse as experience itself: language, logic,
the use of tools to scan the skies, the earth, the eye.

—Madeleine Grumet
"Existential and Phenomenological Foundations
of Autobiographical Methods"

Preface

Imagine a living narrative—an evolving story told with words, moving
images, and sounds. This book portrays young people's *thinking attitudes*
in computer-based learning environments, and it describes how the practice of ethnography is changing using networked media. I liken this form
of interaction to a double helix, where learning and ethnography are intertwined to tell an emergent story about partnerships with technology.

I invite you to partake in this journey through my descriptions of videotaping two school computer cultures by using both this book and the
website site, <http://www.pointsofviewing.com>. The two schools described are not only separated by geography—one being on the east coast,
in New England, and the other on the west coast, in British Columbia on
Vancouver Island; they are also separated in many other ways. Hennigan
Elementary School is an ethnically diverse Boston inner-city school which

has struggled for decades to provide students with equal opportunities for success in an often unfair social system. Bayside Middle School is a rural, predominantly White, middle-class, well-endowed school surrounded by grass, trees, and a mild climate, located in Brentwood Bay on Vancouver Island. The two places seem as opposite to each other as is possible while still being called schools. Yet, they are joined by a strong thread—a change in their respective cultures with the advent of intensive computer-use on the part of their students. Both school communities have watched their young people gain literacy and competence in constructing computer representations of classroom projects. Not only have their tools changed from pen to computer, video camera, multimedia, and the Internet, but their way of thinking about themselves as learners has also changed. Learners now see themselves in the director's chair as they piece together new connections between diverse and often unpredictable worlds of knowledge.

Reading how young people talk about what they do in schools, you may come to believe that we need to change some of our beliefs about how children learn. Using digital media environments, young people have begun to carve out their own pathways, becoming accepted and respected as capable learners with their own intellectual passions, theories, and ways of understanding. Within these electronic spaces, they take on personalized thinking attitudes—ways of thinking that are not fixed and impenetrable, but rather flexible to their way of making sense of the world. These attitudes are continually gaining depth, breadth, and variation as they overlap under different circumstances. Young people are able to shift their ways of knowing with ease as they try on different attitudes that fit them, if only temporarily. These more flexible thinkers can participate as co-constructors in designing educational curricula.

To address how both learning and ethnography change in a digital world, I set a framework for this book that contains three related parts: Storyreading, Storymaking, and Storytelling. In Part I, Storyreading, I describe the schools, teachers, students, and my methods of observing, recording, and using digital media to "read" these stories. I ask how emerging technologies change our readings of representational "texts" that consist of visual and text vignettes. These digital video images sitting on a server computer and accessible through the Internet can be messy and slippery pieces of stories. How do we, as authors, interpret and layer stories to form partnerships with readers? How do we partner with various electronic media? Is the terminology of cultural and reflective partners too strong to describe our relationship with our stories, our media objects? And if *partner* is not the right term, then what other term could we use to address the intelligence that is being assigned to these media objects that will eventually become our robots and agents?

Chapter 1, titled "Looking Through Layers," explores how digital media enable authors to forge connections both with those they study and with their readers. Situating this issue within an anthropological discourse, I combine and extend Clifford Geertz's notion of *thick description*, James Clifford's *partial truths*, and Mary Catherine Bateson's *disciplined subjectivity* within the realm of electronic media. I show how layering video stories produces a richer, more textured, understanding of events while facilitating a greater partnering with those whose voices have been unheard or silenced. I address (and agree with) the notion that the ethnographer can no longer be viewed as solitary observer; she is a member of many discourse communities, sharing authorship and authority with those she studies and with those for whom her books are written and video portraits are designed.

Chapter 2, "Pastiche," introduces the computer cultures at Hennigan Elementary School and Bayside Middle School. Beginning the chapter with the more recent study at Bayside, in the here and now, I reflect on my previous study of the Hennigan School. The word *pastiche* is an artistic piece or musical motif that borrows from a combination of sources; it is derived from the French, "pasticcio" and from the earlier Latin "pasticius," which means paste. And, indeed, I literally paste the stories of these two schools together to draw attention to the changes that have occurred in these growing computer cultures.

Chapter 3, "Gatekeepers of a Horseless Barn," describes the teachers in these two schools. I suggest that teachers may want to learn how to juggle diverse roles rather than function as gatekeepers of knowledge. A new generation of teachers is emerging; a generation with teachers who are able to be both navigators and artists, and who look forward to the process of enabling the next generation of learners to work with them as knowledge partners.

Part II, chapters 4 and 5, is titled Storymaking. These chapters are an account of my becoming a video ethnographer and creating digital tools for analyzing the video. Chapter 4, "ReViewing Knowledge as a Video Ethnographer," deals with how we become participating video recorders. I examine the following themes: studying "exotic" other; creating cultural viewpoints; returning the gaze of the video eye; and extending the documentary genre. I also address the question, "How do you know the kids aren't performing for your camera, Ricki?" by explaining how performance is part of our day-to-day life, a product of being in the company of self and others. Videotaping does elicit the performance of some people and inhibit the performance of others, a factor that needs to be accounted for when drawing conclusions, writing up stories, or constructing video-based portraits.

Chapter 5, "Designing Digital Learning and Research Environments," describes the creation of digital tools for analyzing and layering video. The first tool, designed at the MIT Media Lab between 1987 and 1989 on a HyperCard platform, was called Learning Constellations. To my knowledge, it was the first multimedia tool used for ethnographic video data analysis. Looking back, it was a useful tool that enabled multiple users to annotate video excerpts stored on six videodisks. Users, including myself, could join chunks of data, called *stars*, into *constellations* in order to find patterns and build theories. The chapter also describes the more recent tool, Constellations, and a CD-ROM, *The Global Forest*, designed at the Multimedia Ethnographic Research Lab, MERLin, which I established at the University of British Columbia in 1991. (For those readers with access to the Internet, Constellations can be downloaded from the MERLin website, <http://www.merlin.ubc.ca>.)

Part III, called Storytelling, which includes chapters 6 through 11, is a collection of stories about the girls and boys I came to know over the last twelve years. These stories may be viewed as portraits, case studies, or they may simply be viewed as chapters dealing with how young people grasp for some deeper connection to their own sources of understanding. In the two chapters concerned with the Hennigan School, I describe a 5th-grade boy of Italian–Irish descent who is struggling to make sense of how things move and work. Josh, as the title of chapter 6 attests, is "Minding Machines" when he asks me how electrons travel through microchips causing words to pop up on a computer monitor. Chapter 7, "Image-ining Our Selves," interprets an adolescent African-American girl's interest in creating images of girls both on the computer screen and in her stories. In this chapter, we follow Mindy's love for "making girls" on a computer and imagine-ing herself as inventor.

The next two stories are presented as group portraits. Chapter 8, "Connecting Points of Viewing," concentrates on the ideas of the predominantly White, middle-class girls at Bayside. They are preteens in grades 6 and 7. Like Mindy, they are also reaching towards a larger understanding of themselves and the world around them. Conducting video interviews and constructing digital stories to share with others, they are gaining expertise in the use of digital video environments, not to play games, but to create meaning. These group portraits challenge notions of both "gender neutrality" (girls and boys need the same experiences) and "gender differences" (girls and boys need different experiences to address their biological differences) in the never-ending search for equity in our educational institutions. In chapter 9, "Science as Friend," we hear the ideas of boys, from a range of backgrounds and physical abilities—one boy who describes science as a friend. They tell me they want to study science in a more grounded, hands-on, and "eyes-together" way. They want to connect to a place and to a topic by putting their hands in the soil; that is, by becoming immersed in an experience. They also talk about how knowledge is increased when you can see from another person's "vantage point." In short, boys and girls both need opportunities for stretching beyond their traditional gendered boundaries. Connecting what they experience in a hands-on way with what they study helps them form gender identities that are constantly being stretched and strengthened by working out the complexity in understanding self in relation to others and others in relation to self.

Part III concludes with chapter 10, titled "Attitudes for Genderflexing." It explores four thinking attitudes: metaphysical, how we make sense of what we experience; historical, how we learn from our past; ethical, how we value different points of viewing; and pedagogical/activist, how we change and help make our world a better place. In the concluding chapter of the book, "Configurations, Confusions and Contentment," I explain *configurational validity*. The complex issue of how we validate our views, given the fact that we all see the same things quite differently, is discussed.

This book and accompanying website were constructed not only to provide answers, but also, to ask questions not yet asked about the connection among epistemology—the nature of thinking, ethnography—a method of understanding ourselves and others in shared events, and digital media. I conducted my research as a participating member with the time to engage in observations and conversations over a period of almost three years in each school. Infused in these studies are video techniques and digital tools designed with the assistance of graduate students and technical staff. My goal was, and still is, to bring to readers a sense of "being with" me in my journey as a digital ethnographer.

Acknowledgments

This book is a celebration of the insights of those who have shared their stories with me. And for these gifts, I thank the young people, teachers, staff, and school administrators at each location who have so courageously given of their time and effort to make their schools a caring home. I consider them to be my partners in learning. Time, place, and life changes have lessened our closeness, but I hope they remember our experiences warmly. I hope they continue to acknowledge their accomplishments as they read my stories. And I hope that, even when I seem to be critical, they understand how deeply I appreciate the challenges they face when using emerging media technologies. It isn't easy being a learner as a new millennium begins to unfold. And, as an ethnographer, it certainly has not been easy portraying these explorers without wondering if the act of representing their views isn't, in itself, breaking with the spirit of the times. Yet, I cannot see any better to way to honor their travels than to introduce and describe them and my process of getting to know them to you, and to present a new approach to postmodern ethnography—providing an Internet environment for you to engage with their points of viewing by adding yours.

To those with whom I have had personal contact, in conversations, and through their writings, films, and interactive media forms over the last decade, I offer my gratitude. I especially want to thank Seymour Papert, Glorianna Davenport, Zvi Lamm, Richard Leacock, Edward Barrett, and William Higginson. The reflections of Gavriel Salomon, Sherry Turkle, Howard Gardner, Mary Catherine Bateson, Elliot Eisner, John Willinsky, Ben Shneiderman, Ronald Baecker, Kellogg Booth, Madeleine Grumet, Jay Lemke, Geraldine Gay, Ron Burnett, Henry Jenkins, Edward Barrett, Marie Redmond, Lucy Suchman, and Allan Collins are embedded in this book's theoretical foundation. To those whose works inspire me, but with whom I have never met, I thank Clifford Geertz, Ivan Illich, James Clifford, and Steven Tyler. To those who read and commented on drafts of this book, I am grateful beyond words. Thanks to Irit Shimrat, John Willinsky, Avner Segall, Susan Mair, Joanne Richardson, Jim Gaskell, Judy Segal, Rob Macleod, Maggie Beers, and especially Lawrence Halff who read the manuscript almost as many times as I did.

Lawrence (Larry) Halff has participated at every level of the construction and layout design of this book and accompanying website. As a graduate student, he assisted in conducting the research at Bayside Middle School and now, as a consultant, he provides technological support, designs and programs software, and maintains the MERLin website. At the base of our collaboration is a deep friendship, one that continues to stretch my boundaries. Monika Marcovici, the first programmer in MERLin, is now president of Made by Magik, Inc. A warm thanks to her and to my current graduate students Adam Gibbons, Maggie Beers, Venkateesh Rajamanikam, and David Penberg who help me see how transformative ideas are.

This work has come into being because of the generosity of several agencies. A 1995–1996 National Academy of Education's Spencer Postdoctoral Award provided a year of academic leave, time needed to focus completely on this manuscript. The foundation also provided an infrastructure to discuss my ideas with noted scholars in my field. I thank them, and the other funding agencies and companies that supported this work: the Social Science and Research Council of Canada, the Natural Science and Engineering Research Council of Canada, Oracle Corp., and the University of British Columbia Teaching and Learning Grants. My research at the Hennigan School was supported by grants from the National Science Foundation, International Business Machines (IBM), Apple Inc., and the McArthur Foundation. The Association for the Advancement of Computers in Education (AACE) under the direction of Gary Marks has, over the years, provided a platform to make my ideas public.

To the Lawrence Erlbaum editorial staff, and most especially Naomi Silverman, I extend my deep gratitude. Not only did Naomi provide thought-provoking comments, she stood close by, prodding and encouraging me. Her kindness and willingness to engage in the essence of the book permeate its contents. To the reviewers who read and commented on the original draft, thank you for your helpful comments. A special thank you to Eugene F. Provenzo, Jr.

I would like to also acknowledge the contribution of several colleagues at the University of British Columbia. John Willinsky encouraged me to write from my heart and soul, closely nurturing the development of this book. Jim Gaskell has been my intellectual partner in arms, both when we discuss gender and science and when we dance the waltz, tango, or foxtrot. Leslie Roman has been my telephone colleague and friend, in spite of our both saying we hate to talk on the phone. Mary Bryson and Suzanne de Castell have provided insightful comments on my work to date. Karen Meyer and Jolie Mayer-Smith continue to bravely push science education into places where no man has gone before. And, over the last six years,

David Robitaille and Saroj Chand with her expert support staff have provided a home for the growth my professional life.

The community of graduate students, faculty, and staff at MIT were, and still are, a constant source of inspiration. A special thanks to Nira Granott, Uri Wilensky, Idit Harel, Mitchel Resnick, Yasmin Kafai, Judy Sachter, Aaron Falbel, Carol Strohecker, Steve Ocko, Fred Martin, Aaron Brandes, Alan Shaw, Paula Hooper, Issac Jackson, Amy Bruckman, Michel Evard, Edith Ackermann, and, of course, Jacqueline Kaaraslanian, educational impresario par excellence! Their intellectual constructions have webbed into my frameworks for over a decade now. The Interactive Cinema Group, headed by Glorianna Davenport, offered me the perfect home away from home—friendship married with the kind of technological mentorship that imaginatively fueled my work. And, of course, a warm thanks to Uri Feldman, Kathy Wienhold, Susan Scott Lucas, and Simson Garfinkle.

Two dear colleagues from the Media Lab died over the last few years. Greg Gargarian taught me how to think about music and cognition. His comments in our group meetings showed unconditional respect to each participant. And, he made some of the best Armenian food I ever ate. A picture of Sara Dickenson remains on my shelf as I write these words. She was around the fringes of almost every invention at the Media Lab. We would meet late at night in the open space by the third floor elevator at the Lab. Sara had a deep coughing laugh that filled empty spaces. Thanks Sara and Greg.

Deirdre Kelly, David Beers and their daughter Nora, my dear godchild, have been sources of great joy. I also thank the women and men of the Beth Israel Synagogue in Vancouver for encouraging my spiritual core to soar. Loving friends Silvia McFadyen, Maureen Ludwig Wiggins, Alberta and Seymour Levitan, Ben and Jackie Linder, Avraham and Ruth Biran, Ted Adelson, Linda Zysblatt, Terry Hoffman, Ilana Shoham Vardi, and John Willinsky are keepers and constructors of stories from which I situate my writing. Their ideas are surely resting between the lines of this book.

I thank my parents, Frank and Lil, and my brother, Barry, and his children for their love and encouragement. I drew from the well of my childhood memories often while writing this book. Uncle Alvin and Dorothy were always in my thoughts.

To Avner Segall, for *being there* and *being with* me while writing this book, thank you. And for your commitment to our relationship with our beloved cats Joey, Smokey, Samantha, and Gracie, I thank you dearly.

To those who read this book, my invitation is to explore the video versions of these stories from your points of viewing at the website and add your layers of thinking as you wander from page to page, from part to part, or, what I often call segments of information, from star to star. And thank you for being with me, even before this book came into being.

—*Ricki Goldman-Segall*

introduction

computers, cultures, and constructions

Old paint on canvas, as it ages, sometimes becomes transparent. When that happens it is possible, in some pictures, to see the original lines: a tree will show through a woman's dress, a child makes way for a dog, a large boat is no longer on an open sea. That is called pentimento because the painter "repented," changed his mind. Perhaps it would be as well to say that the old conception, replaced by a later choice, is a way of seeing and then seeing again.... The paint has aged now and I want to see what was there for me once, and what is there for me now.

—Lillian Hellman
Pentimento: A Book of Portraits

Pentimento: Partners for Reflection and Construction of Culture

I position my light carefully as I walk around the face of this book, deciding what to hold on to and what to let go. Now, after the fact, I look at what I have written and rewritten, thinking about how to present this object in a way that will enable you to see it through your own eyes as well as through mine. How I celebrate brightness and expose shadow in this last reshaping will determine how what I have experienced in two computer-rich school cultures is communicated to you, the reader. Even as this book goes into print, I wonder about my role as multimedia storymaker in an academic community fraught with epistemological contradictions at the end of the millennium. The debate over the authority of texts has moved from text to author to the virtual (electronic) space that lies between viewers and artifacts. We can no longer talk about the meaning of an event without asking: "Whose meaning?" We can no longer accept the role of the solitary creator of textual forms without questioning the collaborative nature of working with the creations and ideas of others. We can no longer assume that there is a "best" description of any subject. Yet, despite the fact that meanings are made through interactions with and between electronic artifacts, surely we have not fallen into unfathomable relativism.

Let us look at the medium with which we have had the most experience—television. Watching broadcast media events, we cannot help but ask ourselves about the truthfulness of stories concerning Anita Hill and Clarence Thomas, Rodney King and the Los Angeles Police Department, Hillary Rodham Clinton and Whitewater, and, of course, O. J. Simpson! Media stories are both forums for uncovering the meaning of controversial events and platforms for acting out the political and social dramas of gender and race that still structure our lives. In making sense of these stories, we have been tempted to rely on the master story, the "one-god-for-all" version of reality.[1] Yet, we know better than that. We ask ourselves whose story is presented on television.

---

1. For a thorough discussion of the problem of the grand narrative, see Jean-Francois Lyotard, *The Postmodern Condition: A Report on Knowledge*, trans. G. Bennington and B. Massumi (Minneapolis: University of Minnesota Press, 1983). I would also refer the reader to Jay Lemke, who says: "I am writing from a particular social position, making meanings that are shaped by all kinds of life experiences people in my position [as a professor and scholar] tend to have. Whatever I write is written from a viewpoint within the culture and subcul-

Do we, as viewers, decide innocence and guilt based on a camera's image, a jury's deliberation, or the ability of "actors" to persuade us through their points of viewing? Or do we decide on our own? Some theorists claim we can only see what we know; in other words, in these media dramas, we see our own stories acted out publicly. But if we can only see our own stories reflected back at us, then how do we learn about and from others? Perhaps storytelling, storymaking, and storyreading are moving to the commons, to that public sphere where they began many thousands of years ago. Multiple versions, multiple layers of interpretations, and multiple points of viewing are now made more possible by digital technologies that can easily break wholes into parts and reconstitute bits into new groupings so that we can all create stories and add them to already existing interpretations. Welcome to the world of the digital commons, where private and public meet. Welcome to the world of making meaning at the beginning of the age of the Net.[2]

Points of Viewing

You might be asking yourself why I have chosen to use the phrase "points of viewing" rather than "point of view." Point of view (POV, in cinematic terminology) suggests that each of us—when we take pictures or write texts—describes the world through a personal lens. Some scholars spend most of their academic careers rubbing out any possible point of view, equating it with bias and, therefore, with skewed results. But in many cinematic professions, and within many emerging academic communities, point of view is both inevitable and critical to making interpretations.

I focus on the multitude of points from which we view both the world around us and the world within us. The notion of points of viewing encompasses where we are located in time and space, as well as how our combination of gender identities, classes, races, and cultures situates our

---

ture to which I belong. I do not, no one can, write from an objective God's eye view. No one sees *the* world as *it is*. We see the worlds our communities teach us how to see, and the worlds we make, always a bit uniquely, within and sometimes just a bit beyond what we have been taught." Jay Lemke, *Textual Politics* (London: Taylor and Francis, 1995), 4.

2. See Ron Burnett, who coined the phrase "age of the net," *Cultures of Vision: Images, Media and the Imaginary* (Bloomington: Indiana University Press, 1995).

understanding of what we see and what we validate. But the notion of points of viewing is not limited to the various positions we occupy. Indeed, the purpose of understanding points of viewing is to enable us to broaden our scope—to enable us to learn from one another. It not only brings together our various ways of seeing and interpreting the world around us, but it also underscores the often digital, atomistic, and random nature of how we construct and combine knowledges. Imagine each of us as a separate galaxy filled with constellations consisting of stars (points) that are being viewed by people from different galaxies. Now suppose that we could build new configurations of stars and constellations by combining those stars in our individual galaxy with those in someone else's galaxy.

Each of us, as an individual entity, has many ways of seeing events, many ways of reading texts. We can no longer be limited to one point of view or even to one point of viewing. We are now aided by emerging tools that enable us to understand events from many perspectives, to see many sides of a story. While Alluquere Rosanne Stone makes the clever observation that technologies are prosthetic devices; I believe that tools extend our boundaries to enable us to see from the perspective of others.[3] We are less interested in the one master story, the so-called truth, and more interested in multiple versions and the connections between them. We want to expand our points of viewing by including others' points of viewing. My "theory" is that we want to see how others see both what we see and what we do not see. You might be asking yourself why I use this word—"theory." It comes from the Greek root, *theoria*, which means viewing or contemplating.

Cultural Partners: Computers

This book has been written for people who are interested in how learners view and interpret their real-life and virtual-life worlds as they work in partnerships within cultures mediated by technology. Each person, regardless of age, has become a researcher exploring known and unknown domains, searching over and over again through layers

---

3. Alluquere Rosanne Stone, *The War Between Desire and Technology at the End of the Mechanical Age* (Cambridge, MA: MIT Press, 1995).

of meanings. Some of us dig up the ruins of ancient civilizations, putting together pieces of a story to describe how our ancestors lived. Others spend years following the path of light through the eye to the brain so that we can better understand how it is that we see any object outside our bodies. In these cases, knowledge of something or someone is constructed by deeply uncovering, observing, recording, and making sense of experience. Of course, it is also constructed by hanging out and talking with other researchers and building common ways of thinking about knowledge and knowledges.[4] Knowing something for ourselves means actively using our inner tendencies to make sense of the bits and pieces of phenomena that others have brought to light and then reconstructing something new from combining their "works" with our internal understanding of the world. We do this by acknowledging our predecessors, recreating their creations, and then offering our creations to others so that the whole process may be repeated. The wheel is reinvented by each of us who wants to travel to the still-uncharted places of our own thinking; we each, in our own way, need to reinvent what has come before us in our own image.

Am I saying that there is no private knowledge, no individual invention that comes from solitude? It is true that solitude may yield depth and perception, often enabling us to contemplate and build new connections among disparate events. But even in solitude we are not truly alone. We live with our past memories of events that play out in our present consciousness. Are we not continually being inspired by people, animals, and plants even when we are not surrounded by them? The images in and around us are the result of the ways in which they are interactively constructed within complex biological and social settings. Interaction consists of conversing with self, others, and the rest of nature, whether in their physical presence or absence. In my view, our computer partners could one day be included as members of a virtual community of minds. Not only could these partners become our agents that carry out functions for our mental processes, members of the society of mind, but they could also become cultural partners whose main purpose is to provide us with multiple points of viewing so that we can stretch our boundaries and build

---

4. I use the plural form of the word *knowledge* to highlight its constructionist nature. The singular form tends to suggest (falsely) that there is only one particular knowledge or body of knowledge, and that knowledge is an external entity to be acquired.

commensurable communities based on diversity and variation.[5] In short, both intellectual engagement with others and the inspiration afforded by interactions with the world around us are the sources from which we build our knowledges.

What does it mean to recreate our creations from other creations, our texts from other texts, our thinking from the clusters of ideas that have come before us? How do we invent ideas if all we can see is another version of what has come before? Consider the words recorded many suns ago in Ecclesiastics by "the son of David":

> The sun also rises and the sun goes down, and hastens to the place from which it rises again.... All the rivers run into the sea, yet the sea is not full: to the place where the rivers flow, thither they return. All things are full of weariness. The eye is not satisfied with seeing, the ear filled with hearing. That which has been, it is that which shall be; and that which has been done is that which shall be done, and there is nothing new under the sun.[6]

Although our conceptual understanding of the universe continues to change, and we know that the sun does not really rise or set, the notion of patterns that create new connections still resonates within our consciousness.

Let us return to my metaphor of each of us being a galaxy of experiences that occur over a lifetime. From our galaxies, we try to make sense of what we see, feel, hear, taste, and smell as our senses are aroused and as we arouse those senses through memories and expectations. We are each composed of many selves, all of which interact with each other as we learn. In spite of the fact that we know that knowledge, as such, is not the sum total of a collection of facts and theories, we still expect every learner to follow specific orbits. Worse, we expect each orbit to follow the same linear path.

In this book, I demonstrate how knowledges are deconstructions, reconstructions, and co-constructions that emerge as a result of the interaction between what is already known and what is yet to be known again, in a

---

5. See Pattie Maes, "Agents that Reduce Work and Information Overload," *Communications of the ACM 37*, no. 7 (1994): 31–40; Beerud Sheth and Pattie Maes, "Evolving Agents for Personalized Information Filtering," *Proceedings of the Ninth IEEE Conference on Artificial Intelligence for Application* (Los Alamitos, CA: IEEE Computer Society Press, 1993): 345–352; Marvin Minsky, *The Society of Mind* (New York: Simon and Schuster, 1986).

6. Ecclesiastes 1: 7–9, *The Holy Scriptures*, ed. H. Fisch (Jerusalem: Koren Publishers, 1977), 876.

new form. More than a decade ago, Josh, a boy from Hennigan School, told me about how people get ideas.

> **Josh:** Well, people, like, get ideas but they have to get it from something. You see a rock, you might think of something carved out of it, or something. But you could never know if there were no rocks. You never think of rock, unless you were trying to think of something new. Like, [if] you were trying to think of a new substance or something. Most imagination; you see a car and an airplane, you put them together in a picture.

Although seeing a rock might give you the idea to carve something out of it, what you do to it is determined by factors that may have nothing to do with the rock per se. This may be why Josh toys with the notion that if a person tries to think of something new, or to invent something, then something other than objective reality may be at play—something that has to do with a collective imagination, your points of viewing.

The knowledges described in this book are flexible, ever changing, and local. They are personal interpretations "tested" against others on a continual basis. As learners, we want to see how closely what we understand is related to what another person understands. We stretch our own knowledges by finding out what others see and know. Each of us does this in our own way, selecting different stars to put into our constellations. We look for different points of viewing with regard to what we thought we once knew. My nephew Nathan, who had just learned to fly, explained this phenomenon in an email message to me in January of 1996.

> **Nathan:** I love to learn new things. I love, after learning how to do something, looking back and wondering what it was like learning how to do it, and looking back and wondering what it was like even before I started to learn. It's like driving. You watched others do it and wondered how they could have complete control and maneuver a vehicle. Now I see how it is done.

What happens when we decide to use computer technologies as cultural partners in our learning? Emerging technologies not only enhance learning and extend our abilities to see, hear, and speak; they propose alternative ways for us to explore the world around us—ways that are not bound by conventions designed for a pencil-and-paper classroom headed by a solitary teacher. In the next millennium, learning will entail traveling through and around knowledge constellations. With the help of their computer partners, learners will connect discrete chunks into groupings and design expressive artifacts that communicate their analyses and interpretations of their voyage to other travelers. They will follow paths, navigate data, and put together textured layers of knowledge within their own learning constellations. Like everyone else, electronic voyagers are always situated within sociocultural frames of reference. Learners construct configurations that are unique to their points of viewing the world—configurations that bring together the various knowledges they have gleaned from living with others. This includes the virtual life lived in, around, and with texts, art forms, and reproductions created by people whom one may have only met electronically.

For centuries many learners have constructed various configurations without an electronic partner. Inventors have always put things together so as to enable a continual dialog with the creations of others. What I am talking about is the emergence of a far more public form of inventing—a form of inventing that is now accessible in most electronic learning cultures. This entails a communal mind-set that is oriented to taking advantage of emerging technologies—one that is amenable to viewing our minds as artifacts that other learners may encounter and respectively build on. In other words, with the use of new computer technologies, we extend not only our technological abilities, but also our various personae—the societies of our minds—in the form of new objects for others to think with.

Reflective Partners: Digital and Analog Video

This book has also been written for people who want to use digital video technologies as vehicles or cultural tools for understanding themselves and others. Consider how pervasive video has become over the past decade. Can anyone go on a ferry, a gondola, a camel, or even a bus without seeing someone videotaping? On a recent bus ride from New York's JFK Airport, an American family videotaped the entire drive along Route 95 to a hotel in Connecticut. The camera, held by the father, was aimed out the front window for one hour. What did he see out there on a muggy, overcast summer day that I did not? Have we all incorporated Andy Warhol's vision of documenting the commonplace as art? Would this family actually sit in front of their VCR to watch this videotaped journey? We have become global recorders (dare I say ethnographers?), focusing on everything from the mundane and vulgar to the humorous, horrific, sensational, and exotic. With our video cameras, we have become a culture of voyeurs-auteurs, viewers and creators. What is this 4- or 5-pound toy that has entered our hands?

Part of the problem in understanding how the video camera has entered our day-to-day lives is that we have not yet developed a culture of critical visual literacy. As a community, we do not really know how to read moving images in order to decode their effect on our consciousness.[7] Parents often focus their criticisms of film, television, and (now) the Internet on the content of what their children are "reading;" what they fail to realize is that it is the medium itself, its demands on our pattern of knowing, and the style in which it enables images to be placed together, that should be the focus of their cri-

---

7. Throughout the century, scholars in media studies and media education have called for a serious examination of the technological changes in communication and education with the introduction of media forms. See Lewis Mumford, *Technics and Civilization: The Interplay Between Artifact and Culture* (New York: Harcourt Brace and World, 1934), and Harold Innis, *Empire and Communication* (Oxford: Oxford University Press, 1950). To begin the more popular route—instigated by the famous aphorism, the medium is the message, one might refer to the work of Marshall McLuhan, *The Gutenberg Galaxy: The Making of Typographic Man* (Toronto: University of Toronto Press, 1962). In a more scholarly vein, Gavriel Salomon asked why we continue to ignore media forms, given their power to exert influences on our thinking. See *Interaction of Media, Cognition and Learning* (San Francisco: Jossey-Bass, 1979). He posed a theory of reciprocal interactionism where mind and media are in constant dialog. Neil Postman added the view that "embedded in every tool is an ideological bias, a predisposition to construct the world as one thing rather than another, to value one thing over another, to amplify one sense or skill or attitude more loudly than another." See *Technopoly: The Surrender of Culture to Technology* (New York: Vintage, 1993), 13. Other challengers to the "media effects" approach are: Len Masterman, who addressed the ways in which media education can lead to a more democratic and emancipatory society by teaching young people how to become media literate—see *Teaching the Media* (London: Comedia, 1985); David Buckingham, who maintained that young people construct meaning from media texts—see "Teaching About the Media," in *The Media Studies Book: A Guide for Teachers*, ed. D. Lusted (London: Routledge, 1991); and more recently, Avner Segall, who stated that media texts are socially constructed environments for learning and critiquing the world rather than merely aids to instruction—see "De-Transparent-izing Media Texts in the Social Studies Classroom" in *Trends and Issues in Canadian Social Studies*, eds. I. Wright and A. Sears (Vancouver: Pacific Educational Press, 1997).

tiques. What they also forget to consider is how good we are at constructing our own meanings from the texts we read. We are not empty buckets to be filled by media objects. Parents and young people need to discuss how content and form are interwoven so as to present meanings that are interpreted through specific sets of cultural understandings, understandings that reside not only outside us but also within us.

While we have thought deeply about our relationship with tools, cultures, and artifacts, we have only begun to think about the contributions that video-based technologies can make to this understanding. Our tools are continually working with us to recreate our cultures, and our cultures are being reshaped by this interaction, which, in turn, reshapes our tools. The relationship is not one of cause and effect; rather it is interactionist. Cultures, tools, and artifacts orbit around each other in unusual patterns. Refining and defining go hand in hand. Artists know this interaction between tool and artifact; educators often ignore it. What we need in education are questions that critique and explore our use of current technologies in light of an awareness that culture is a mutable construct. Culture changes and culture changes us.

The medium (or tool) is not merely a vehicle to transmit the message, even the cultural message. This limited view of media as direct conveyor belt of ideas has led to the "media effects" theory of media: "Television programs cause my children to be violent," parents lament. Media and medium theorists—Harold Innis, Marshall McLuhan, David Buckingham, John Fiske, and Susan Douglas—have argued against media effects theory.[8] What goes in does not just come out the other end. We create meaning from what we see; we become co-directors. However, even Innis and McLuhan overstated their proposition that the medium, in and of itself, is the message. The medium opens a path for a different set of partnerships among viewer, author, and text—a set of partnerships that revolves around, and is revolved around, our constant reconstruction of culture. A video segment (in text form), for example, is the representation of a cultural moment in

---

8. See Harold Adams Innis, *The Bias of Communication* (Toronto: University of Toronto Press, 1991); Marshall McLuhan, *The Gutenberg Galaxy*; David Buckingham, *Children Talking Television: The Making of Television Literacy* (London: Falmer Press, 1993); see also John Fiske, *Understanding Popular Culture* (London: Routledge, 1989); John Fiske and John Hartley, *Reading Television* (London: Methuen and Company Ltd., 1987); and, for a provocative blend of feminist scholarship with pop culture, Susan J. Douglas, *Where the Girls Are: Growing Up Female with the Mass Media* (New York: Times Books, 1994).

the making of cultures. A video object is a cultural object, something to turn around and reshape. And, just as we change it through our manipulation, so it changes both us and our cultural possibilities.

Culture is not merely the sum total of what we inherit from our parents and social groups; it is what we create with others in the context of our lives, with or without various technologies. In the early days of anthropological research, influential thinkers such as Franz Boas, the anthropologist to shift the discussion from race and move it to one of culture, collected the artifacts of indigenous peoples and encouraged ethnographers to describe the "authentic" context of the collected objects before they disappeared as a result of Western infiltration.[9] This led, as we know, to a gathering, by museums and galleries, of the art of indigenous peoples around the world.[10] By collecting, categorizing, and analyzing, Boas thought that ethnographers could witness and accurately document the last remains of vanishing exotic cultures. The goal of museums of that time was to preserve cultural artifacts so that we could all benefit from them; and, indeed, we have, at the expense of those from whom they were taken.[11]

Our notions of culture have changed, as has our notion of what it is acceptable to examine within a given culture—even within a school culture. We no longer see culture as a static collection of rituals waiting to be transmitted, although these rituals are alive and well in the often hidden part of our curriculum guidelines. As educators, we are now permitted to question how cultural rituals are sanctioned and contested by those who live together in certain environments. We can look at the school not only as a place that disseminates culture to those who have no choice but to partake in its rituals, but also as a place where cultures emerge and are created, layer upon layer. The school is its own culture, and it contains many subcultures, each with its own past, present, and future. The young people and adults who share the same physical and psychological space for 8

9. James Clifford, *The Predicament of Culture: Twentieth Century Ethnography, Literature, and Art* (Cambridge, MA: Harvard University Press, 1988), 228.

10. For a critique of the role museums of anthropology and natural history have played as collectors of other people's artifacts, see James Clifford "On Collecting Art and Culture" (Clifford 1988). His description of Lévi-Strauss and his contemporaries in the New York City of the early 1940s underscores the period's passion for accumulating cultural objects (see pp. 236–244).

11. See John Willinsky for a discussion of the place of the museum within the educational legacy of imperialism in *Learning to Divide the World: Education at Empire's End* (Minneapolis, MN: University of Minnesota Press, 1998).

to 10 hours a day are the makers of that culture, not merely its recipients. (Obviously, some participants still have more authority to direct the artifacts that get produced. The privilege of the privileged.) Bringing new tools, even those as simple-looking as video cameras, into the school changes its extant culture. Such tools enter into students' lives in a way that breaks conventions. For example, Josh once jumped onto the edge of his father's truck, holding my video camera, and videotaped his father painting a house. Suddenly, he realized the power of this tool for telling stories about what happens to him in school.

> **Josh:** Ricki, follow me for one whole day and you'll hear all the yelling and screaming. You'll see what life is like for us. I have a better idea; you give me the camera and I'll do it. I'll direct it. It will be called, *A Day in the Life of Josh*.

Are we ready to let young people create their own portraits of schools? Are we ready to bring our video images of school cultures into the larger arena of educational discourse? With the advent of the Internet, the doors to an international arena have sprung open. Little by little, bits and bytes of digital images are fluttering around the Internet, available for all to read. More and more, these images are being created and monitored, not by teachers and other guardians of cultural rightness, but by students. At a middle school on Vancouver Island, which I describe in detail in the following chapters, students conducted video and multimedia portraits of their school by interviewing each other. With the help of their teacher, Joe Grewal, they designed a HyperCard portrait called *Welcome to Bayside Middle School*. As a community of inquiry, researchers, teachers, and students studied an endangered rainforest called Clayoquot Sound; we also designed a CD-ROM called *The Global Forest*, which, through digital video and text stories, describes our investigation of the socioscientific controversy surrounding Clayoquot Sound. What does this mode of inquiry do to our previously held notions regarding "culture," "tools," and "artifacts?" Isn't it time to flex our minds and examine emergent learning cultures growing and changing in the context of distributed media technologies?

part I
storyreading

If we then ask about the nature and role of ... the reader's conception of what kind of story or text he is encountering or "re-creating"—we are in fact asking not only a morphological question about the actual text, but also a question about the interpretive processes that are loosened by the text in the reader's mind.

—Jerome Bruner
Actual Minds, Possible Worlds

The Double Helix, or Two Lenses on Two Stories

Why are two overlapping bodies of knowledge—multimedia ethnography and the nature of children's thinking in two computer-rich school cultures—integrated in this book? The simple answer is that putting them together forms a new entity, a kind of double helix that is strengthened by a close, spiraling connection. Each focus moves around the other, each informing the other. What you have access to in this book are linear text descriptions that have emerged from video "data" collected at two schools—data selected and made into digital video portraits, predating my written portraits. You can see segments of these digital portraits at <http://www.pointsofviewing.com>, and I guarantee that they are quite different from what we in qualitative research traditionally call case studies. The text case studies, as they are written out in Part III of this volume, are yet another layer of interpretation covering the events that I videotaped.

In traditional ethnographic approaches, text-based fieldnotes are constructed into text-based stories or case studies. But video fieldnotes are continually being manipulated into smaller chunks until they become video stories that can be retold as text portraits or can "live in" some video format. At each point, new layers of interpretation are produced as one selects and cuts in order to build a new artifact. And yet more layers of interpretation are added as the story moves from one media form to another. Layers of interpretations are added because data are analyzed by multiple users, including those persons whom I videotape. And, as others view my portraits, I change my interpretations. (Yes, such a process is recursive and often exhausting due to its conceptual open-endedness.)

Video data enables a finely grained description that concentrates on minute details, such as the turn of a head, the raising of an eyebrow, a slight twitch of the nostrils. What emerges is a story that often reads like a stage play.[12] Readers can become virtual actors, knowing about the gesture, the colors in the room, the harshness of light reflected off the desktop. In fact, one day we might have networked ethnographic accounts that enable the viewer to virtually "be there" and to interact with the people

---

12. For a discussion on designing computers as expressive tools, see Brenda Laurel, *Computers as Theater* (Reading, MA: Addison-Wesley, 1993).

being described as the research is being conducted. Or we might just have the end of ethnography and the beginning of a new way of knowing others.

However, in the past, textured and visual details were offered without video. In the 1930s, anthropologist Raymond Firth described his journey on the ship the *Southern Cross*, providing the viewer with a strong sense of "being there." Consider the visual (and phallic) image depicted in his textual description:

> In the cool of the early morning, just before sunrise, the bow of the *Southern Cross* headed towards the eastern horizon, on which a tiny dark blue outline was faintly visible. Slowly it grew into a rugged mountain mass, standing up sheer from the ocean; then as we approached within a few miles it revealed around its base a narrow ring of low, flat land, thick with vegetation. The sullen gray day with its lowering clouds strengthened my grim impression of a solitary peak, wild and stormy, upthrust in a waste of waters.[13]

Visual anthropology is a field that dates back to the late 19th and early 20th centuries. Photographs and film are not new media forms within ethnographic accounts.[14] However, earlier text descriptions, photographs, and films are all linear media forms and, hence, are not as slippery and potentially collaborative as are digital media forms, which can easily be reconstructed and distributed in malleable forms.

Two lenses to tell two stories. My meditations on multimedia ethnography, although innovative, would lack substance if the stories of the children using emergent technologies were not present. The cultural life of the schools constitutes the soul of these stories, bringing theories of culture, technology, and learning to light; the methodology becomes one of the core stories. Readers can weave their thoughts about how boys and girls use computers as culture makers. This enables

---

13. For an analysis of Raymond Firth's use of language to evoke the sense of *being there*, see Clifford Geertz, *Works and Lives: The Anthropologist as Author* (Stanford: Stanford University Press, 1988), 11–13; and Marie Louise Pratt, "Fieldwork in Common Places," in *Writing Culture: The Poetics and the Politics of Ethnography*, eds. J. Clifford and G. E. Marcus (Berkeley: University of California Press, 1986), 35–37.
14. See chapter 4 of this volume for an historical account of visual anthropology.

children, teachers, researchers, and readers of texts to form emerging communities of inquiry. Thus, the more complex answer to the question which I posed earlier ("Why are two overlapping bodies of knowledge—multimedia ethnography and epistemology—integrated in this book?") is that this integration enables you, as reader, to become part of the resultant double helix as you journey through the schools with your multimedia ethnographic lenses.

Looking Through Layers: Views of Digital Video

Laura Dern, one of the leading actors in *Jurassic Park*, lovingly told the audience at the American Film Institute's presentation of the 1995 Life Achievement Award to Steven Spielberg how he entertained her one evening when they were caught in a life-threatening hurricane while making the film. He held a flashlight first above his face, then below his chin. As he repeated these actions, he said: "Love story; monster movie. Love story; monster movie."

Love Story, Monster Movie

Infusing a work with points of viewing is something we cannot avoid. This is why I, as author of this volume, am so careful to place my light on the issues that I want you, as reader, to see. As author, I say: "Multimedia ethnography; children's thinking. Or, multimedia thinking; children's ethnography," depending on how I hold my flashlight. Moreover, this director wants to share the flashlight with you, her readers and viewers. I want to provide you with the tools to join me in my research, so that, eventually, we can share rhetorical devices and tools while constructing our creations and infusing them with points of viewing. Not an easy feat, in spite of how advanced we believe our digital tools to be.

Central to using digital video technologies is asking how we know that the video we are watching is somehow representative of the body of video that was initially collected. In other words, can we trust what we see of these digitized videotaped events, even if we know that the videographer included and selected as much as she could and was as comprehensive as possible? Certainly including a lot of stuff, even a lot of good stuff, does not guarantee the validity of any endeavor. Telling a good story touches on issues concerning point of view (POV), or what I call *points of viewing*. It also touches on issues concerning how we come to decide that a certain representation is robust enough for us to believe it, whatever the story's genre might be. For example, we know that even the cinematographer of fiction must convince her viewers that what they are viewing is believable. Each representation of a genre or combination of genres has an audience to convince. Thus, we need to rethink previously held notions of what we hold to be valid, truthful, and trustworthy accounts.[15] We need to uncover, by looking through layers of interpretations, conceptual devices that address the complexity of using video for making, telling, and reading believable stories—stories that are based on a version of reality that we are constantly negotiating with our peers.

One way of opening this discussion is to ask ourselves: Is there a difference between bias and point of view? Is the distinction, as interactive cinematographer Glorianna Davenport has maintained over the years, based on whether we agree or disagree with the point of view of the author or filmmaker?[16] According to Davenport's argument, it is easier to think an interpretation is biased (and therefore not to be believed) when we do not agree with it. Consider Oliver Stone movies as examples. If we agree with Stone's interpretation of Nixon or JFK, we think his story is interesting; if we do not, we think it is biased. However, what happens when we acknowledge that a story is biased and yet still feel informed by it? In the documentary film *Roger and Me*, directed by Michael Moore, the viewer travels with Moore in and around Flint, Michigan, while he attempts to get an interview with Roger Smith, who was then chair of General Motors. Those who agreed with Moore's point of view thought the documentary to be a fair representation of Flint; those who disagreed with his POV thought it biased and not representative. However, another community of viewers, one which includes myself, thought the filmmaker's cynical point

---

15. The theory of configurational validity is discussed in detail in chapter 11 of this volume.
16. To understand how interactive documentary filmmakers build entry points for viewers to become analytical participants in understanding media events, see Glorianna Davenport, Thomas A. Smith, and Natalio Pincever, "Cinematic Primitives for Multimedia," *IEEE Computer Graphics and Applications* (July, 1991), 67–74.

of view contributed to making the movie believable. Regardless of whether he told a complete story about life in Flint, I learned something about the character of the town and the people who live in it. Everyone in the movie—from the woman who sold rabbits for "Pets or Food" to the wealthy townsfolk partying in a local prison on a Saturday night—had a quirky story to tell about the local culture. To view the actions of corporate America in small-town America through the eyes of a political activist with a sense of humor was, in and of itself, a treat. The issue here is the way in which the POV of one author, or the points of viewing of multiple authors, infuses an artifact—whether it be a movie, novel, or website—with layers of interpretations. After all, to what do the words POV refer but how filmmakers, not to mention film viewers, infuse whatever they create with meaning?

Perhaps a more productive way of looking at the question of bias would entail examining how POV influences what is supposedly objectively reported as news. In CNN's (January 26, 1996) coverage of the events surrounding Hillary Rodham Clinton's historic subpoena to answer questions concerning her role as a lawyer in what has come to be called the "Whitewater Affair," a TV anchor naively asked two commentators whether there was a Republican agenda to keep this issue alive for as long as possible. The Republican-sympathetic reporter winced, avoiding the question; the Democrat-sympathetic reporter reveled: "Yes, why is so much money being spent on this issue when there is a huge budget crisis in the U.S. that the Republicans themselves say they want to address?" As educated viewers, we ask ourselves why our journalists are not being asked to reflect more about their roles as propagandists and political partisans. Why do they not openly address their points of viewing so that we can properly critique their stories? You might argue that this is a matter of becoming media literate; all we need to do is to educate viewers about how to read televised media events. But it also points to the more embedded mystique surrounding notions of objectivity. For example, there are still some journalists who tend to believe that they are simply telling the story as it happens; that they are not interpreting, but merely carrying the message.

Video recording in the world of educational research can be naive in the same way. Of course educational video ethnography is as infused with the author's POV as is political reportage. Even in the most "objective" projects (with the camera on a tripod at the back of the room), the researcher chooses where to place the camera, how "tight" (close up) or "wide" (far away) the shot will be, at what angle the camera will record, and who will be in its view. One tends to think that the less the camera is manipulated, the more objective the result. But this may be missing the central issue. Even the hidden camera in the 1960s television program *Candid Camera* was placed in accordance with the filmmaker's perspective.

Thus, when video ethnographers, as participant recorders, view cultures, it is their relationship to those cultures that is captured on videotape. Both ethnographer Mary Catherine Bateson and filmmaker Richard Leacock address this issue. Bateson states that you come to terms with point of view by reviewing and documenting your own personal responses, not by trying to avoid them: "If you are doing ethnography or natural history, you record carefully what your attention has allowed you to see, knowing that you will not see everything and that others will see differently, but recording whatever you can so it will be part of the cumulative picture."[17] Leacock simply states that filmmaking is the "observer's perception of what happened in the presence of the camera."[18] But, to some degree, both Bateson and Leacock are the intellectual products of a traditional scientific paradigm. Neither is quite willing to admit that POV—bias, if you want to be blunt—is where we start in our understanding of media texts, whether these texts are constructed with words, images, or sounds. Digital media forms that can be reconstituted make this problem an adventure filled with surprises, for we now have the power to share our points of viewing and the construction of our artifacts with readers while we are in the process of interpreting what we understand of any given moment in time.

Let me step back a bit and rework Leacock's statement to ask: Is video ethnography the video ethnographer's perspective of what takes place in front of the camera when the camera is turned on? Multimedia ethnography is difficult to define because, as of now, not enough people are conducting this kind of research for us to know either what the genre looks like or what constitutes multimedia connoisseurship.[19]

---

17. Mary Catherine Bateson, *With a Daughter's Eye: A Memoir of Margaret Mead and Gregory Bateson* (New York: Pocket Books, 1984), 203.
18. Richard Leacock, "Ethnographic Observation and the Super-8 Millimeter Camera," in *Principles of Visual Anthropology*, ed. P. Hockings (Paris: Mouton, 1973), 148.
19. For a description of connoisseurship in qualitative research, see Elliot Eisner, *The Enlightened Eye: Qualitative Inquiry and the Enhancement of Educational Practice* (New York: Macmillan, 1992).

Ambiguity and Digital Video Data

There are advantages and disadvantages to using digital technologies in ethnography. An obvious advantage to the video ethnographer is that she can supplement her video with text, documents, fieldnotes, and other data both in order to gain insights into what to shoot and to provide other users with a kind of description that builds on, but also deviates from, Clifford Geertz's notion of *thick description*.[20] Disadvantages stem from the fact that digital video data are notoriously messy, slippery, and elusive.

For those who have difficulty dealing with ambiguity and messiness, digital ethnography will not be a comfortable method to use in studying others. Just reading this book may be confusing to those who have spent their lives justifying margins and finding containers in which to place the data, and, sometimes, vice versa. Those trained not to ask questions may become uncomfortable with what will seem like the rambling of children as they search for their meanings. However, the largest barrier to becoming a digital video ethnographer is that video data are open to many interpretations, many points of viewing. Data are as slippery as the tape upon which they are recorded.

Video data, digital and analog, are particularly subject to the infusion of POV. It is important to know who the video researcher is—who shot (or who directed the shooting of) the video, when, where, and for what purpose; thus, it is important to pay particular attention to the context in which the event was recorded. It could be that the video recorder—let's call her Kate—and the user are the same person. However, Kate may experience the data quite differently when she analyzes it (several months, weeks, or even hours later) than she did when she shot it. Upon repeated viewing, Kate may have a number of differing interpretations. It could also be the case that Kate uses footage shot by her colleague, Leroy. In fact, Kate and Leroy could be working together on the same research project. When working on a collaborative video analysis project, Kate and Leroy can share views with each other and with other "readers" in various locations. Sharing interactive documents on distributed networks could enable other users to interact with Kate and Leroy's ideas in a way that allows them to become part of the interpretation process. Clearly, the notion of fixed interpretations is part of our pre-electronic past.

---

20. Clifford Geertz, *The Interpretation of Cultures* (New York: Basic Books, 1973).

You might be saying to yourself, surely we do not read print texts in the same way when we read them again. Yes, we read texts differently the second time around. We know this from rereading novels. However, the difference with video data is that with video, one "feels" closer to the original event on reviewing it. When I watch the video of a child talking about inventions, I have access to a plethora of visual stimuli that can never be translated into words in text, whether in 1 or in 100 viewings. While conducting my own data analysis, I find layers upon layers of detail that transport me to the time of the event. My visual data seems fresher to new analyses. (That said, I would infer that others more sensitive to the variety of text might have a different opinion.)

It is also true that video data are more elusive and mutable than are text data. In short, video compounds ambiguity although appearing to do the opposite.[21] I say this in spite of my respect for the research on Anchored Instruction Theory conducted by the Cognitive Technology Group at Vanderbilt, which posits the notion that learning should be embedded in authentic learning tasks and that video makes these authentic tasks clearer.[22] In its research on the use of visual representations, this group contends that, because video data are dynamic and spatial, they allow viewers to form clear mental pictures of complex situations—pictures that are closely related to real objects and events "in the real." In simple cases, where seeing an image aids understanding, this is true. To use this group's example, a child seeing a bird put stones in a glass to raise the level of water in the glass understands this action more clearly when seeing it, recorded or not, than she does when reading about it. But according to the research conducted by Jim Gaskell and his colleagues at the University of British Columbia, it seems that what is retained and understood differs according to media form used.[23] In their study, secondary students who were presented

---

21. For a discussion on multimedia as an organizational memory tool that can lessen ambiguity, see Kai Lim, *Multimedia as an Enabling Technology for Enhancing Organizational Memory to Support Memory Systems*, Ph.D. diss. (University of British Columbia, 1996).

22. Cognitive Technology Group, "Examining the Cognitive Challenges and Pedagogical Opportunities of Integrated Media Systems: Toward a Research Agenda," *Journal of Special Education Technology 12* (1993a): 118–24. See also Cognitive Technology Group, "Integrated Media: Toward a Theoretical Framework for Utilizing their Potential," *Journal of Special Education Technology* 12 (1993b): 71–85.

23. P. James Gaskell, Reg Fleming, Renee Fountain, and Alfred Ojelel, "Socioscientific Issues," in *British Columbia Assessment of Science Technical Report III* (Victoria: Ministry of Education, 1991).

with a story about a socioscientific issue in printed news format were more likely to frame it in terms of a conflict between different points of view than were students who were presented with the same issue in a video news format. Students who watched the video tended to describe the issue from a single point of view (theirs) and to downplay any controversy. At the same time, many of those students who were presented with the print format disengaged from the story and skipped the written questions, whereas those who were presented with the video format kept watching and often used a dramatic image as a basis for discussion. The point is that, in general, students engaged differently with, and constructed different meanings from, the two media formats.

What most of us, including Rand Spiro and his colleagues, seem to agree on is that digital data, as used in most hypertext or multimedia environments, can provide flexibility for the reader.[24] Digital data enable viewers to "get the picture," one might say, of what was occurring when the video was shot. We know, from the rich literature on situated cognition, how critical it is to have an understanding of the context of any given event.[25] Moreover, we know that media can be used successfully for learning and instructional purposes.[26] But that is not the end of the story. For all the blanks that are filled by seeing the image represented, other ambiguities arise.

I once compared a 5-minute text transcript of an interview with Josh, a 10-year-old from the Hennigan School, with a 5-minute video interview. These data come directly from my first multimedia ethnography, conducted from 1986 to 1990. The text transcript could be easily coded, annotated, filed, stored, and retrieved using either pen and paper or a computer. Analysis of the text data follows a linear path, even if one creates hyperlinks. However, let us suppose that I am looking at the text transcript and trying

---

24. Rand Spiro, Paul J. Feltovich, Michael Jacobson, and Richard L. Coulson, "Cognitive Flexibility, Constructivism, and Hypertext: Random Access Instruction for Advanced Knowledge Acquisition in Ill-Structured Domains," *Educational Technology 31* (1991): 24–33.

25. See John Seely Brown, Allan Collins, and Paul Duguid, "Situated Cognition and the Culture of Learning," *Educational Researcher 18*, no. 1 (1989): 32–42; and Jean Lave, "Cognitive Consequences of Traditional Apprenticeship Training in West Africa," *Anthropology and Education Quarterly 8* (1977): 177–80.

26. For a discussion of emerging media in schools, refer to Robert Kosma, "Learning with Media," *Review of Educational Research 61* (1991): 179–211; and Robert Kosma, "Implications of Instructional Psychology for the Design of Educational Television," *Educational Communications and Technology Journal* (1986): 11–19.

to understand Josh's use of the word "amazing." I ask: "How is this word used to link ideas? Does saying the word 'amazing' give Josh time to think about the next topic? Does this word show curiosity about the world?" We can easily imagine searching through 20 pages of text, checking for instances of the use of "amazing." It would not be difficult to search and link relevant annotations of other researchers who may have commented on Josh's use of "amazing," although linguists will testify that text analysis is fraught with webs of intricate paths.

Imagine the additional complexity involved in analyzing the same 5 minutes of a video stream. To analyze it, we need to be able to interpret not only what Josh is saying when he uses the word "amazing," but also what he is doing—hoping that what he does will give us clues about what he means, and hoping that we have understood his taxonomy of what these gestures mean to him. A 5-minute digital video stream digitized at a sampling rate of 15 frames per second contains (15 frames per second x 60 seconds per minute x 5 minutes =) 4,500 frames that could show subtle variations of gesture. Josh shifts his body forward, sighing, "Amazing!" Does this show excitement, a sense of wonder, or a slight fear of the unknown?

Yes, in certain circumstances, video does lessen ambiguity; after all, it offers us both visual and auditory modes on which to base our analyses. However, this assumes that we have common codes for interpreting signs, gestures, and intonations.[27] And, as anthropologists have pointed out over the last century, individuals from various cultures vary greatly in their use of gestural language, as do individuals within the same culture. In short, the greater context that video provides becomes yet another challenging code to decipher.

Reinterpreting Thick Description

Throughout my past 10 years as a multimedia ethnographer, I have found myself returning again and again to Clifford Geertz's notion of thick description.[28] Geertz used the notion of thick description to convey the fact

---

27. An Israeli flight attendant visiting Italy for the first time told me about how he once put his fingers and thumb together (facing upwards) and shook his hand slightly at the Italian ground crew. In Israel, this gesture means, "Please wait for a minute; be patient." In Italy, he was cursing them! Same gesture; different meaning.
28. Clifford Geertz, *The Interpretation of Cultures*.

that descriptions are always multilayered. His book, *The Interpretation of Cultures*, was published in 1973. Since then, even the most avant garde postmodern ethnographer continues to theorize about Geertz's work because it compels one to ponder the meaning of events which often seem so terribly random. His focus over the last decade has been on the writing of culture and the anthropologist's role as author. By 1988, Geertz had published *Works and Lives: The Anthropologist as Author*.[29] This book was quite a departure for a person who was trying to find ways to make ethnography into a better scientific endeavor—an endeavor in which, if truth remained evasive, one could yet gain a measure of validity through analyzing descriptions that were layered, textured, contextual, and, of course, convincing. In his more recent work, however, Geertz returns to the soul-searching question, "Where has all the science gone? Floundering through mere happenings and then concocting accounts of how they hang together is what knowledge and illusion alike consist in."[30] Does he utter these words with sadness—for both the demise of ethnography as science and the seeming relativism of postmodernity—or does he simply state the obvious? Knowledge and illusion are synonymous. Science is gone. At least, science as we knew it, or thought we knew it.

Geertz brought the notion of thick description to life in the field of anthropology, and the concept quickly spread throughout diverse knowledge domains. For the record, it was Gilbert Ryle, the Oxford philosopher, who first coined the term. Ryle's concern was to uncover the levels of accomplishment demonstrated by a person's actions. He sees the analysis of layers of description, moving from thin to thick, as a means by which we can determine the purpose and the intention of any given action. As he says about a number of people sitting still, chin in hand, each on his or her own rock:

> Notice that in each case there is a thinnest description of what the person is doing, e.g. penciling a line or a dot on paper, and that this thinnest description requires thickening, often multiple thickening, of a perfectly specific kind before it amounts to an account of what the person is trying to accomplish.[31]

---

29. Clifford Geertz, *Works and Lives: The Anthropologist as Author* (Stanford: Stanford University Press, 1988).
30. Clifford Geertz, *After the Fact: Two Countries, Four Decades, One Anthropologist* (Cambridge, MA: Harvard University Press, 1995), 3.

Ryle poses the problem of distinguishing between a man sitting on a rock with his chin in his hand and a man who is a "thinker of thoughts." For example, a person sitting on a rock counting vehicles driving by is not a thinker of thoughts. A person listening to a distant band is not choosing what he hears and, therefore, is also not a thinker of thoughts. A third person is going over a tune in her head, but the tune is not of her creation. In contrast, a person on an adjacent rock is creating a poem or composing a song; here is a thinker of thoughts. Ryle states two conditions for determining who is and who is not a thinker of thoughts. First, the thinker must be detached from the immediacy of his or her circumstances; second, the thinker is in control of his or her "own bottom-level moves and motions."[32]

Thus, according to Ryle, it is necessary to apply the notion of thick description in order to understand different levels of thought. Consider the way in which he uses "thinnest" in the following passage:

> Euclid trying to find the proof of a new theorem is working on a higher accomplishment-level than Euclid trying to teach students his proof when he has got it; and trying to teach it is on a higher accomplishment-level than that on which his students are working in trying to master it.... None the less it may still be true that the only thing that, under its thinnest description, Euclid is here and now doing is muttering to himself a few geometrical words and phrases, or scrawling on paper or in the sand a few rough and fragmentary lines. This is far, very far, from being all that he is doing; but it may very well be the only thing that he is doing.[33]

Ryle created the notion of thick description as a means of differentiating between what is really happening when the same action occurs under different circumstances. Let us remember that, in Ryle's time, psychology and other knowledge domains were riddled with notions of stages, levels, and developmental sequences.[34] Society as a whole was consumed with the notion of ever-increasing growth; even spiritual growth was discussed as a transcendental movement from lower to higher states. So it is not

---

31. Gilbert Ryle, *Collected Papers*, vol. 2 (New York: Barnes and Nobles, 1971), 498.
32. Ibid., 499.
33. Ibid., 496–97.

surprising that Ryle would search for ways to differentiate between what is knowing and what just appears to be knowing.

Geertz's contribution to Ryle's notion of thick description was to add to it the notion of intention—a notion that would bring his readers closer to the events being described. Or so he hoped—so we all hoped.[35] For Geertz (in the early 1970s), the purpose of doing ethnography was to sort out the layers of inference and implication with regard to any given event. Separating the thin from the thick description sets up a hierarchy of meaningful structures, enabling one to gain a deeper and richer view of whatever culture one is studying. Geertz is not establishing hierarchies of accomplishment, as is Ryle; rather, he is establishing hierarchies of meaning. These hierarchies of meaning lead to commensureability, the ability of one culture to translate (i.e., to find a reasonable facsimile for) another culture's web of significance.[36]

According to Geertz, if we are to gain insight into the meaning of a particular culture, then we need to understand that all its events, behaviors, and institutions are imbued with signs. In describing a certain event thickly, we begin to get beyond the surface interpretation. We enter a deeper (i.e., thicker) layer of interpretation as we attempt to determine what a particular gesture—for example, a person sitting on a rock with her chin resting in her hand—means to that person. When it is described thickly, we can begin to understand what this gesture signifies. We can determine whether it means that she is simply resting her head, pretending to look like she is deep in thought in order to impress the person next

---

34. Within the last hundred or more years, theories about thinking have followed a developmental theme—Sigmund Freud's oral, anal, genital; Eric Erikson's eight stages of human development; Jean Piaget's pre-operational to formal operations. Theoreticians in the humanities have relied upon science to construct their models for understanding the nature of the human mind.

35. In the earlier phase of my work, I was convinced I could "get close" to the meaning of the event. See Ricki Goldman-Segall, "Thick Description: A Tool for Designing Ethnographic Interactive Videodisks," *SIGCHI Bulletin 21* (1989): 118–22. However, after spending years as a practicing video ethnographer while reading Stephen Tyler, among others, I am now less convinced that I can find the truth and report the real meaning. See Stephen A. Tyler, "Post-Modern Ethnography: From Document of the Occult to Occult Document," in *Writing Culture: The Poetics and the Politics of Ethnography*, eds. J. Clifford and G. E. Marcus (Berkeley: University of California Press, 1986), 122–140.

36. Geertz uses Max Weber's notion of "webs of significance." See Clifford Geertz, *The Interpretation of Cultures*, 5.

to her; making fun of another person who is sitting in a similar fashion on a rock down the beach; or rehearsing for some part in a play.

Geertz uses Ryle's example of the contraction of the eyelids (winks on winks on winks) to show how easy it is to misinterpret the meaning of a wink. This gesture could be a twitch, a wink, a parody, or a rehearsal of a parody. According to Geertz, signifiers—twitches and winks—are symbolic acts, which, when textured enough to render meaning, eventually create a language through which they may be communicated to others.

I use the notion of thick description in analog and digital video analysis to share my interpretations with those I study. I want to enable others to add their layers of interpretation to a platform for *multiloguing*, a term I use instead of dialoguing. Users can access data and add their points of viewing as well as, eventually, their own data. This platform is where we can share our collective views with viewers who may live in a research cyber-community on the Web. These viewers might only visit our site once, or they might decide to hang out and do their own studies. Thick description, as reinterpreted in a digital video environment, provides authors, viewers, and new user/authors with a way of adding meaning to what has already been recorded. Yet the age-old problem with observational methods, that they "tend to resist any kind of systematic evaluation" and that they are "imprisoned in [their] own immediacy," continues to perplex us.[37] Perhaps distributed digital video data cannot solve the problem of data being "imprisoned in [their] own immediacy," but they can open the doors of the prison of solitary interpretations. No longer do we have to imagine the solitary, vibrant young Margaret Mead going off to Samoa because her mentor, Franz Boas, discouraged her from conducting her doctoral work anywhere that did not have a regular postal delivery![38]

In short, although ethnographic events will always be events that occurred in the past and only remain with us through our recollections and reconstructions of fragments of memories, we are still interested in

---

37. Ibid., 24.

38. Mead and her husband, Gregory Bateson, used the still and movie camera extensively in their work. (If she were alive today, Mead quite possibly would be delighted to use the Internet to post her images and fieldnotes.) See Margaret Mead, "Visual Anthropology in a Discipline of Words," in *Principles of Visual Anthropology*, ed. P. Hockings (The Hague: Mouton, 1973), 3–13. For a more detailed discussion of this issue and the use of the still and movie cameras in ethnographic reporting, see chapter 4 of this volume.

communicating with others what we observe and construct. We can now build platforms of video artifacts (for the Internet) that take on "lives" of their own and yet remain representations of what we have shared in our nonvirtual life among other cultures. No, it does not solve the problem of finding the best meaning for an event or of eliminating ambiguity and messiness, but it could create a different climate for research with others, and with our tools.

Partnering with Video Recordings: "After the Fact"

You might ask yourself how using videotape data and multimedia tools can enable you to gain insight into your projects. In my experience, videomaking encourages self-expression, communication, and learning—both in the videographer and in those she videotapes. Videomaking encourages a conversation with the camera and with the video data. I talk to them as you might talk to your word processor, car, or telephone. Yes, I have anthropomorphized my camera, the multimedia tools I use, and the artifacts they help me construct; I think of them as sharing a life with me.[39] The most apt phrase for the relationship I have with my mode of observation and analysis is a partnership of intimacy and immediacy. Andrew Lippman defines the interactive relationship with computer tools as being one of mutual activity and spontaneous interruptibility; Alluquere Rosanne Stone goes one step further, referring to the partnership with machines as "a prosthetic device" for constructing desire.[40] I prefer not to think of these tools and their products as my prostheses for constructing and representing desire, however seductive this idea might seem.

When I work with a video partner, a camera for instance, I have to think with the camera while I conduct interviews, knowing that the camera can be an invasive instrument that may shape the way the interview is conducted. I start off with comments that elicit responses. I

---

39. Anthropomorphizing is a topic Sherry Turkle discusses in *The Second Self: Computers and the Human Spirit* (New York: Simon and Schuster, 1984).

40. Andrew Lippman, "Lippman on Interactivity" in *MacUser* (March, 1989); Alluquere Rosanne Stone, *The War Between Desire and Technology at the End of the Mechanical Age* (Cambridge, MA: MIT Press, 1995).

often reflect back to the young people what they say, as psychologist Carl Rogers suggested many years ago in a theory called *active reflection*.[41] I repeat what young people say, trying to mirror and reflect without judging. (I am not always successful!) The questions I ask stem from my interest in what young people are thinking when they are putting together and creating new computational constructions. Due to the possible invasiveness of videotaping, my first step is either to be invited by the young person to see what she is doing or to ask permission to participate with her while she is working. If I am conducting an interview, young people are always invited to participate, and if they decide not to be interviewed, I do not feel my results will be skewed. I am not making conclusions based on random sampling. The young people choose whether to participate. There is no sense in forcing young people to partake in an interview aimed at helping them to articulate their own ideas about their learning. Therefore, when I sit down beside a child who is working, I ask whether she wants to tell me (and the camera) what she is doing or thinking. If the answer is "No," then I do not record. If invited, my questions are aimed to provoke reflection.

I use the recording capacity of the video camera to capture moments that I would not be able to remember if I had to write them down after the fact. Geertz reminds us that "what we can construct, if we keep notes and survive, are hindsight accounts of the connectedness of things that seem to have happened: pieced together patternings, after the fact."[42] "After the fact" means after the event, but it also means we are now beyond the belief that "facts" are anything more than social constructions. The ethnographer who does not use film or video to record events has to reconstruct the story from fieldnotes or audio tapes. The video ethnographer is at an advantage; she can concentrate fully on the person and on the subtleties of the conversation without having to worry about remembering every detail. When I do not have the camera with me, for example, I spend most of my time trying to write things down worrying that I am missing what I cannot see when I am writing. I also try to "memorize," or at least capture, the key ideas, words, and gestures. Knowing that the camera, as my partner, is doing that job, I can relax and fall into the motion of the

---

41. Carl Rogers, *On Becoming a Person: A Therapist's View of Pyschotherapy* (Boston: Houghton Mifflin, 1961).
42. Clifford Geertz, *After the Fact: Two Countries, Four Decades, One Anthropologist*, 2.

interview.[43] Videomaking requires that I concentrate fully on what the young person is trying to communicate to me. Instead of saying, "Yes, mm-hmm," I "nod" with the camera; I encourage them by silently focusing on a hand gesture, the flicker of an eye, or a sigh. With the camera in my lap, on my hip, or at chest level, my eyes only rarely glance at the image in the viewfinder. I become a participant recorder.

Sharing the Role of Ethnographer with Those We Study

When thinking about using emerging video technologies to conduct an ethnographic study, the tendency is either to discredit the possibilities or to exaggerate the potential. One tends to forget that even a well designed tool is only as good as its user. It is not enough to use more sophisticated technologies merely to do the same things. Technologies enable people to change, to create new roles. And these new roles make possible a different set of interactions.

The video camera and multimedia technology are not merely good research tools; they are tools that extend the already developing culture of moving images. Multimedia cultures grow in the context of advanced "moving" technologies. Papert maintains that we need to think about emerging technologies in the same way that we think about art or transportation. Thinking about trying to produce a better form of Impressionism did not bring about Cubism.[44] When we think about technologies, we need to think about how they enable new kinds of things to happen to people.

I have found that girls and boys appropriate my research quite easily. They become ethnographers of their own culture, crafting artifacts to represent themselves. Children appropriate the camera in two ways. In my first study at the Hennigan, Josh decided to direct my work and to make me his "cameraperson." As director, he told me what shots to take and what paths to follow. I remember one day in particular, when I was driving him home from school. It was a sunny New England autumn day, and

---

43. I use the word "motion" because I believe that my camerawork responds to the tone and feel of the children's search for ideas. When a young person I am videotaping pauses to find the next idea, I pull out of a tight shot position on my camera and move to a wide shot, giving more space for finding the next idea.

44. This phrase is excerpted from a documentary video by Ricki Goldman-Segall, *Thinking about the Future* [video] (Cambridge, MA: Cambridge Center for Adult Education, 1987).

we stopped to look at a maple tree in full crimson glory. He suggested that he be an announcer on a TV broadcast station. He would report "live from Jamaica Plains." In a playful mood, he spoke into his mike, saying, "Me and my CAMERA-person" (referring to me). Similarly, at the Hennigan, he often invited me to videotape what he was doing. He would make a "come here" gesture with his arms and then show me on what to focus my camera. Josh, the director.

In contrast to the Hennigan, when I first arrived at Bayside Middle School in 1993, many of the young people had already had some exposure to video cameras. Although some of them had never actually used one, the technology had already been demystified. In the Bayside study, my little Hi8 camcorder often traveled from person to person. The students conducted interviews with each other or just fooled around, videotaping upside down and so forth. It was the preteen girls who seemed particularly excited about handling the camera and making their own videos and multimedia segments. The students were creators of their own cultural artifacts. I tried then, and still do, to create a culture of videotaping in which one of the symbols of power and control, the video camera, could be used by anyone who wanted to use it. To encourage this, I leave a camera in the classroom at all times. For example, on a field trip to Clayoquot Sound, the grade 7 class, their teachers, parents, and I took 5 video cameras and about 15 still cameras. We conducted interviews and videotaped purple starfish as well as a basketball game we played one evening with the kids from a local school. Again, the young people were the culture-makers and recorders. (See chapter 5, pp. 135–140.)

Some questions I have asked myself over the years are: Can these young students conduct their own cultural analyses of their schools? How do their descriptions differ from mine? Surely I can never be the expert on someone else's culture, even if I am an experienced videographer. And where are the boundaries that so clearly separate my culture from theirs? At some point, we begin to share our different areas of expertise, and then we both begin to change.

I have also asked myself whether the multimedia story pieces that children construct can be thought of as ethnographies or whether they are more akin to cultural artifacts. In my approach to digital ethnography, I assume that neither my story nor theirs is the best story, the master story, regarding what life is like for students in schools with emerging technologies. Ethnography in the postmodern era of the Net has to include the multiple voices of those with whom we work and play—voices that are heard in a context of gender, ethnic, and power relations—as well as the voices of those who view our artifacts. The boundaries between "us" and "them" have to be both acknowledged and deconstructed, or we will merely reinforce the hierarchical relations embedded in notions of "studying down," as Laura Nader has discussed in Del Hymes' *Reinventing Anthropology*.[45]

In short, I try to make the video camera a pervasive tool, accessible to students and adults. I pass my camera around just to make sure that no one thinks it holds any secret powers, and, as much as possible, I try to enable the students to co-author my final video and text representations. Sometimes I leave my portable computer at the back of the class, with my fieldnotes file open to receive their comments; sometimes I work with them on their multimedia projects and they work on mine. I cannot say that authorship is shared equally, but it is co-constructed.

Lateral Editing: Enabling Distance Participants

In the editing of video recordings, you might ask yourself how much layering and manipulating of the original is enough and how much is too much. While editing video data, both the videotape and the remembered "products" come together in the editor's mind to create different video slices of the initial experience. Many directions emerge, each with its own partial truth, each contributing to a yet more textured description of what was going on at the time of recording. Hyperlinking, threading, or building strands through digital data opens the possibilities for layering. For example, consider what happens during traditional linear editing. An editor could place a shot of children's fingers typing at a keyboard beside a shot of children's fingers. Viewers might think this scene explores children's typing styles. However, if the purpose is to show the body language of children using the computer, the editor could follow the video segments of the fingers with shots of different parts of the body taken from different angles, directions, and distances. Each of the two sequences would have a different meaning, depending on the placement of the video segments.

---

45. Laura Nader, "Up the Anthropologist: Perspectives Gained from Studying Up," *Reinventing Anthropology*, ed. D. Hymes (New York: Pantheon, 1972).

Manipulating sequences is best described by Ken Dancyger.[46] Dancyger cites a study by two filmmakers, Pudokovin and Kuleshov, who juxtaposed a shot of an actor "with three different follow-up shots: a bowl of soup standing on a table; a shot of a coffin containing a dead woman; and a little girl playing with a toy. Audience responses to the three sequences suggested a hungry person, a sad husband, and a happy adult, and yet the first shot was always the same." This illustrates how, in linear, nondigital editing, meaning is easily affected by sequence.

Imagine what happens in digital editing, when any bit of data can be manipulated or even simulated. Consider what happens when ethnographers decide to add images of people to backgrounds, as was done in the movie *Forrest Gump*. (Forrest shakes hands with President Kennedy.) Is this so different from what Trinh Minh-Ha has done in her film, *Surname Viet, Given Name Nam*? In this "documentary," she interviews Vietnamese women who lived through communist rule and the Vietnam war. The film is woven together from different threads, the most prominent two being interviews supposedly conducted in Vietnam, but actually staged in the United States, and "unstaged" interviews with the Vietnamese-American women who performed the interviews in Vietnam. Minh-Ha does not expose the fact that she staged some of her scenes until the end of the movie, where she discusses what she refers to as "re-enactment":

> To come back to the choice of staging these interviews, usually in documentary films re-enactments are used mainly when people want to break away from the monotony of talking heads.... But here re-enactment is used precisely for the part that usually people would not think of re-enacting, which is interviews. It is used to deal with the notion of interviewing itself and with the interview as a cinematic frame, thereby refusing to reduce its role to that of a mere device to authenticate the message advanced.[47]

One advantage of nonlinear multimedia ethnography is that layers of video can be juxtaposed and layered by placing video pieces laterally instead of linearly and by allowing viewers to choose what to see.

---

46. Ken Dancyger, *The Technique of Film and Video Editing* (Boston: Focal Press, 1993), 16.
47. Trinh T. Minh-Ha, *Framer Framed* (New York: Routledge, 1992), 164.

For example, Josh is talking about the baseball player Roger Clemens. In another video clip, Josh's teacher, Linda, is watching the video of him while being interviewed herself. In yet another video clip, Linda is using the video data analysis tool *Learning Constellations* to watch both Josh and herself. In my own research, I have found that interpretations do not remain fixed when we conduct *lateral inquiry*. They change as we talk about what we are watching; they change as Josh watches himself and as Linda watches herself; they change as I write about them now, after the fact. What emerges as I look through the layers of different digital video cuts is a thickening of description, and this point of viewing enables viewers to add their interpretations to what they are seeing and to become distance-participants.

In short, digital video ethnographers build video descriptions of persons, places, or events in order to communicate their interpretations of what was happening at the time the video was recorded. They know they will not wholly succeed and that, at best, they will convince, persuade, or compel viewers and readers to believe what they have filmed or written.

Both in video and in text-based ethnography, the video ethnographer is always working with the "material stuff" on a piece of tape as well as with the "remembered stuff" pertaining to the original experience of the event. What might happen if I could take Margaret Mead's text and film fieldnotes and build my description of Samoa? Could I contribute to Mead's interpretations of Samoa by working, not from her finished books, but from her raw data? For those of us already deep in the trenches of digital ethnography, this kind of question is the place at which we now reside. We finally have the tools and bandwidth to put modest video portraits on a website and to invite those who visit them to view and comment on what they see. Yes, they can add links to their websites and build the story exponentially. Purists may say that this is not ethnography! After all, ethnographies are well-constructed stories—stories that have their own inner integrity and are not fragments. They are highly crafted in order to give the reader that sense of "being there." However, I ask you to think about the ability to extend bandwidth for real-time video transmission over the coming years. Think about our ability to use these media forms to build stories that contain rigorous interpretations and well-crafted stories, that are indeed fragments of other stories.

Digital ethnographies, chunked out in parcels for visitors to manipulate at a website, will become a pervasive mode of studying others.[48] Ethnography can no longer be characterized by an image of the solitary researcher out in the field, receiving mail service once a month. James Clifford, George Marcus, and Stephen Tyler, among others, have already delivered the fatal blow to anthropological traditions that once treated descriptions of events as truths by changing the written discourse. Now it is up to those of us exploring networked digital environments to build on the fragments, to share our stories of others, and to develop collaborative cultures on the Internet.

---

48. See the MERLin website <http://www.merlin.ubc.ca/publications> for online graduate student publications.

Pastiche: Two Computer Cultures, Time and Space Apart

There is a famous story about a Chinese master painting a landscape. Just as he is nearly finished, a drop of ink falls on the white scroll, and the disciples standing around him gasp, believing the scroll is ruined. Without hesitating, the master takes the finest of his hair brushes and, using the tiny globe of ink already fallen, paints a fly hovering in the foreground of the landscape.

—Mary Catherine Bateson
Composing a Life

Bayside Middle School: First Encounter

The *Spirit of British Columbia* weaves its slow path into a narrow passageway called Active Pass. The deep horn of the ferry sounds while a young girl, a fellow passenger, whispers her life story to me. I sit spellbound on a cold white storage bin, listening and looking for patterns in her life—patterns that teach me about my own life. The journey to Bayside Middle School is a journey to places I knew as a preteen. I enter with a passport that has the word "Expired" stamped on it in bold. Yet I see myself in every interchange of ideas. I see the patterns in the mixing and creating of cultural identities, different as they are for each generation.

It is easy to forget how reflective a girl of 13 can be when she encounters an interested stranger. We do not listen enough to young people. Sadly, the school culture listens even less. My fellow traveler's windblown whispers continue, the ferry blows its horn again, and she is gone. Yes, I would be a "stranger" in the school, I would be the "other." What secrets would the children of Bayside want to tell me about their lives? How would I tell their story so that others would be able to read, hear, and see what life is like for them in a semi-rural Canadian community on an island jutting out into the Pacific Ocean? Would my video camera help me create new levels of understanding for myself, while enabling me to share with others the texture of life at Bayside Middle School? How would I portray a story that is both theirs and mine? Will my readers and viewers be interested in my reflections, videos, CD-ROMs, and in this, my book, as I become closer to this culture?

This state-of-the-art school was built in 1992. The staff and students had just moved into their new environment, which was equipped with computer labs and had computers in many of its classrooms. A strong collaboration between the school and the Ministry of Education's Educational Technology Center (ETC) laid the basis for the integration of new technologies across the curriculum.[49] The majority of Bayside teachers were not high-tech specialists; they had merely been transferred to their

Kelli (May 1993): I love your work so far. It's so true. The only thing I would change would be if you called us young people instead of children.

new site from their old one, Mt. Newton Middle School. Throughout the transition process, my colleague and friend, Ted Riecken, a professor from the University of Victoria, conducted action research projects with the students at Bayside. He invited me to the school to see the kinds of research his group was conducting in a technology-rich school. Little did I know in 1993, when I spontaneously said, "Yes, I'd love to visit," that the next 3 years of my life would entail many trips through that narrow passage on my way to and from Vancouver Island. Right before the ferry docked, I remember trying to contain my nervous excitement, telling myself: "Ricki! Schools are schools." Meanwhile, the seagulls continued to search for food, squawking wildly as they zoomed in and out of my focus while I stared into the patterns of waves left by the rhythm of the ferry.

My car rolls up and down hilly country roads spotted with horses and cows, passing little farms situated on long, lush, Irish-green land. Dark green,

---

49. ETC, once under the directorship of Michael Hoebel, is now the Educational Distance and Learning Branch of the British Columbia Ministry of Education and is, at the time of publication of this manuscript, directed by Barry Carbol. Mike, Barry, and Peter Donkers have been instrumental in providing the school with the technological expertise and encouragement needed to get a multitude of research projects completed.

almost navy, evergreens outline the clear blue sky with wispy, dark, triangular designs. Four hours after leaving Vancouver, I reach Brentwood Bay, fifteen miles north of Victoria. It's a glistening, sunny day in an otherwise gloomy Pacific Northwest spring. I drive up a long driveway toward a neoclassical Greek structure standing creamy white amongst an encircling coniferous forest. Aha, an outpost of Western imperialism here in British Columbia, near the Pacific Ocean, standing "Silent, upon a peak in Darien."[50]

It is not common for educational researchers to describe emerging computer cultures in semi-rural communities; we describe the lives of children in the urban metropolis.[51] Stereotypically, researchers have labeled rural communities as less technologically advanced than urban communities. We think it is in the cities that young people and "high tech" interact. To date, when advanced technologies are brought en masse into schools, the latter are often located mostly in very affluent or extremely poor urban communities. Yet I ask myself what I can learn about these students' approaches to designing and using technological tools in what appears to be a group of young people more interested in horses and horseback riding than in computers.

Students stroll outside Bayside Middle School despite the fact that classes are in session. A group of girls meanders back from an outdoor sports activity, carrying their lacrosse gear; others are sitting with pen and paper, writing, talking, or relaxing in the sun. After a month of rain and clouds, some fresh air and sunshine seem like a good idea to me, a person who once lived in Israel and worshipped the sun gods. I ask myself, "Where are the playground monitors?" Granted, this is not an inner-city elementary school, but I still expect "security" for the students. All I see is languid body movements, big floppy T-shirts, and one guy with jeans so big that two people could inhabit them. Why do these young people in Brentwood Bay exude such confidence? Do they know or sense the extent to which adults have worked to build a learning environment for them?

---

50. John Keats, "On First Looking into Chapman's Home," The *Norton Anthology of English Literature*, ed. M. H. Abrams, vol. 2 (New York: Norton, 1962), 347.

    Or like stout Cortez, when with eagle eyes
    He stared at the Pacific—and all his men
    Looked at each other with a wild surmise —
    Silent, upon a peak in Darien.

51. Tom Barone's ethnographic account of the Appalachian community in North Carolina stands out as a excellent counter-example. See "Things of Wise and Things of Beauty: The Swain County High School Arts Program," *Daedalus 112* (1983): 1–28.

Does this sense of comfort have to do with the fact that they are from fairly affluent semi-rural communities? Is life just easier and slower here than it is in urban areas, or does it merely look that way to my harried city eyes?

When I think about getting to know these young people and their teachers, it seems as much a challenge as did trying to find ways to understand the racially and ethnically diverse school populations in Boston's Hennigan School.

Hennigan School: Coming Back a Stranger

When I first arrived at Boston's Hennigan School (an elementary school) in 1985 to do my first video ethnography, I was fresh "off the boat" from my life as a new immigrant, an "olah chadasha," in Israel. I had been a lecturer at the Hebrew University in Jerusalem and an English teacher who had taught in classrooms filled with young people from diverse ethnic and socioeconomic backgrounds. But I was an outsider at the Hennigan. Why did I find it so hard to connect with the students and teachers there? How could I be an outsider back in North America, where I was born? Was I in awe of the African-American and Hispanic cultures? How would I be able to tell their story? Was it hubris to think that I could cross racial and ethnic boundaries, even to visit? And how would I bridge the gap between my university culture at MIT and a school culture on the edge of a struggling, racially tense neighborhood? It did not seem fair that we, that I, had the privilege of studying them. Thus, my initial goal was to find ways to communicate without either invading their culture or losing my identity in it (if, indeed, we can be said to have singular "identities"). My hope was to talk and write about our interaction while looking for common interests.

The community of eager and ambitious researchers to which I belonged would itself have made an interesting story. We were a particularly complex mix of about 15 MIT graduate students, research associates, and faculty. Most of us came to this community with already established areas of expertise in education, psychology, artificial intelligence, computer animation, music and cognition, or art. (The Media Lab's philosophy was to bring together epistemologists, artists, and scientists under the rubric of media technology.) Finding ways to talk to each other across disciplinary boundaries was a challenge in those first months. Just reaching a tentative agreement on how to conduct our study or what to look for when making ethnographic fieldnotes was a major decision that was negotiated for many weeks. Seymour Papert, author *of Mindstorms: Children, Computers, and Powerful Ideas*, was the head of our MIT group, Epistemology and Learning. Sylvia Weir, author of *Cultivating Minds: A Logo Case Book*, along with Sherry Turkle, already world-renowned for her book, *The Second Self: Computers and the Human Spirit*, were also investigators and researchers with us at the Hennigan School, as were Edith Ackermann, professor at the Media Lab, and visiting scholar from Queens University, William Higginson.[52] Supported by grants that were given to the Media Lab from a consortium of computer and communications companies, we packed up our diverse resources and then unpacked ourselves and over 100 personal computers one autumn Sunday afternoon into the open-area pods at the Hennigan School.

Looking back, I realize I was probably in culture shock during those first months, overwhelmed by expectations and frozen by being thrust into a school with an agenda that was not yet mine. We were graduate researchers attached to large grants under a world-renowned thinker. We wanted to please our faculty advisor, yet we wanted to carve a new path; we wanted to present our culture in a positive light, yet be scholarly and critical of its limitations; we wanted to be open to changing our points of viewing, yet be cognizant of our own nearsightedness. Little did I know how those early experiences with the children, their teachers, and my colleagues would change my life. And, although Papert's words still play and replay in my thoughts, his ideas have taken me to a different shore than even he had foreseen. I learned to juggle and reconfigure contradictions and discrepancies between theory and practice and find the broader patterns that weave new stories. Being lost on that foreign shore during those early months forced me to find a different voice, one that would enable me to launch a 3-year video ethnography of this emerging school-university partnership.[53]

---

52. Seymour Papert, *Mindstorms: Children, Computers and Powerful Ideas* (New York: Basic Books, 1980); Sylvia Weir, *Cultivating Minds: A Logo Case Book* (New York: Harper and Row, 1986); Sherry Turkle, *The Second Self: Computers and the Human Spirit* (New York: Simon and Schuster, 1984).

53. Seymour Papert, at that time, was influenced by Carol Gilligan's work. See Carol Gilligan, *In a Different Voice: Psychological Theory and Women's Development* (Cambridge, MA: Harvard University Press, 1982). Our research group examined how and if girls' intellectual

The Growth of a Culture

Whenever two cultures interact, both are changed. Within the first few months, we brought to the Hennigan School: personal computers, a programming language (Logo), a word processing program, BankStreet Writer, and ourselves. I see these "gifts" as our peace offerings. Project Headlight was the name we ascribed to this cultural meeting of minds from the Hennigan School and the MIT research community and our machines. From the very beginning our goal was to participate in the culture of the school in order to make incremental changes to the lives of both children and adults through the use of new technologies. Yes, it now sounds almost patronizing: "Researchers Bring Tools to Poor Schools." But, in 1985, it seemed a fair exchange of precious gifts.

A year earlier, in 1984, Papert, Weir, and Turkle decided to seek out a school within the Greater Boston School District to try out the tenets of the constructionist philosophy implicit within *Mindstorms*, Papert's 1980 treatise on computers and education. Two teachers at the Hennigan School, supported by their principal and vice-principal, responded to his search; theirs was the only proposal Papert received that did not originate from a school administrative body. The Hennigan School was also selected because it was not a model school but, rather, a typical inner-city school coping with the same problems as were other schools across North America—problems such as how to help children at risk, how to cope with drug problems, how to provide equal choices and opportunities for children from diverse ethnic and socioeconomic backgrounds, and how to encourage learning in mathematics and the sciences. The Hennigan School, located in a Boston community called Jamaica Plains, had the open-style architecture typical of the politically active 1960s large-area "pods" and classrooms divided by sliding walls. The school's physical structure was perfect for the technological innovations we were proposing.

One of our dreams was that constructionist technologies would be able to address widespread social and educational problems by enabling students to

---

development was softer, more negotiational than was previously considered to be the case. In an article, Papert stated: "Just as Gilligan describes another voice for moral discourse, perhaps we are seeing another voice for mathematical discourse—indeed, for the whole spectrum of intellectual endeavor." See Seymour Papert, "The Conservation of Piaget: The Computer as Grist to the Constructionist Mill," in *Constructivism in the Computer Age*, eds. G. Forman and P. B. Pufall (Hillsdale, NJ: Lawrence Erlbaum Associates, 1988), 12.

be architects of their own knowledge. Just looking at the research literature from a few of the education and technology research centers around
North America indicates the importance of situated and contextual knowledge cultures. The Banks Street College research group, inspired by inno-
vators Jan Hawkins, Kathleen Wilson, and Margaret Honey, was (and still
is) conducting research and designing computer-based learning environments for children's social construction.[54] John Seely Brown, Allan Collins,
and Paul Duguid developed a theory of situated and cognitive apprenticeship in computational learning environments based on Jean Lave's semi-
nal 1977 work.[55] Roy Pea, director of the Institute of Research and Learning (IRL), situated between Stanford and Xerox PARC, laid down the
foundation for research project-based based learning using "cognitive
technologies."[56]

In the meantime, John Bransford and his colleagues at Vanderbilt were
working on video-based units in an attempt to involve students in scientific inquiry.[57] In fact, Bransford wanted to build a tool, similar to Logo,
that would enable young people to become producers of their own videos.

---

54. See Kathleen Wilson, "The Palenque Optical Disc Prototype: The Design of a Multimedia Discovery-based Experience for Children," *Children's Environments Quarterly* 5, no. 4
(1988): 7–13. See Margaret Honey, Babette Moeller, Cornelia Brunner, Dorothy Bennett,
Peggy Clements, and Jan Hawkins, "Girls and Design: Exploring the Question of Technological Imagination," *Center for Technology Education (CTE) Technical Report 17* (1991).
55. John Seeley Brown, Allan Collins, and Paul Duguid, "Situated Cognition and the Culture of Learning," 32–42; Jean Lave, "Cognitive Consequences of Traditional Apprenticeship Training in West Africa," *Anthropology and Education Quarterly 8* (1977): 177–80.
56. Roy Pea, "Beyond Amplification: Using the Computer to Reorganize Mental Function-
ing," *Educational Psychologist 20* (1985): 167–82. Several years later, Pea, as Dean at North-
western University, established the Collaborative Visualization Project (Co-Vis), a National
Science Foundation-supported initiative to enable young people to learn about science by
conducting science as scientists do. Designing tools for visualizing data, such as global
weather patterns, was a large part of the initiative to encourage students to participate in
data gathering and in the data analysis of visual and computational learning environments.
See also, Roy Pea, "The Collaborative Visualization Project," *Communications of the ACM
36* (1993): 60–63; and Roy Pea and Louis Gomez, "Distributed Multimedia Learning Environments: Why and How?" *Interactive Learning Environments 2* (1992): 73–109.
57. See the following articles: John D. Bransford, "Computer, Videodisks and the Teaching
of Thinking," (paper presented at the 1985 American Educational Research Association,
Washington, DC); John D. Bransford and N. S. McCarrell, "A Sketch of a Cognitive Approach to Comprehension: Some Thoughts about Understanding What It Means to Com-
prehend," in *Thinking: Readings in Cognitive Science*, eds. P. N. Johnson-Laird and P. C.
Watson (Cambridge, England: Cambridge University Press, 1977), 377–99.

The tool that emerged was called Producer.[58] (Bransford and his colleagues are cognitive theorists, and they examine the effects of video on comprehension, perception, and mathematical problem-solving.)[59]

With a strong Artificial Intelligence orientation, computer scientist Elliot Soloway at the University of Michigan built tools to enable children to construct hypermedia documents.[60] In his more current work, Soloway and his colleagues participate with communities of students as they explore science through the design of sophisticated technologies developed for distributed knowledge construction. Similarly, Marlene Scardamalia and Carl Bereiter, along with their research team at the Ontario Institute of Studies in Education, built a text-based collaborative writing tool called CSILE.[61] CSILE is a tool that enables children to construct collaborative texts and to annotate each other's works. They also promoted a theory of cognitive structures called *intentional learning*. Similarly, at the University of California, Berkeley, Marcia Linn and Andy diSessa developed theories of knowledge construction.[62] Linn analyzed the cognition of students who wrote programs in the computer language Lisp, and diSessa worked with students who were learning physics using his object-oriented program called Boxer. For diSessa, physics deals with "a rather large number of fragments rather than one or even any small number of integrated structures one might call 'theories.' Many of these fragments can be understood as simple abstractions from common experiences that are taken as relatively primitive in the sense that they generally need no explanation; they

---

58. John D. Bransford, Robert Sherwood, and Ted Hasselbring, "The Video Revolution and Its Effects on Development: Some Initial Thoughts," in *Constructivism in the Computer Age*, eds. G. Forman and P. B. Pufall (Hillsdale, NJ: Lawrence Erlbaum Associates, 1988).
59. Ibid., 180–89.
60. Elliot Soloway, Mark Guzdial, Kathy Brade, Luke Hohmann, Iris Tabak, Peri Weingrad, and Phyllis Blumenfeld, "Technological Support for the Learning and Doing of Design," in *Foundations and Frontiers of Adaptive Learning Environments*, eds. M. Johns and D. H. Winne (New York: Springer, 1992).
61. Carl Bereiter and Marlene Scardamalia, "Cognitive Coping Strategies and the Problem of Inert Knowledge," in *Thinking and Learning Skills*, vol. 2, *Current Research and Open Questions*, eds. S. S. Chipman, J. W. Segal, and R. Glazer (Hillsdale, NJ: Lawrence Erlbaum Associates, 1985), 65–80; Marlene Scardamalia and Carl Bereiter, "Computer Support for Knowledge-Building Communities," ed. T. Koschmann, *CSCL: The Theory and Practice of an Emerging Paradigm* (Mahwah, NJ: Lawrence Erlbaum Associates, 1996), 209–249.
62. See Marcia C. Linn, "The Cognitive Consequences of Programming Instruction in the Classrooms," *Educational Researcher 14* (1985): 14–29; Andrea A. diSessa, "Learning about Knowing," in *Children and Computers*, ed. E. Klein (San Francisco: Jossey-Bass, 1985).

simply happen."[63] I always thought this to be a good definition of the kind of learning that took place both in the Hennigan School and in Bayside Middle School. His theory of physics resonates strongly with the notion of *bricolage*, a term first used by Claude Lévi-Strauss to describe a person who builds from pieces and does not have a specific goal at the onset of the project.[64]

Robert Lawler, another leader in the field of computational learning environments, points out that the *bricoleur* is always involved in a process, even if that process is not directional.[65] Lawler, actively involved in the study of cognition and computers, conducted a formative and in-depth study of one child's learning in a computer culture. He was also a regular visitor at the lab in those days, and he often discussed his ideas, which were inspired by Piaget's focus on the child as a model for cognitive development. Lawler coined the term *microviews* to describe the cognitive process of knowing within *microworlds* (a term he attributes to a 1972 Marvin Minsky and Seymour Papert progress report that defines the internal and external nature of intellectual structures).

> The important idea encoded in the term micro is the centrality of fragmentation in the process of knowing: the external world can only be experienced as a collection of microworlds.... Microviews are internal, cognitive structures built through interacting with such microworlds and reflecting that fragmentary process of knowing.[66]

Throughout the 1980s and early 1990s, a plethora of research articles and books were published on epistemology, culture, and knowledge. Eugene F. Provenzo, Jr. addressed popular culture issues concerning young people's construction of knowledge in electronic learning environments.[67] David Jonassen looked at constructivism and the "technology of instruction" through the hypermedia lens. In fact, Jonassen walks the middle ground between purist constructionists (such as Papert), who situate

---

63. Andrea A. diSessa, "Knowledge in Pieces," in *Constructivism in the Computer Age*, eds. G. Forman and P. B. Pufall (Hillsdale, NJ: Lawrence Erlbaum Associates, 1988), 52.
64. See Claude Lévi-Strauss, *The Savage Mind* (Chicago: University of Chicago Press, 1966).
65. Robert W. Lawler, *Computer Experience and Cognitive Development: A Child's Learning in a Computer Culture* (West Sussex, UK: Ellis Horwood, 1985).
66. Ibid., 193.
67. Eugene F. Provenzo, Jr., *Video Kids: Making Sense of Nintendo* (Cambridge, MA: Harvard University Press, 1991).

knowledge construction as an internal condition that gains richness through making and manipulating objects, and the instructionists, who design learning environments as knowledge packages to be used by learners. Jonassen, who once developed instructional techniques that lead learners through what he has called "frames" toward "a planned set of responses," now links constructivism more closely to the technology of learning.[68]

A breakthrough article titled "Partners in Learning," by Gavriel Salomon, David Perkins and Tamar (Tami) Globerson captured the spirit of the 1980s and early 1990s insofar as computers and epistemological issues were concerned.[69] Globerson, before her untimely and tragic death, was a central player in our culture at MIT, where she had spent her sabbatical, so I was quite familiar with her theory of computers in education. Salomon, provoking Papert by demanding more proof for his constructionist theories about children's epistemological pluralism, was invited to present and debate with Papert on a few occasions.[70] And Perkins, just "down the Charles River at that other university" was an inspiration for those of us (Idit Harel and Yasmin Kafai, in particular) who were studying knowledge as design (which happens to be the title of his 1986 book).[71] Salomon, Perkins, and Globerson influenced a generation of thinkers about the *effects with* and the *effects of* a technology. *Effects with* occur when people work with technologies—the technology becomes a partner that can do things people cannot, whereas *effects of* occur when "cognitive residue" can be used after we stop working with a technology. "Extending the reach of minds," or what Salomon often refers to as *mindfulness*, is what can happen when people are engaged in their learning, an idea I return to in chapter 10.[72]

Our MIT constructionist community of the late 1980s was sometimes referred to as a *closed shop*, one not interested in outside inspiration. Part of that impression is well-founded; the level of intellectual fervor is high at MIT and is likened to trying to take a sip from a fire

---

68. David Jonassen, *Programmed Instruction: A Program* (Greensboro, NC: University of Greensboro, 1976). See also Thomas M. Duffy and David Jonassen, *Constructivism and the Technology of Instruction: A Conversation* (Hillsdale, NJ: Lawrence Erlbaum Associates, 1992).
69. Gavriel Salomon, David N. Perkins and Tamar Globerson, "Partners in Cognition: Extending Human Intelligence with Intelligent Technologies," *Educational Researcher 20* (1991): 2–9.
70. Gavriel Salomon, *Interaction of Media, Cognition and Learning* (San Francisco, CA: Jossey-Bass, 1979); Gavriel Salomon, *Communication and Education* (Beverly Hills, CA: Sage, 1981).
71. David Perkins, *Knowledge as Design* (Hillsdale, NJ: Lawrence Erlbaum Associates, 1986).
72. Gavriel Salomon, David N. Perkins, and Tamar Globerson: op. cit., 2.

hose. Moreover, our project, which began in 1985, was one of the first to entail large teams of researchers conducting observational investigations in computer-rich school cultures, so we had few exemplars to examine. We were one of the exemplar projects finding our own path. Our financial backing (from such groups as the National Science Foundation, IBM, Apple Corporation, the McArthur Foundation, and the LEGO Corporation) provided a level of support that was unheard of in those years. If one looks at the faculty and students from the Learning and Epistemology Group—the name of our MIT research group, it seems clear that the work that was done in this particular research culture spread to a range of academic and industrial settings, furthering the theoretical basis of constructionism into deeper permutations; but let me step back a bit, to the fall of 1985.

Culture Shock

By the fall of 1985, our group began investigating the use of Logo at the Hennigan School, while at the same time teaching the teachers, the students, and ourselves how to program in this computer language. ("Teaching" is probably not the best word. What we did was to develop a style of talking about the microworld of mathematics through programming in Logo.) Project Headlight involved one-third of the school—16 teachers and approximately 250 students from grades 2 through 5. Four of the teachers taught regular classes in English; four taught the advanced work classes (classes for students who were able to move quickly through the curriculum and thus have time for other projects); three were special education teachers; and five taught bilingual classes in Spanish. The teachers, along with the principal and vice-principal, visitors, and the MIT researchers, attended Project Headlight planning meetings every couple of weeks. They also participated in 3-week summer workshops held either in the school or at the Media Lab.

In the center of each pod are the computers, arranged like a Y with equal arms. My first reaction is that the exposed wires and the cramped spaces around the joining of the tables are dangerous for children. The structure situates the teacher as the leader, rather than the facilitator. I envision a pod with the computers arranged in circles, with wires enclosed, promoting both freedom of movement and collaboration. The teachers and my co-researchers agree. We move the computers into large circles.

Branching off from the wide hall connecting the pods are the teachers' lunch room and a room that became known as Turtle Cove. Turtle Cove is the space our MIT group uses as a common office, workspace, cloakroom, and meeting room. This windowless concrete space, sometimes visited by an overly friendly rodent, acts as much as a meeting place as it does as a storage room. It contains our camera and computer equipment, a blackboard, several child-sized chairs, and a slab of plywood—once a door—that functions as a large work table.

Fieldnotes (September, 1985): The school is a sprawling two-story concrete building with graffiti covering the outside walls. I walk into the building without sensing that I have come inside; the inside corridors have the same empty, wide feeling that the outside of the building has. I follow the stairs to my right and proceed up a long graduated concrete ramp to find myself in an open space connected to another open space by a wide corridor. These two open spaces are what we call the pods, with classrooms jutting out around each of the two pods. The spaces are quite open, bare and gray—concrete walls exaggerated by the cold tones of overhead fluorescent lighting. Posters of children's projects hang on the walls, providing a welcome invitation for future possibilities.

To this day, I remember my fear of being assaulted while walking the two blocks to the school from the "T," the Metropolitan Boston Transportation Authority (MBTA). After the first week I always arranged a lift with a colleague. I remember the bold red and black graffiti covering the low, gray concrete building where parents would leave their children for the 7-hour day. And I remember the hallways—the long hallways where children would be told to walk in straight lines to their classrooms and to the cafeteria, often being yelled at to keep quiet. The corridors magnified voices.

In spite of the yelling, and teachers yelled a lot, they were dedicated to making the school better. After all, they carried out the arduous task of attempting to teach children who were in great need of positive experiences and encouraging feedback. Looking back, I now think my most disturbing thought was that we would never be able to change the yelling and anger, and that I would be not able to enter this culture without a heavy heart. Although I have been an insider in school cultures, teaching school and university both in Canada and in Israel, I was not secure in my role as a researcher, a participant observer, an "outsider." I knew I would always be gazing through a looking glass, a filter, or, as Henri Giroux says, I would be peering past a border crossing.[73]

In October of 1995, 10 years after we entered the Hennigan for first time, I returned to talk to some of the teachers. The cold gray concrete had been painted in warm pastel colors. The teachers had a few more lines on their faces, streaks of gray hair, and they looked softer and more graceful than they had before. It was as if nothing had changed, and yet so much had changed. This group of teachers, once the pioneers of school computer cultures, were in a constant battle for technologies that would keep their students networked and retooled. They asked about one of the more fashionable researchers, who, to them, seemed as shining with energy as a movie star. What was so-and-so doing now? And how was that tall guy who had long hair, the one who fixed all the computers? I couldn't resist taking photographs. Not video. I wanted to capture moments, moments with young children sitting at computers working on Logo programs. I tried to reinvent with my still camera what life had been like once I had stopped feeling like a stranger at the Hennigan. I now look at these somewhat grainy photographs with a bittersweet sadness for the ragged edges I might have smoothed. The photographs are not a study of what was, but a representation of my wiser eyes looking back on my life with the children at the Hennigan. Oddly, many of the boys and girls that I photographed there in 1995 reminded me of the children we worked with in the late 1980s. They were enthusiastic about what they had made in Logo; they wanted to share their thinking about these objects. Who says you can never go back? You can, if you are open to what is the same as well as to what is different, and if you can see the past through the lens of the present.

Graffiti: Artifact of Revolt

Our research team worked with one wing of the school, consisting of 16 teachers (and their classes), the principal, and the vice-principal. My focus was fine-grained. I wanted to study the culture of computers at the Hennigan by developing portraits emerging from long-term relationships with several students. I wanted to know if a computer-rich culture could give these children and adults the physical, social, and intellectual space to understand their own thinking, about both the things they imagine and the things they create. I also wanted to maintain my sensitivity about the

---

73. Henri Giroux, *Border Crossings: Cultural Workers and the Politics of Education* (New York: Routledge, 1993).

interaction of the school culture with the MIT culture. To accomplish these goals, I conducted formal and informal videotaped conversations with the children in order to make sense of what happens to their thinking within an emerging computer culture. (From 1985 to 1988, I visited the school approximately twice a week, observing, videotaping, and working with children and teachers on their projects.) I developed a style of videotaping that described what was happening in the computer pods, in classrooms, and during extracurricular music, art, and science activities. I tried to capture the spectrum of life in the school.

I did not think that the Hennigan was a model learning environment in the fall of 1985, and I do not think it is now. What I observed in my first visits was a school beset with rituals of discipline—rituals that span the history of schooling. As I reflect back on the school, the image that comes to my mind is one of graffiti. The graffiti were a most fitting response to the intransigence of a rigid physical and social structure infused with archaic forms of controlling unacceptable behavior. The front of the building was bereft of any form of greenery. A grassy field, however, lay at the back of the school. In a far corner of this field there were a few climbing structures upon which the children could play at recess. The girls, mostly African-American and Hispanic, played skip rope on the asphalt of the parking lot, directly under the graffiti. Smaller groups of girls and boys in gender-based groups often hung out by the climbing apparatus, climbing or playing games. The boys used the open field for kicking a few balls around and running.

At recess, playground supervisors monitored the children. In my 3 years at the Hennigan, I never saw a classroom teacher outdoors playing with the children. The lines separating teachers and young people were clearly drawn, as one would expect in a traditional school. In the name of maintaining order and protecting the children from harm, playground supervisors became expert in resolving conflicts. The method most commonly used was that of singling out certain children in order to monitor a particular group's behavior. Josh, the precocious 10-year-old I mentioned earlier, told me that, when yelling at a group of children, certain adults would make up a name, saying something to the effect of, "Casandra, stop talking!" Even if no one's name was Casandra, the children would freeze into attention for fear that their names would be used next. At the end of recess, a hand bell rung by the head playground supervisor informed the children that it was time to return to their classrooms. Either their teachers would come to fetch them or the recess supervisor would lead them in lines to their classroom. The children then walked in scraggly lines through large hallways from the open-area pods into their classrooms.

Bayside Middle School: Walking the Corridors

How differently from the Hennigan School does Bayside Middle School welcome strangers. Walking into the bright sky-lit corridors, with children's art covering every possible blank space along the upper half of the walls, I am struck by the openness of the physical space. Smells of cooking draw me to a kitchen-like classroom, where teenage girls and boys are baking sweets. Girls and boys are busy in what we used to call "Shop," now referred to as Technology Education. In British Columbia, both girls and boys are assigned to these courses. The disadvantage is clear: There is less choice for those who do not want to take a given "elective." On the other hand, both girls and boys get to try on new roles and to stretch their abilities. (This is certainly more equitable than it used to be. In my school in Winnipeg in the early 1960s, boys took Shop and girls took Home Economics—a fancy name for baking, cooking, and sewing.)

I meet Ted Riecken, my colleague from the University of Victoria, and the vice-principal, Keven Elder, in the school office. Keven is a happy, outgoing kind of administrator with a crop of gray hair outlining his young face. He tells me he's finishing his doctorate and has written several reports on using technology to engage children in their school practices.[74] He encourages others to participate fully in the culture of the school—a school that seems to have many overlapping activities. The first thing Keven asks me is whether I want a cup of coffee. When I accept, he pours the coffee into a cup and passes it to me. "I'm home," I say to myself.

After the friendly introductory chit-chat, Keven gives me his tour. The school is divided into four main pods: North, South, East, and West. A pod at Bayside is a collection of classrooms that are connected to each other; it is what, at the Hennigan, was called a wing. The school has 750 students, aged 11 to 14, in grades 6 through 8; 45 teachers; 3 administrators, and several support staff. It's a small school, much smaller than the

---

74. Keven Elder, "Education and Technology: Today and Tomorrow," *Royal Commission on Education Report*, 1988.

Hennigan. Keven and Wayne Hunter, the principal, have worked hard to build a sense of community with each of the pods. Classes within a given pod share many activities and engage in competitive sports as a group. The pods seem like mini-schools within a school, providing shelter for students on their journey through adolescence. There is something comforting about being in the middle, I think. Maybe this thought reflects my own phase of life. No longer young; not yet old. Somewhere in the middle.

Each classroom at Bayside has a door leading outside. Having these doors contributes to the feeling that the classroom is a home rather than a guarded enclosure. I see these open doors as indicating that classes are no longer cut off from the world—they no longer exist as cloistered islands. Access to the Internet has opened the doors for many students, who regularly post their school projects to outsiders. Shared learning is not a fantasy for the future. These kinds of learning experiences are happening in educational centers throughout the world, even if what is being produced still looks a bit messy.

Annotation: Imagine the security problems open doors would create for children in inner-city schools! Could schools in urban communities have open doors and playgrounds without fences? Schools across North America ensure their students' safety by asking them to pass through a metal-detector on their way in. Would teachers and children in an inner-city school feel safe in a school built like Bayside? On the front page of the September 30, 1996 *Vancouver Sun*, Ian Haysom (Southam Newspapers) reports that "every one of the 635 schools in the Los Angeles district is surrounded by three-meter high chain-linked fencing; hand-held metal detectors and body searches are used to keep knives and guns out of the classroom, and the school district operates it own police force, placing an armed officer on every high school and junior-high campus."

Students at the Bayside Middle School created a rudimentary website describing their study of Clayoquot Sound. (You can view some of the products of their study at the MERLin website or on *The Global Forest* CD-ROM.) Gerri Sinclair of the ExCITE Laboratory at Simon Fraser University conducted the Barkley Sound Project, which enables students to connect with scientists.[75] Students work with scientists in both the Jason Project and the CoVis Project.[76] And teachers communicate beyond their walls. The Latitude 28 School House is just one small example of a space that provides a wealth of resource materials for teachers. Most recently, educators from sixty countries met at the Media Lab to form a working

---

75. See <http://www.excite.sfu.ca>.
76. See <http://www.jasonproject.org> and <http://www.covis.nwu.edu>.

community, 2B1, focused on "bringing computers to children in techno-logically isolated places."[77]

At Bayside, many (although not all) of the teachers are delighted with these possibilities. As we wander down corridors, I notice that every two classrooms share a small adjoining room. In the class I first visit, Joe Grewal's, the extra space has been converted into a computer workroom for special projects. This workroom is about 7 feet wide and runs the length of the classroom, connecting Joe's class to that of his colleague. Glass walls from desk level to ceiling give this space a unique connection to the class-room; they also create a sense of privacy. From Joe's class, I can see into the adjacent classroom, or, rather, I could have if the teacher had not hung posters on the glass walls. In this workroom, there are several computers and video workstations, each with enough space for five or six people. Joe's students design their HyperCard projects in this space, and it is here that I will spend a great many hours in conversation with them. The teach-ers have used their extra workroom spaces to work on lesson plans, to talk on the phone, to read and respond to email, or to just sit quietly with a few students to discuss projects.

One of Bayside's 1993 innovations was to get each teacher a computer with networked email. The network was then still internal, but, by 1996, the teachers in each classroom had access to the Internet. For example, when I call Keven from my home in Vancouver and ask him which teach-ers might like to work with me on a collaborative study of an endangered rainforest, he dashes off an email message to his faculty asking them to get back to him. They do, within the day (or hour!). But what surprises me most is that the public announcement (PA) system still blares into the class-room, interrupting work. "Will Jessica Grant please come to the office?" Why don't some technologies ever get thrown out?

Each pod, consisting of 10 classrooms, has its own Macintosh computer lab (the size of a regular classroom), with one computer for, at most, every two students. These labs are not project-based environments. In these rooms of wall-to-wall computers (color Mac Classics), the students learn how to use HyperCard, Claris Works, MS Word, and other software programs. The school's computer club uses one of these labs for more advanced projects. Moreover, every person in the school has the right to an email account and has had access to the Internet since 1994. This was certainly

---

77. Nicholas Negroponte, "2B1," *Wired 5*, no. 6 (1997): 184.

not the case at the Hennigan. When I think back to 1985 through 1987, I remember how hard it was just to get our internal network set up to share Logo tools. Transferring stuff electronically has not always been as easy as it is today. But if we couldn't easily move data across our internal networks in 1985, we could walk around the computer pods sharing our conceptual tools. And we were passionate and engaged in our work, or, as one of the students called it, our "hard fun."

Hennigan School: The Watering Well

The students involved in Project Headlight at the Hennigan had a fair degree of freedom to meander around the computer pods during their daily computer time. The wide corridor between the pods was often used for large group activities, ranging from spreading out huge sheets of paper for painting to making papier maché objects to having weekly teachers' meetings with Papert, Weir, and a representative group of researchers. The computer pods were similar to the watering wells of ancient villages—they were places where people could congregate and share ideas. At the Hennigan, the pods were places for adults to help the children with their programming ideas and to talk with them as they worked at their computers. They were also meeting places for the myriad visitors who came from all over the world to see our experimental project. But the most wonderful thing about the pods was that they provided a place for students to observe and to discuss each other's ideas. Often, students would walk around the circles, hunting for new ideas and engaging in conversations that would lead to new collaborations. To my eyes, the pods were a welcome sight/site. I stopped focusing on the graffiti and started focusing on the students' eagerness to tell their stories of programming in Logo.

Often I would videotape the students from afar. Curious about their gestures, I found myself watching them as they worked alone or together. Some students hovered, half standing, by their computers, one knee bent on the chair, the other supporting their body weight. Others moved excitedly from side to side on their chairs, leaning into the computer. Children who frequently worked together gestured a lot when communicating ideas to each other. "No, Josh, it should look like this. Not like this," Thomas would shout, waving his arms and acting out the movement of a car they had programmed using Logo. And Mindy would talk to Thomas, both with her voice and with her hands, while looking at the computer. Most of the students were soon able to talk to others while staring at their monitors. Most probably the video-game culture, just beginning its rise in popularity, contributed to this ability.

Typing, or what we now call keyboarding, was never formally taught to the Hennigan students. A computer program for teaching typing skills was available, but few ever used it. They created their own ways of typing that, eventually, came to resemble standard styles. But, in the beginning of the project, you would see kids rigidly pointing one finger from each hand toward the keyboard. Or you would see two fingers moving rhythmically all over the keyboard. Our Logo community had a wild mix of all kinds of styles of doing and thinking. However, what seemed most strange to me at that time was to see boys and men keyboarding. Keyboarding had none of the gendered meanings that had been associated with typing in the 1950s, 1960s, and 1970s. These boys did not think that only girls learned to keyboard. The gender-specific stereotype surrounding typing died with the advent of the computer. And why not? The computer is not a typewriter; it is a machine for increased power and dexterity.

Bayside Middle School: Places to Meet

When I review the video of Bayside Middle School that I have shot more recently, I realize that the computer labs, in addition to being used for staff development and mentoring, are instructional places for learning programs and completing assignments.

Often, students' real-life desktops are gathering places for reference materials, articles, magazines, and binders. The computer is the central tool they use to bring together ideas obtained from these other, more linear, media forms. While

Annotation: Rolling around the room in their wheeled chairs creates a distinct "look and feel" to the space. I have often wanted to shoot this scene using a time-lapsed camera. I would place the camera on the ceiling to capture the crisscrossing of linear movements that seem both random and patterned; a real life manifestation of a virtual reality hyper-linking program.

they work, they chat, discuss ideas about their projects, and generally work in a relaxed manner. There is an animated calm in the labs. The chairs the students sit on have little wheels on the bottom, and they can roll over to visit a friend across the aisle.

Bayside has many less formal places than the Hennigan for the exchange of ideas and for social interchange, such as the locker dugouts and the bathrooms, where students tend to gather for furtive chats. But the school auditorium, which also serves as the general lunchroom, and the gym are the places where most of these close-encounters-of-a-second-kind occur. The auditorium is situated to the left of the entrance to the school, the gym to the right. The architects and school board envisioned the auditorium as the center of community activities. So, before you even arrive at the school office, you pass the auditorium with its large glass doors inviting you into the common space. This room, overlooking the landscaped school yards, is big enough to seat 250 people. In the years that I visited Bayside, I attended concerts, dances, lectures, and community information days (with booths set up by the local police, health clinics, and others)—all in the auditorium. The soft wooden floor of the stage provided a good foundation for curricular and extracurricular dance programs. And the acoustics, along with the wired audio at the podium, provided a professional sound system for invited lecturers. The lectures I arranged with experts concerning the issues surrounding the rainforest at Clayoquot Sound, such as David Cohen, the dean of the Faculty of Law at the University of Victoria, were attended by an audience of about 150 grade 6, 7, and 8 students.

The social time for most of these students occurs during lunch in the auditorium. Teachers eat in the teachers' room, and lunchtime monitors are hired to supervise the students. The kids sit with whomever they choose, a decision that is often negotiated before lunch. After our field trip to Clayoquot Sound, Natalie invites me to spend time with her at the lunch table on every visit I make to the school. I appreciate being given the time to "break bread" with her and her friends. From time to time, as I eat one of the mustardy hot-dogs, the stories of the day emerge. The students run the cafeteria in the lunchroom, even taking care of the cash register. A very kind woman from the neighborhood prepares hot food. At lunch one of the young women who sits with me is content to eat a few cheesies and drink a coke. She is very skinny, with long brown limp hair, an elfin smile, and big brown soft eyes. We talk about her image of being a girl and other issues that seem to relate to how she treats her body. She is twelve years old, eats food with little nutritional value, and seems unconcerned about what she is doing to her body, despite suggestions from her peers and from adults.

Hennigan School: Digesting and Appropriating

Lunchtime at the Hennigan was (and still is) a gregarious and almost chaotic time. Sounds from the big old auditorium filled the adjoining open corridors, where they echoed mockingly. On many occasions, I would walk in line with the children to the auditorium for lunch. Hot meals were edible but not tasty. Some of the children brought their own lunches from home, in spite of the fact that the school lunches were free. The tables in the auditorium were arranged in rows, which were easily monitored by the same persons who monitored the outdoor recess period. Adult supervisors paced up and down the aisles and around their tables while the children ate. When spoken to at all by adults, the children were addressed in loud voices and told not to talk during lunch time. This was curious, as the place was full of the sounds of kids who know that they can play outside as soon as they finish eating. Those children whose tables had been "good" were the first to get permission to leave the auditorium after finishing lunch. (Throughout the day, the auditorium was used as a detention hall. Thus, being detained there may, for some of the children, have denoted punishment.) Children were regularly warned that if they talked they would be the last to go outside after lunch. This warning rarely changed their behavior, as they continued to bump into each other "accidentally on purpose" while sitting at the long arborite tables. Annie, particularly upset about the way she was treated by the lunchtime monitors, told me it bothered her to have adults yelling while she was eating.

After my first few visits to the Hennigan, I realized that hanging out in the auditorium allowed me to observe the dynamics of the hidden curriculum. While routinely having the cooks and kitchen staff pack my styrofoam plate with school food, I came to understand the receiving-of-stuff culture of the school. Children in schools are receivers—receivers of knowledge, of acceptable ways of behaving, of homework assignments, and, when available, of food. In school, food and standards of behavior are combined, as they often are at home, in restaurants, and in friends' homes. The difference is that, at home, people often make an effort to combine enjoyable social intercourse with satisfying the biological need for food. At the Hennigan, children were given food, the "raw materials," without being provided with an environment that would encourage them to feel, "this is mine; I want to make it part of me, I can appropriate this." *Appropriation* refers to a situation in which a person takes in an idea so fully that it is recreated in another form—internally.

Where were the teachers? They ate their lunch together in small groups throughout the different sections of the school. Often the teachers used this time to have a break from the children, to talk with their colleagues, and to catch up with constant bureaucratic demands (e.g., filling in grade sheets and attendance records). Our group of Headlight teachers was often engaged in a series of discussions during lunch, in addition to all those other meetings we scheduled with them! Special "brown-bag" sessions on mathematical thinking, Logo projects, or other related activities were held. One could say that the extra time needed for the full participation in Project Headlight did not encourage the teachers to spend routine time with the children, and one needs to ask what kind of message this sent them. The separation of teachers from children during routine functions reinforces the existing hierarchical structure within which the separate levels of school life fit. Teachers, children, staff members, and even principals are separated from each other by demarcation lines that maintain an illusion of order, safety, and stability. In a structure based on dominance, no one feels secure.[78] No one is really at the top of the pyramid; everyone, from cook to principal, is locked into a "receiving" grid, having too little room for appropriation and creativity. In other words, in traditional school cultures the adults, as well as the children, are receivers. The stuff they receive is different, but their roles are just as clearly delineated: cooks cook; teachers teach; janitors clean up; children obey rules and are expected to learn the unwritten curriculum—and we all lose out by not being allowed to give and receive our best and by not being given the chance to try on new roles. The receiving-of-stuff culture of the school stifles the possibility of children contributing to adults and to other children.

Although, over the last decade, I have focused on the learning experiences of children and adolescents as they engage in activities that seem to unravel the traditional instructional curriculum, I have always known that, in order to understand school cultures introducing computers, I need to understand the adult members of schools. However, I do not necessarily

---

78. Michael Apple is well known for his inclusion of those who take care of our schools. In several talks, presented at the American Association for Educational Research, he has recommended that janitors and cooks become part of school curriculum committees. To explore his ideas of power more fully, see Michael W. Apple, *Education and Power* (Boston, MA: Routledge and Kegan Paul, 1982).

agree with many of my colleagues, who believe that the only way to change schools is to change teachers. Yes, to some degree, teachers do have the power to make changes. And they need to be supported for the changes they make as well as respected for their knowledge and expertise. However, the kind of change I am addressing in this book has to do with the introduction of electronic technologies, a learning phenomenon that is occurring throughout the world, involving both adults and children. In other words, a societal change is occurring, both inside and outside the school walls and between all learners.

I want us think about education in ways that do not put learners of any age into pre-established roles but, rather, enable them to take chances while constructing and deconstructing knowledges through the use of technological partners. This can be done if we learners—researchers, parents, teachers, and students—work as communities of inquiry to layer our knowledges of ourselves and the world around us. Yes, it is true that, until very recently, only a handful of pioneering and enterprising teachers have been willing to make these changes—temproal and spatial changes wherein students wander around in "cyberspace" unchaperoned! But their risk has been worth the effort. These teachers are now ready to let go of their previous positions as gatekeepers and are defining roles that enable them to see the relationship between themselves and their students as one of partnership in learning. Let me tell you about some of these pioneering adults at both the Hennigan and the Bayside schools as the pasticcio thickens.

3
Gatekeepers of a Horseless Barn: Teachers in Transition

Learning is the human activity which least needs manipulation by others. Most learning is not the result of instruction. It is rather the result of unhampered participation in a meaningful setting.

—Ivan Illich
Deschooling Society

Teaching Beyond Borders

Teachers in the electronic era of global communications are currently deciding how best to bring what is "out there" into their classrooms.[79] International conferences at which educators share their innovations in virtual teaching have become commonplace. Government grants are not only supporting the infrastructure that will port all this knowledge around the globe and back again—at a price, of course—but are also facilitating research that addresses the future of classrooms without walls, universities without permanent faculty, and businesses without office buildings. Is anyone questioning how we will promote the

---

79. For more on educational changes using virtual classrooms and distance learning, see Jim Cummins and Dennis Sayers, *Brave New Schools* (New York: St. Martin's Press, 1995).

inspiration that teachers can bring when we are all hooked up to a windowless, and perhaps teacher-less, classroom?

The networked computer is changing the lives of teachers. Teachers are eager to have their students access electronic information so that they can engage in international communication. However, teachers know that meanings are attained through the integration of inner and outer experiences, and that students learn by making meanings, not only by receiving data. Many teachers are walking a tightrope, balancing instruction with construction, routine activities with spontaneous activities, and safety with risk. Traditional meanings ascribed to work and play are changing. Teachers, like the rest of us, can shop, bank, travel (virtually), read, socialize, and congregate in political groups without ever leaving their homes. If these teachers are experiencing boundary blurring in their personal lives, then will they not begin to teach differently? And let us not be naive enough to think that change is always good. It may be inevitable but it is neither necessarily nor intrinsically good for humanity.

I have often likened the role of the teacher to that of the artist. The artist produces an artifact that we, as audience, walk around, examine, and critique. We see the "real" world differently after we have read a poem with a teacher who knows how to show us what we missed in our own reading. The teacher creates a poem—a place that lives in our minds— and sometimes this poem takes on a life more multifaceted for us than it was for the poet. A good teacher makes an art form out of something that is already an art form. She builds on what exists for her, through her eyes, and presents it to us as a precious gift—something to learn about, to turn over in our minds, and to reshape for new reconstructions.

My goal is to give you a glimpse into the lives of several teachers I have come to know at both the Hennigan and Bayside schools. These people are not models, exemplar teachers, or experts for you to emulate. I present them as inspirational artists working with the technologies of our times. These are people who are not perfect, but whose commitment to teaching extends far beyond the use of any given technology. Their stories illustrate how, given the introduction of technologies into the school system, teachers can address the human issues of taking care of the intellectual, social, and emotional lives of young people. They show how teachers grow and change, becoming ever-active members of these emerging computer cultures.

The Changing Roles of Bayside Teachers

Joe's eating a sandwich is not the only sign that this class is not typical of most classes, even of those at Bayside. Joe's class feels more like a community than like a typical classroom. Tables are drawn together so that the students are able to work in groups; they do quite a bit of group work. They sit in clusters of four with their desks touching. Yet one senses space rather than clutter. Joe's desk is tucked away in a corner beside huge windows overlooking the forest and outdoor space (suggesting that he, too, is permitted to have private thoughts in a public space). His desk does not command authority in the traditional way. Joe finishes his sandwich and the lesson continues. His voice is gentle, warm, firm, and almost inaudible when he speaks to his class. You want to listen.

Fieldnotes (May 1993): I haven't finished drinking my sparkling mineral water but it's time to visit Joe Grewal's class for my afternoon at Bayside. I close my drink tightly and place it in my purse. Walking into the room, the first thing I see is Joe, wearing shorts and a sweatshirt, sitting cross-legged on a table drinking a bottle of sparkling mineral water and eating a sandwich. He is explaining an assignment to the young adults in his class. (He later explained that he had just come from gym class and had not had time to eat lunch. I guess he felt that I needed this explanation.) I ask myself how many times I have been in a class where the teacher was eating a sandwich. Never, is my answer. Schools are schools? Maybe not. Maybe Bayside is not about adults feeding children.

Joe's voice blends into the sounds of the rustling of shoes, the moving of paper, and the scraping of chairs as the students move from one position to another. Joe seems to be everywhere, even when he is not in the classroom. He is "present in his absence," as Madeleine Grumet so poetically writes.[80] At the same time, his presence does not appear to rule the class. Someone is always moving or working on a current project. The movements in the class are fluid, and no one looks to Joe for approval when moving or talking. Shoulders are low; heads shift from side to side; arms are active, engaged; and even the students' legs seem to fold slowly into soft angles. Moving and talking are part of the rhythm of the class. Many activities seem to be taking place, even when Joe is giving his instructions for a particular assignment. Joe, according to my camera's eye, has turned his classroom into a community.

Jon and Wendy (May 1993): Mr. Grewal does yell a lot and his voice is as gental as a donkey!

---

80. Madeleine Grumet, *Bitter Milk: Women and Teaching* (Amherst, MA: University of Massachusetts Press, 1988), xiii.

I watch Joe and the students and am struck by their level of engagement. Jen, Amber, Heather, Kelli, and many more find ways of weaving in and out of each other's thoughts, chatting continuously, obviously engrossed with each other's perspectives on the project at hand. I wonder how much of this has to do with the presence of computers (which play a large role in Joe's classroom) and how much just has to do with Joe's tender and inviting personality.

Even the more traditional teachers at Bayside realize that, in the last part of the 1990s, it is too late to keep the horses in the barn. The roles of teachers have always been in flux, but never as much as they are today. Sometimes teachers' roles change because the needs of society change, especially in times of war or political upheaval; sometimes the field takes on its own internal revolution, as in the 1980s' "reflective practitioner" phase.[81]

Kelli (May 1993): Dear Ricki, I love your computer, it's "way cool." Well, I guess I have to write something about your notes so I found your notes very interesting, they were deep, way deep! They went straight to the heart. Your words were very descriptive. DID YOU oops Did you like our carnival? I did, but they got a little to much cotton candy (but it did get me hyper!!!!!!) anyways back to my note. Well I think thats about all, but the rest of it was totally awesome!!! Love, Kelli

Most often, however, internal and external influences mirror each other, creating their own refractions.

It is often hard to pinpoint any exact source of change. Teachers are ready for the technologies that have entered their lives, and their field has undergone a constructionist shift. Knowledge is no longer thought of as a "substance" to be poured into children's heads. In the late 1990s, many educators are concerned with how learners put ideas together and how they break them apart to form new constructions, depending on the circumstances. And they are concerned with managing the various projects in which their students

Amber (May 1993): Ricki, I really enjoyed your, what should I call it, Story? Anyway I enjoyed it. I liked the constructive critisisum and of course, the good comments. It was neat how you made Mr. Grewal—or "Joe" actually sound like a nice man (just kidding). I'm quite a nosy person, so I like to hear about other peoples' lives. This could also be helpful towards our Bayside Multimedia project. I don't know what else to write about so I'll be seeing you soon?

are engaged. How many collaborative group projects can you have in a classroom without having an experienced, guiding adult to provide overviews, ask enticing questions, and, yes, to inspire others to initiate journeys? As important as it is for teachers to become researchers

---

81. See Donald Shon, *The Reflective Practitioner* (New York: Basic Books, 1983).

and facilitators, shaping material into forms that are interesting for others is still what good teachers do best.

Juggling: Teachers with Dexterity

Joe Grewal, Jordan Tinney, and Keven Elder (Bayside's vice-principal) are the teachers I worked with the most on the Clayoquot Project. Keven has a doctorate in education and also teaches courses in computer applications. He is a jovial and inviting person, who always has time (in spite of the fact that he is the busiest person I know). As long as it benefits the students in the school, his attitude is, "Let's do it." I mentioned in the previous chapter that the Clayoquot Project would have remained a dream if it had not been for Keven's attitude. He oversaw every detail of the planning, which included inviting teachers to participate, running planning meetings, and ensuring support from the school board for the speedy execution of research applications. If ever there is a prize for excellence in juggling, Keven should receive it. Without his ability to integrate the various threads of the Clayoquot Project into the overall theme of the school, this project would not have materialized. Unfortunately, because Keven's main contribution was "behind the scenes," it is not possible for me to describe his day-to-day activities. The mystery of the administrator. However, one of the teachers with whom I worked regularly was also an expert juggler.

Jordan Tinney is fast, efficient, and extremely accomplished in several knowledge domains. He has a degree in electrical engineering and a passion for science and technology. He completed his teacher education program at the University of Victoria a few years ago, and, at the time of the Clayoquot Project, he was completing a Master of Arts degree in Education. He's the new kid on the block at Bayside, and he is already applying for the job of vice-principal (anticipating Keven beginning his new job as vice-principal in the neighborhood high school). Jordan is one of those persons we all admire for having boundless energy. He also put the finishing touches on the school's electronic infrastructure, which made the networking fully operational. Along with Keven and Joe, Jordan has been one of the movers in the school's technology push.

As a researcher I have learned a lot from working with Jordan; much more, I think, than he has learned from me—although he questions my saying this. In a talk with Tara Goldstein, a visiting professor from the University of Toronto, and myself, Jordan says, "I really want to ... make sure the kids understand how to record observations and how to reason from those observations and to be able to present them in a manner that they can argue." Tara responds, "The process of observing, looking for data, collecting data, was really a lot of your project, no?" "Yes, yes," Jordan says, becoming animated.

> **Jordan:** Knowledge skills and attitudes are the important areas I'm working to cover now. I think they're attitudes we can work on all the way along. It's the knowledge base ... and the skills that I need to concentrate a bit on from here. That's why they're doing this, because they need some knowledge of force, mass, gravity, inertia, before they can create.

> **Tara:** Do you feel you've been neglecting ... the core curriculum?

> **Jordan:** Yeah. Because, I mean, the curriculum, despite all the talk about the good points and the bad points, has been devised by good teachers over the years. It didn't just float down.... Are we neglecting that stuff to work far more on the attitudes and the values? Yes, integrating a theme is a good idea, but it really comes down to "less is more." And is less more?

Jordan is struggling to balance the need to provide a "strong knowledge base" with the need to provide students with the means of developing a good attitude toward their learning. Not an unusual struggle for a teacher who is embarking on a journey in which some students are beginning to undertake independent explorations. It is the struggle between form and content in yet another guise.

Having grown up in a logging community, and having put himself through university by logging, Jordan is concerned about the communities that are affected by the closure of mills and logging companies. He favors the smaller logging companies in BC who have changed their practices over the years. It seems ironic that I would initiate a project to study the Clayoquot Sound dispute (i.e., whether logging should be allowed in this particular temperate rainforest) with someone who was once a logger and who grew up in a logging community. But then, one of my purposes in initiating the rainforest study is to provide students with the conceptual and computational tools to look at controversial data from diverse points of viewing. With the central teacher in my study sympathizing predominantly with the logging industry, and with me feeling more supportive of the environmentalists, our collaboration was able to provide students with different points of view concerning the data they collected. And with regard to the goal of providing students with choices, Jordan and I were of like mind.

Both Jordan and I believe that students need to have access to information and that they need to critique what is given to them in charts, graphs, videos, and/or articles. Working with Jordan means analyzing both the data and the media forms through which they are delivered. So we work on literacy issues, trying to enable students to become sophisticated interpreters of the various forms of media (ranging from newspaper articles to electronic databases, videos, photographs, lectures, diagrams, etc.). We gather, select, and analyze data for our group and individual portfolios. Of course, nothing is neat in this project. Jordan and I, like many researcher/teacher teams, stumble through our collaboration, many of our dreams remaining unrealized. Much of our work is still limited by time constraints—it took hours to digitize video with computers that never seemed to have enough RAM. I was always schlepping a scanner, a video camera, or a hard-drive from MERLin, my research lab at UBC, to Bayside. Once we spent months teaching the students how to digitize their movies,

Jordan Tinney (April 1995): Science is too often seen as a passive body of knowledge rather than an active process of questioning and seeking answers to problems. This view is furthered by the curriculum in science often not being relevant to students. Virtual Clayoquot, our study of Clayoquot Sound, helps students see an issue that is very relevant to their daily lives and the role that science plays in the exploration/management of our natural resources. Students who witness the impact of logging on the temperate rainforest often form their own questions and seek answers through a variety of means. The gathering of data through a variety of media allows students to form multimedia documentaries, sharing their view of a sensitive environmental issue with other classmates and with learners in distributed locations. The traditional view of a scientist leads to some of our students seeing science as not being relevant to their lives. Since they do not envision themselves in a lab coat with glasses and a pocket protector, they feel that science is not for them. Students' studies of Clayoquot Sound allow them to see the roles that science is playing in the management of natural resources. Students are able to meet scientists who are actively reviewing the ways in which we manage our resources, and see that they are often young, female or male, and living in the region exploring the impact of logging on the environment of our coastal rainforests. These scientists are often viewed as role models and the research they are undertaking is seen as adventurous rather than boring.

only to find out that we had not used the appropriate compression algorithm and had to redo weeks of work. But, looking back on the two years of the Clayoquot Project, I appreciate the range of activities Jordan undertook in modifying the grade 7 science curriculum to include the voices of many students as they intensely followed the rainforest issue.

What strikes me now is how Jordan juggled the various aspects of being a teacher at a school dedicated to creating computer cultures. Not only has he participated in the Clayoquot Project, but he also runs the computer club and collaborates with my colleague Ted Riecken on the Camelot Project.[82] In this project, Ted's university students and Jordan's computer club students take on anonymous roles as famous characters from medieval times and carry on conversations that emulate virtual communications more commonly played out on MUDs (multiple-user domains, in which a person logging onto the Internet can interact with others by taking on various personae).

One has to call into question what being a teacher means in these electronic spaces and places. Can we define what teaching is like in school-based computer cultures? It is no longer possible to think of training teachers to merely follow prescribed curriculum guidelines. Teachers need to know how to deal with many different roles as they approach the 21st century. And encouraging teachers to be jugglers raises many confusing questions. Yet, if the curriculum is opened to a larger range of issues, will teachers ever be able to know what young people know? Should they care? What happens to standards and testing in a world where what children learn and how they learn are intrinsically different? Perhaps we can look to other environments, such as the Hennigan School, for better ways to ask these questions.

Teachers and Teacher/Researchers at the Hennigan School

The Logo culture in Project Headlight was not directed at children's receiving knowledge from teachers, but at their constructing it. In fact, the

---

82. Ted Riecken, "The Camelot Project: Developing Students' Historical Understanding Through Interactive Electronic Storying," in *Wired Together: Computer-Mediated Communication in K–12*, vol. 2, eds. Z. L. Berge and M. P. Collins (Cresskill, NJ: Hampton Press, 1997).

entire community tried on new roles: teachers reflected on teaching as did researchers; children became both designers and researchers; researchers took on teaching roles and learning roles; and school administrators learned Logo programming. In the Logo culture, the students created their own projects. We provided the tools, expertise, and ideas about how to get pieces (procedures) to work well in wholes (programs). And we (teachers and researchers as a community) provided a context, an environment in which these projects could develop.

For example, Aaron Falbel, using Ivan Illich's theory of convivial tools, worked as a colleague with children to create animation from original drawings and to think of themselves as convivial learners.[83] In Falbel's project, children created animation projects using transparencies, whereas in Judy Sachter's project, they explored their understanding of 3-D rotation and computer graphics.[84] Lise Motherwell conducted one of the first gender and technology studies.[85] Rena Upitis, a visiting scholar from Queens University, created musical performances in which the students made music, first by using their bodies, and then by working with the computer.[86] Mitchel Resnick, along with Steve Ocko and Fred Martin, derived design ideas from watching children play with LEGOLogo™ bricks.[87] These "objects" seemed to live in the virtual spaces between the LEGO pieces they held in their hands and the ideas they manipulated in their minds. Making these LEGO "creatures," complex mechanical objects that could be programmed to move in certain ways, led to Resnick's theory of *distributed constructionism*, Fred Martin's notion of how children build constructionist concepts while writing programs to control the actions of robots, and Steve Ocko's reinterpretation of *deconstructionism*—kids deconstructing objects that already work before they put something new together.

---

83. Aaron Falbel, *Friskolen 70: An Ethnographically Informed Inquiry into the Social Context of Learning*, Ph.D. diss. (Massachusetts Institute of Technology, 1989).

84. Judy E. Sachter, *Kids in Space, Exploration into Spacial Cognition of Children's Learning 3-D Computer Graphics*, Ph.D. diss. (Massachusetts Institute of Technology, 1990).

85. Lise Motherwell, *Gender and Style Differences in a Logo-Based Environment*, Ph.D. diss. (Massachusetts Institute of Technology, 1988).

86. Rena Upitis, *This Too is Music* (Portsmouth, NH: Heinemann, 1990).

87. Mitchel Resnick, *Turtles, Termites and Traffic Jams: Explorations in Massively Parallel Microworlds* (Cambridge, MA: MIT Press, 1994); Fred Martin, *Children, Cybernetics and Programmable Turtles*, M.A. thesis (Massachusetts Institute of Technology, 1994).

Meanwhile, in a research project initiated by Idit Harel, children designed software to help other children learn about fractions.[88] This idea that children could be designers of their learning environments was developed further by Yasmin Kafai, who introduced computer design as an environment to understand how girls and boys think when playing and designing games, a topic of great interest to video game designers.[89] All of these projects worked within the culture that teachers had already established. And for those teachers and children who "lived" in and around the computer pods, the variety of research projects often dovetailed quite well with their teaching innovations.

I knew that the Hennigan would not dramatically change from the first day I walked into its gray stone hallways, but I never gave up hope. I had hoped we would move to a less instructional environment where learning was, as Illich has said, "unhampered participation in a meaningful setting."[90] Yet the intransigent rituals of schooling as acted out in the playground, the lunchroom, the library, and the classroom, remained somewhat untouched, or at least unchanged. So what made the Hennigan special? There were moments when the teachers broke through the glass ceiling and, in spite of the fact that the school did not transform itself, the lives of many individual teachers and children did change as they learned to take charge of their learning through planning, designing, building, and reflecting on their inventions as a community. Who were these adults and how did they enable others to change? I now describe two from the team that invited me into their classrooms.

Teachers in Transition

When we introduced the Logo culture at the Hennigan, we (teachers and researchers) were making a major attempt, through the introduction of electronic media, to change the way children learn. However, many of the successes we had were not only because of the computers. They were linked to how teachers humanized the work children did

---

88. Idit Harel, *Children Designers: Interdisciplinary Constructions for Learning and Knowing Mathematics in a Computer-Rich School* (Norwood, NJ: Ablex Publishing Corp., 1991).
89. Yasmin Kafai, *Minds in Play: Computer Game Design as a Context for Children's Learning* (Hillsdale, NJ: Lawrence Erlbaum Associates, 1995).
90. Ivan Illich, *Deschooling Society* (New York: Harrow Books, 1972).

on the computer. How they supported young people to follow inner thoughts and feelings while they worked on the computer. One such teacher was Marianna Siva.

Marianna had a special flair for creating an inviting atmosphere in her classroom. On one particular day, I observed four groups working simultaneously in her small classroom: Steve Ocko, a researcher, was working with a teacher's aide, explaining LEGOLogo to him, while a young boy sat close by, listening and watching the two men; some children were drawing at their desks; others were doing homework; and Marianna was teaching a small group beside the stand-up blackboard. With some teachers, working in groups is what they learn in their teacher training; with Marianna, it seemed to be an outgrowth of her gregarious nature. The class was "structured" like a home, with many simultaneous activities scattered around the room. Marianna established a straightforward and unconditional atmosphere to which the children responded with grace.

The classroom community seemed to have so many special needs that at first I felt a great sense of guilt over not being able to fulfill them. I have always suffered from a fear of not being able to solve the problems I see around me—which is why I knew I would never be a doctor. Teaching seemed to offer hope, until I was confronted with so many suffering children. Learning is not always the easy, joyous, and fluid phenomenon we teachers try to make it; it is often a painful process, during which deep personal fears are released from the bottom of a jammed well.

Marianna and I often discussed one particular girl in her classroom, a small child named Jane, who had a peculiar inability (or unwillingness) to speak. The specialists could not find any physiological reasons for her lack of speech. She would sit in her quiet world, timidly smiling when our eyes met. Jane could speak with her eyes, with the delicate tilt of her head, with her soft mannerisms, and sometimes with her small, questioning voice. Jane was physically frail and small; she reminded me of a wounded baby

Fieldnotes (January 1986): Today I sat with Jane in Marianna Siva's classroom. This is the first time that Jane has initiated anything by herself at the computer. We sat together and she quickly showed me that she knew FD 100 RT 90. Last week she seemed to grasp what we were doing together, but I was not sure if she understood that RT 90 turns the turtle cursor 90 degrees to the right and FD 100 moves the turtle cursor 100 turtle steps in the direction it is facing. As usual, Jane made her CASA picture and was quite animated the whole time. Usually she sits at the computer without any significant body movements. This time, she did not stop moving! Marianna walks around the room visiting us from time to time, encouraging us to continue. She responds to Jane's animated responses with a flourish.

bird that still had a sparkle in its eyes but no strength to vocalize its pain. She weighed very little, her straight hair was held erratically by a barrette, her skin pallid. She looked two years younger than she actually was. Jane was seeing a school therapist, with whom I spoke several times. According to this therapist and Marianna, Jane was living with her grandmother, a kind woman, in her 50s, coming to terms with being the primary caregiver.

Jane and the other children of Project Headlight were surrounded by adults who were interested in understanding them. We participated in the children's projects and helped them plan new activities. As researchers and teachers, we worked with the children as they built new things. Jane was very much a part of an emerging Logo culture. She often spent time in the computer pods, sitting on the lap of a researcher or teacher in front of the computer. At first her response was minimal, but within a few weeks she would smile with glee, just typing in a number and watching how far the turtle would go. She also loved to change the colors on the screen. Her favorite activity, which she did over and over again, was to build a Logo illustration called "CASA." Making a square and a triangle was not very interesting to her; but using squares and triangles to build herself a home fulfilled a personal need. It was not long before Jane was sitting by herself, confident in her ability to create her own home, here *casa*, in the school.

Jane's story seems to crystallize what Papert was trying to accomplish in those years: the use of mathematics as a tool for thinking. In my fieldnotes of January 31, 1986, I describe what I was experiencing as a researcher whose task it was to explore the thinking of children.

What I admired most about Marianna, as a teacher, was the way she "listened" to Jane's body language and heard the little messages. A week before Jane's birthday, Marianna invited me to her classroom party. When I asked Marianna what small gift I could bring Jane, she instantly answered, "stickers." Jane's face beamed with excitement as she took a love sticker, wrote her name next to mine, struggling with each letter, and gave me her gift. It was then I realized that by allowing children the right to bring their experience and knowledge of the world to others, we can enable them to be active participants in their communities. Marianna, and many teachers like her, know when to provide the right "tool" to elicit children's participation and membership in constructionist communities.

Pausing to Reflect

Linda Moriarty, a 4th and 5th grade teacher, welcomed the MIT "invasion" with remarkable enthusiasm. She was reaching a turning point in her professional life and was eager to change what she had been doing in the school for the last 10 years. Although her main areas of expertise were language and literature, she took to the Logo culture, in which turtle icons trace designs on a computer monitor, like a turtle to water. The possibility of participating in an important technological change was a guiding force for her throughout the following three years. Linda describes herself as follows:

> **Linda:** You know, I so believe in technology. I so disagree with "back to nature" or that kind of stuff. It's just that we're distorting things because we're not paying attention to our trade-offs that we're making as we're moving along. But how can you stop the mind from moving? The whole idea is so absurd! Of course people are going to create and create, and get more technology. It has to happen, or we'll stop the brain.

Linda's desk was located by the entrance to her classroom; the children's desks were usually set up in semicircular rows facing the chalkboard. Two children sat at each desk, and this encouraged collaboration. Children would come to her desk to ask her for assistance when she was not in front of the class teaching, or working with those in the computer pods.

Linda was as comfortable in front of a classroom explaining Logo commands as she was kneeling on the floor beside a child, working one-to-one on a programming difficulty. She used a combination of directness and humor to organize her class. On one particular visit I made to the class, she was teaching Logo programming. She did not usually teach Logo, but several children were having trouble with how to use four turtle cursors, so she was explaining the function of a command called "SetPosition." As usual she stood, very upright and comfortable, in front of the overhead projector—carefully articulating every word. In so doing, she kept the students focused on her instructions. Her manner of presentation also included consciously pausing after every three to five words in order to emphasize her directions. This made her sound very much like someone giving street directions to a foreign visitor (which may not be a bad metaphor for explaining how to get from one place to another in Logo).

> **Linda:** If you're using turtle 0 [pause], then make sure [pause] that you push that one [pause] over [pause] before you ask for the position, so it uses the same turtle that you began with [pause]. Suppose you had it like that [pause]; just move your turtle over [pause] and then [pause] type: [pause] Position. [pause] Then [pause], in your procedure [pause], you use [pause] the command [pause]: Set [pause] Position. [pause] You're going to set it now [pause], and you use those same two numbers [pause], except only you put brackets around them [pause] because it's a list [pause]. If you have more than one word [pause], you must have the brackets.

Linda regularly paused and used facial expressions to make a point. Her head would turn to the side almost flirtatiously; her eyes would dart from side to side and her eyebrows rise; and her shoulders would lift as she breathed in and then fall when she expressed what she was thinking. Linda brought her whole self to the teaching experience. Nonetheless, she occasionally missed something important. For example, one of her advanced-level pupils, Andrew, fell through the cracks, as educators often say. Linda told me she believed that if she had taken more time to listen to Andrew more closely in the classroom, as she did the following summer when she sat in my office watching hours of videotapes, she would have been better equipped to help him:

> **Linda:** You know, Ricki, you're just limited in the classroom and you do not hear the kids individually talk a lot. When I've heard him talk—unfortunately it was in a circumstance he was in trouble that time—I was just floored at how verbal he was and how he understood his behavior.

Teachers have too little time to follow the ideas of individual children in any depth, when their time is taken up in preparing them for examinations, and keeping up with the extra curriculum allotment for special classes. Linda mentioned that the only time she could listen to the children was when they were answering the questions she asked or when they asked a question related to the subject being studied. After watching and listening to Andrew on video, Linda decided that the following year she would plan a time during the day for children to tell their own stories to the rest of the class. Unfortunately for Andrew and for the school, Linda left the Hennigan to take a position as an administrator at another school. She needed a change in perspective, a different set of responsibilities, and new colleagues in order to preclude total burn-out. Linda left her position believing that she might have been able to work things out with Andrew had she taken the time to listen to his stories and to integrate his style of learning into classroom activities. Her advice to Andrew's teacher for that coming year was to give him the opportunity to use his verbal skills in ways that would give him a platform for inventing stories.

Producers and Directors of the Learning Play

Although many teachers still see themselves as the gatekeepers of knowledge, I believe those days are gone. And I believe that the teachers briefly described in this chapter also know that they can no longer confine learning to their classrooms. Irrespective of their seeming power, teachers, principals, staff members, and visiting researchers cannot hold children back from conducting their own explorations. Whether we like it or not, they will find information that many adults do not want them to find, listen to music adults think is just noise, and wear clothes that adults think make them look sloppy. They will do what we did; what our parents did. Except they will do it with much more access to worlds within worlds of information at their fingertips.

What I suggest is that teachers give up trying to keep the barn doors closed. I suggest they take a look at what's on the outside of the barn first. Then they need to find ways to explore, with those children with whom they live throughout the day. They need to navigate new territories, learning how to construct larger groupings of human experience from the plethora of possibilities and points of viewing. Needless to say, after they have gathered their constellations around given topics of exploration, they need to analyze, critique, and deconstruct the wholes to identify the partial knowledges that are often silent or silenced by what is mainstream and common knowledge. The need to put them together again in ways that honor and contest how others see the world. The changing role of teachers is not to become the school technologist; it is to enter into the discourse with children about what it is to know something in any given culture, even a computer culture. It is to become part epistemologist, part ethnographer, and, always, to become a learner.

Therefore, to reiterate the questions posed earlier: will teachers ever be able to know what children really know in these mediated cultures? And what happens to standards and testing when each child's learning is encouraged to be intrinsically unique? My answer to the first question is "no." The second question I answer with a better question, "What else do *you* think could replace uniformity and conformity as the measure of learning?"

part II

storymaking

Composing a life through memory as well as through day-to-day choices seems to be the most essential to creative living. The past empowers the present, and the groping footsteps leading to this present mark the pathways to the future.

—Mary Catherine Bateson
Composing a Life

Composing Portraits

In a darkened theater hall where my video stories were presented, I would hold my breath waiting for the audience's response, waiting to see if my assemblage of images would resonate and be understood. Would they laugh with the young girl who, rolling her eyes, tells me her favorite thing about attending this high-tech school is that she likes the "FOOOOD?" Would they feel empathy for the homeless, toothless man smiling so sweetly at me outside the White House as he waits patiently for his free food? My anxiety was sweet and immediate. They would laugh or they wouldn't. They would be moved or bored.

Now my multimedia stories live on CD-ROMs and on websites as objects for others' refabrications. I have much less visceral feedback on how, if at all, audiences view what was once a tender, painful, or joyful moment, in spite of the fact that on the website they can annotate as soon as I post a story. Yes, I worry that those whose lives I videotape and digitize may be adversely affected by having *bytes* and *bits* of themselves living forever in cyberspace— frozen in time, as the expression goes.[91] Yet children do not seem to think of their digitized images as being fixed or limiting. They see networked media as their playground for co-construction, their platform for multiloguing. So why do I question my role as author of media texts that can no longer be either mine or theirs? Is Roland Barthes correct when he says that as a work leaves the author's pen (and even before), the *author is dead*? That the life of a work is with those who read it?

> [A] text is made of multiple writings, drawn from many cultures and entering into mutual relations of dialogue, parody, contestation, but there is one place where this multiplicity is focused and that place is the reader, not, as was hitherto said, the author.[92]

Composing portraits from moments shared with others and placing them on a digital platform has been a joyful and fearful endeavor. I often ask

---

91. New York based artist Ardele Lister produced the video *Hell*, in which people were trapped in videodisks floating in a dark universe, their stories held within an encapsulated sphere, a modern interpetation of Dante's Inferno. See Ardele Lister, *Hell* [video] (New York: Museum of Modern Art, Video Collection, 1985).

92. Roland Barthes, *Image-Music-Text* (New York: The Noonday Press, 1977), 148.

myself if my chosen field of study in digital ethnography answers the already noted problems of ethnographic inquiry, such as authorship, ownership and censorship, or merely creates more complicated versions of the same questions. How do I examine my authorship as a multimedia designer of interactive media texts if interpretation is subject to the reader's prerogative?[93]

Being a digital ethnographer combines groping through myriad videotaped conversations and finding connections between and among them, fumbling through data, catching the nuance in a smile, and finally producing a work that seems whole, even though, as author or co-author, one always has a feeling of partiality. Every time I create a story, even a 3-minute digital video sequence describing a class field trip to Clayoquot Sound, I am confronted with what is not there—with what I did not or could not show others about what "really" happened.

Working with analog and digital video data can shift the nature of ethnographic inquiry, redefining its boundaries by blurring the distinctions that previously separated those who are the subjects of inquiry (informants and participants), those who do the recording and interpreting (ethnographers), and those who read the texts (audiences). With distributed telecommunications, diverse individuals can meet, discuss, debate, and critique each other's versions and visions. Email chat groups already invite this layering of ideas. In North America, many people have access to video cameras and can videotape moments of their lives. This video can then be digitized onto a computer and shared with others, who can add their views to it, thus creating something quite different from the original context. People might not yet be sharing digital video, but it is only a matter of months, or maybe a few years at most, until distributed desktop video is as common as is sharing text.

Becoming an ethnographer using digital media also means repositioning oneself as a member of a community of inquiry—one voice among many. The ethnographer, the video technology, and the total environment within which the researcher and the children interact are inseparable. Becoming a multimedia ethnographer also means building groupings or

---

93. To explore the issue of authorship in the use of electronic media, see Ricki Goldman-Segall, "Whose Story Is It, Anyway? An Ethnographic Answer," *IEEE Multimedia 1* (1994): 7–12.

configurations of "data" based on a range of ways of viewing events, people, and places. It means creating a culture for shared collaborative "authorship" and for distributed co-constructionism.

Annotation: Imagine contacting the *Southern Cross*, the ship that took anthropologist Raymond Firth to Polynesia, to have a chat with Firth, check out his views about the locals, and tell him about yourself. Imagine sending Margaret Mead an email note about your child rearing practices or being able to call up her latest digital movie filmed by Samoans. Or sending her home-video you shot of your children.

This technology is still in the hands of those with privilege and powers; but access to information networks is becoming commonplace within many community groups. Saturation of society with video-based tools is a matter of time, not only of power. Similarly, the field of ethnography, like the field of education, has had its doors opened to the public. Anyone who has access to the Internet can scrutinize the posted video research data in this book, for example, and contact those in the video directly.

Public access invites two possibilities. The first is that we can choose to work as communities of inquiry to shape positions that reflect diverse points of viewing. Voices that were once traditionally silenced, because they lacked a seal of approval that could only be bestowed by membership in professional associations, can now be heard. Or, we can continue to be gatekeepers, privileging views that reflect the "common good" as defined by those (of us?) with power.

4
ReViewing Knowledge as a Video Ethnographer

Today's young citizens have grown up with the new freedom of the 16 mm synchronous sound filming, the impact of television transmission, and the possibility of computerized videotape storage of records. This technological revolution has facilitated the development of ethnographic film from the fragmentary and idiosyncratic to the systematic and thorough. We now turn our cameras on ourselves for a good hard look at our own societies, thus redressing an imbalance which the "native" subjects of ethnographic films have found highly offensive.

—Emile de Brigard,
"The History of Ethnographic Film"

Becoming a Video Ethnographer

During my first rainy yet colorful New England autumn, I would get a ride to the Hennigan School with either a faculty or another student researcher. I mark the beginning of my ethnography from the times I spent at or en route to the Hennigan without a camera. My eyes were the first lens I used to capture the Logo culture; my ears the first receiver to filter the high pitched tone of the school. Yet, looking back, I realize how my decision to take a course in Interactive Filmmaking with documentary filmmaker Richard (Ricky) Leacock and interactive cinematographer Glorianna Davenport changed my academic life. What started as a playful class project, to document children's creation of a computer culture at the Hennigan School, turned into a research approach that would hold my intellectual attention for more than a decade.

In this chapter I describe how I became a video ethnographer by addressing issues that emerged from my decision to use video. In a sense, this chapter is both a narrative and an ethnography of my research methods. I choose to explain the theory in narrative form. This is because my years of speaking with teachers, parents, graduate students, and faculty have taught me that they are less convinced by a taxonomy or list of "what to do" (the prescriptive method), and become more involved with their own thinking about their methods when relating to my practice. In short, they learn about their practice and theory, their *praxis*, from my story. Therefore, I present my story about becoming an analog and digital video ethnographer as an invitation to others, not as a prescription.

The issues I discuss are: finding a topic to study; developing a postmodern cinéma vérité style; becoming a participant recorder; developing technical skills for multiple photographic gazes; and accepting the performance in front of my lens as "research" data.

Early Documentary Filmmaking

My formal study began when I learned how to hold a video camcorder, when to turn it on and off, what to videotape, and, most important, how to approach the children with this invasive tool. As Gerald Temaner and Gordon Quinn state: "Every filmmaker, or anyone behind the camera and in front of the editing table, faces three questions. What to shoot? How to shoot it? How to put it together?"[94] I was still at the what-to-shoot phase, but quickly discovered that if I did not think about how to put it together, I would not be able to find a cogent story. Luckily, I had access to video editing suites, where I could quickly find out what was missing from my seemingly random video segments—segments that I started calling *chunks* or *stars*.

Back at the Hennigan school, my camera lens first focused on the whole learning culture, and especially on the teachers. Believing as I do that educators are akin to artists, creators of mental images in the minds of the children they inspire, I naively went into the environment in order to "capture" it—perhaps only slightly less purposefully than did the Christian missionaries and others who photographed the "exotic other" of colonial cultures during the late 19th and early 20th centuries![95] However, reviewing my footage convinced me that I had videotaped something quite

---

94. Gerald Temaner and Gordon Quinn, "Cinematic Social Inquiry," in *Principles of Visual Anthropology*, ed. P. Hockings (The Hague: Mouton, 1973), 56.

different from what I had originally thought. Far from appearing to be artists, the teachers I observed were people struggling with how to do the best job they could. They figured out how children could learn in this kind of computer culture, resolved pecking order conflicts as they arose, and, reaching beyond these personal politics, had some fun along the way.

In the meantime, my focus shifted to the children. I could sit with children, talking, laughing, and working with them. Like them, I was learning Logo. My not being the expert who would solve their computer problems meant that they did not see me as the bearer of knowledge. How did they see me?

To become a member of the children's community, I had to be able both to play while I worked and to work while I played. I tried not to be perceived as someone who would evaluate them or exert control over their behavior—unless, of course, they were in any kind of danger. My gut feeling was that, if

> **Fieldnotes (March 1986):** In the process of becoming friends with the children, the sharing of feelings and thoughts has begun. Josh treats me like his playmate. I worry that he doesn't respect me enough. Yet I feel we are becoming friends. He calls me over to hang out with him whenever I walk into the computer pod. Other children pick up on his openness and also seem to relate to me as someone to talk to, to play with, and someone who cares about them. While I videotape Josh and Thomas working, James gets upset with me because I don't come over to play with him! I say, "James, I have to work now." He looks at me with total confusion in his eyes and says, "Ricki, I thought you came here to play!" Well, in some sense, he's right.

they were going to want to share their ideas with me, then I could not be viewed as someone who instructed, monitored, or supervised. In short, these first months were spent in what ethnographers call *establishing rapport*, or what Mary Catherine Bateson often calls *resonance*. I was locating within myself where the children's lives resonated with my memories of elementary school.

---

95. For a comparison of three late 19th-century and early 20th-century photographers in Papua, New Guinea (R. M. Williamson, traveler and amateur anthropologist; Reverend Harold Dauncey, missionary with the London Missionary Society; and F. W. Barton, colonial administrator of Papua), see Martha MacIntyre and Maureen MacKenzie, "Focal Length as an Analogue of Cultural Distance," in *Anthropology and Photography*, ed. E. Edwards (New Haven: Yale University Press, 1992), 158–63. An intriguing postcolonial discussion of the problematic issues surrounding the representation of others through the eye of the journal *National Geographic* can be found in Catherine A. Lutz and Jane L. Collins, *Reading National Geographic* (Chicago: University of Chicago Press, 1993). By showing how race, gender, and privilege position the photographers' framing of images, Lutz and Collins tell the history of *National Geographic* from a feminist perspective.

At this point in the Hennigan study, I realized that my results might not be as clear and crisp as I had hoped they would be.[96] I would always be looking through the shadowy lens of my past—my childhood in Winnipeg—trying my best to keep a continuous flow between my inner world and the world I was bringing to life on the screen. Unlike Bateson's, some of my compositions would be made up of the interplay of words, visual images, and sounds; like Bateson, I would always be responding to what I felt, what I recorded, and what opportunities my lens offered me with regard to understanding emerging cultures:

> You dream, you imagine, you superimpose and compare images; you allow yourself to feel and then try to put what you feel into words. Then you look at the record to understand the way in which observation and interpretation have been affected by personal factors, to know the characteristics of any instrument of observation that made it possible to look through it but that also introduced a degree of distortion in that looking.[97]

Developing a Postmodern Cinéma Vérité Style

Developing a style for video ethnography was my next phase, a phase as complex as developing a writing style. The style that emerges as you compose your artifacts reflects who you are, who you were, and who you are becoming. And it becomes part of the ever-changing genres that make up our current cultural climate.

If you want to develop your own voice amid the genre, you cannot merely imitate a style and then impose it on the data—although surely you are constantly influenced by others and by the styles they choose. What happens is experimental and messy. First you get a sense of what's

---

96. This form of empirical research is messy. The rationale for my work is to build neater piles of retrievable data. However, I have come to realize that these tools cannot force categories and themes, nor can they force a theory to emerge. The computer tools help the data look tidy, but these new structures open yet unseen messy spaces. Nevertheless, by problematizing the process, I have learned that what I once thought to be a simple pattern-finding act is, in fact, a complex activity that has challenged me to articulate the veracity of my chosen method.

97. Mary Catherine Bateson, *With a Daughter's Eye: A Memoir of Margaret Mead and Gregory Bateson* (New York: Pocket Books, 1984), 198.

happening and what the story means to you; you hang around and video-tape moments that seem interesting. You expect the unexpected. And you expect that you will recognize the story when it "appears." Moreover, you learn to accept that sometimes the "best" story emerges in your writing of the text or in the making of a (digital or analog) video work. As James Clifford reminds us, ethnographers do not "claim that ethnography is 'only literature.' They do insist that it is always about writing."[98] In a similar fashion, the video ethnographer often creates the story in her working with the video. As she constructs the story, she attempts to persuade, influence, be understood, and, if necessary, seduce the reader with the stylistic and rhetorical devices that best connote meanings.[99]

To develop a video ethnographic style, it is important to develop a critical respect for the visually-based genres through which our eyes have come to know the world around us. Then, by confronting what our eyes have grown accustomed to, we challenge those genres. I remember sitting in film classes with Richard Leacock as we each presented our weekly rushes in class. A big gruff guy with a bounce in his step, Leacock could see through insincerity in our video works. Almost ruthless, he would bring us to our visual senses, reminding us that we couldn't make a scene happen simply because we wanted it to. We learned to draw from what was recorded when the camera was turned on. Those were the days when I still believed that the camera was an observational eye. Later, I would come to recognize my own participant eye.

For Leacock, filmmaking is social commentary on ordinary events. Once hired by *The Saturday Evening Post* to cover the birth of quintuplets in Aberdeen, South Dakota, Leacock and Joyce Chopra turned the camera on the members of the media who had descended on Aberdeen to cover the event. Instead of producing a movie that increased the hype, they produced a critique of American mass media. In *Happy Mother's Day,* reporters and film crews, along with local businessmen, react to Mr. and Mrs. Fischer as fertile commodities to be paraded in an open car, waving at the

---

98. James Clifford, "Introduction: Partial truths," in *Writing Culture: The Poetics and the Politics of Ethnography*, eds. J. Clifford and G. E. Marcus (Berkeley: University of California Press, 1986), 26.
99. Harriet Bjerrun Nielsen, writing about the effects of texts on the minds of readers, theorizes that all texts are seductions in "Seductive Texts with Serious Intentions," *Educational Researcher 24* (1995): 4–12.

spectators.[100] Leacock and Chopra cross the borders between art and observational documentary. Although Leacock's dream has always emulated Tolstoy's ideal of "recording life as it happens," he never for a moment believes that what he is recording is the "truth."[101] He knows he is telling *his* story about the quintuplets, his story about the media's appetite for whatever is considered edible at any period in time.

Annotation: Those of us who attempt to describe the lives of others are, to some degree, complicit in a power game that underscores certain events and dismisses others—not to mention the fact that we expose those who share moments of their lives with us to the gaze of an unknown audience. Yet, should we not read *National Geographic* because we think it represents a colonial world view, or not see the film *Happy Mother's Day* because media breeds more media? Surely we can recognize the contradictions while remaining committed to challenging positions of privilege by including the voices of those who are silenced. As communities of inquiry, we can work together to provide a larger platform for discussion without removing the uniqueness of the artistic voice and the continual development of genres that inform us through their rhetorical placement of images and sounds.

We learn many things from an examination of Leacock's cinéma vérité genre. Along with his contemporaries, trained in Europe during the Second World War, his filmmaking style is similar to the one found in war-time newsreels —follow-the-action from trench to trench shooting. While avant garde fiction filmmakers such as Jean Luc Godard began to incorporate interviews into their fictional movies, the documentary filmmakers were moving "further towards its subject and further away from fiction."[102] As Douglas Harper points out, the early 1960s saw an increase in the use of visual media to inform society about its inequalities. Harper notes that cinéma vérité gave birth to visual sociology. Visual sociologists in the late 1950s and 1960s thought that subjects such as poverty, inequality, countercultures, migrant farmers, and so on, could be best described and aided through the use of the still camera; leading visual sociologist Howard Becker, for example, thought that photographers should be conscious of what directs their photography and illustrate these positions in their work. Harper, in 1994, asks us to reflect on the kinds of research traditions that employ cameras, pointing out that we need to look not only at how our

---

100. Richard Leacock and Joyce Chopra, *Happy Mother's Day* [film] (New York: Pennebaker Inc., 1964).

101. Richard Leacock, "Personal Thoughts and Prejudices About the Documentary," unpublished paper (Cambridge, MA: MIT Media Lab, 1986).

102. Colin Young, "Observational Cinema," in *Principles of Visual Anthropology*, ed. P. Hockings (The Hague: Mouton, 1973), 65.

understanding of the "scientific truth" of the photograph has changed, but also at how science itself has come into question:

> It has been said by many that the camera is a telling symbol of modernism: a machine that advances the purposes of an empirical science ... a science whose existence itself is the result of the liberal agenda of social reform. But the assumptions that underlie sociology, documentary photography, and ethnography have shifted since Becker wrote what was a clarion call for sociologists to take up cameras. The larger mandate of science itself is questioned.[103]

Film historian Emilie de Brigard believes that ethnographic film began as a "phenomenon of colonialism."[104] According to de Brigard, Felix-Louis Regnault, a French physician who became interested in anthropology in the late 19th century, was the first person to make an ethnographic film—a film about an African woman making a pot. Soon after Regnault's film, which actually launched a lucrative motion picture industry in France, the Germans and the English took center stage. Alfred Cort Haddon led an expedition to the Torres Straights, using a full range of recording devices. His colleague, Baldwin Spencer, then undertook a 30-year study of aboriginal peoples in Central Australia, where he collected 7,000 feet of film. However, it is the autobiographical and commercial films of the Lumière family that moved the film industry furthest. This family produced a series of *documentaire* romances, stories filmed against exotic backgrounds—a theme with which we became all too familiar during the Rudolf Valentino era.

Early in the 20th century, the Edison communications firm, "sent camera-persons to film Samoan dancers at Barnum and Bailey's Circus, Walapai snake dancers in the pueblo, and Jewish dancers in the Holy Land."[105] But perhaps the most infamous ethnographic film is Edward Curtis's *In the Land of the Head-Hunters*, which depicts the Kwakiutl of the northwest

---

103. Douglas Harper, "On the Authority of the Images: Visual Methods at the Crossroads," in *Handbook of Qualitative Research*, eds. N. Denzin and Y. S. Lincoln (Thousand Oaks, CA: Sage, 1994), 406–07.
104. For a concise history of the use of film in ethnography, see Emilie de Brigard, "The History of Ethnographic Film," in *Principles of Visual Anthropology*, ed. P. Hockings, 15.
105. Ibid., 18.

coast of British Columbia. Curtis dressed the Kwakiutl in ritual clothing they no longer wore, and staged all of his scenes.

Early film ethnographers tended to be explorers who wanted real life reenacted in front of their cameras' lenses. They enjoyed "discovering" and "capturing" their subjects on film. Often, it was the adventure that drove them to the far ends of the earth. Arctic and South Sea adventurer Robert Flaherty produced the famous films *Nanook of the North* and *Manoa* as "drama, education and inspiration combined," or so said a spokesperson for the Asian Society.[106] De Brigard develops this idea further, stating that "Flaherty's gift was not that of a reporter or recorder, but rather that of a revealer."[107] In spite of the fact that his works contain great visual detail and acuity, and his panchromatic film became the industry standard, the authenticity of his films are still under question. (But then, what does "authenticity" mean in these postmodern times

Annotation: The first time I watched *In the Land of the Head-Hunters*, I was visiting the British Columbia Provincial Museum in Victoria. Surrounded by First Nations artifacts that indigenous peoples want returned to their tribal communities, I felt the full weight of telling others' stories. It was doubly jarring to watch Curtis's staged ritual of a sacred hunting expedition in a museum filled with bought or stolen artifacts. Humiliation upon humiliation, I thought.

when constructions on constructions, such as staging performances for documenting the lives of Vietnamese women, are felt to be more "truthful" than cinéma vérité reporting?)[108]

One could, sarcastically, say that Soviet propaganda films of the 1920s and 1930s are authentic in a political sense—they accurately describe what those in power wanted the public to see and believe. The documentary genre was used by the Soviet Union to portray the drama and beauty of the worker. A typical close-up is an image of a plain young woman, her hair blowing freely in the wind, her head tilted up gazing into the future. She is situated in the fields, with thrashers and other big machinery nearby. She is the architect of her future, taking part in a social revolution. Nevertheless, the straightforward message with the twist of irony from Soviet filmmakers such as Eisenstein, Pudovkin, and Vertov inspired a generation of cinéma vérité filmmakers around the world—although David

---

106. Robert Flaherty, *Nanook of the North* [film] (New York: McGraw-Hill Films Inc., 1922); Robert Flaherty, *Manoa, A Romance of the Golden Age* [film] (New York: Museum of Modern Art, Department of Film, 1922); Emilie de Brigard, op. cit., 22.
107. Emilie de Brigard, op. cit., 23.
108. Trinh T. Minh-Ha, *Framer Framed* (New York: Routledge, 1992).

MacDougall tells us that Vertov was more concerned with the perceptual psychology of the observer than with the events being filmed.[109] However, within anthropological circles, it is the works of Margaret Mead and Gregory Bateson, followed by those of Timothy Asch, John Marshall, and Frederick Wiseman, which often stand out as examples of the science of documentary filmmaking.[110]

Mead (who usually directed) and Bateson (who usually filmed) conducted film ethnographies as early as the mid-1930s. Throughout this period of their research, Mead and Bateson explored visual methods for conducting anthropological research. Unlike their predecessors, they were both established professionals. When they employed visual media, they had a pretty good idea what they would find. In other words, they did not use these media to elicit meanings, but to record, catalog and gather data. After gathering 25,000 photographs for their book *Balinese Character*, they sorted them according to such topics as orifices, play, siblings, and so on.[111] Not very inspiring, but this research was conducted in what was then considered to be pushing the boundaries of anthropological tradition.

I suggest we accept the notion that genres, even the documentary genre, are in flux and may not only be reflections and images of the world *out there*. Viewers and makers of media forms interact with multiple versions and visions of cultures—cultures that are also in a state of constant permutation. Clearly, we have moved our lens from the strict documentary, recording the world as it reveals itself to the filmmaker, toward a keener interaction among multiple points of viewing. As times change, we change and our genres change. We move with and against the styles of our times, quoting the quotations of those who have come before in the hope of finding some new key to unlock the secrets of the people and stories we study.

---

109. David MacDougall, "Beyond Observational Cinema," in *Principles of Visual Anthropology*, ed. P. Hockings, 109.

110. In 1989, John Marshall spoke to our film class at the Media Lab. After twenty years in the field, his commitment to the Bushmen in Africa was clearly evident. He spoke about his support for their effort to fight encroaching "civilization." Park wardens with good intentions were threatening the Bushmen's ritual giraffe hunts. See John Marshall and Lorna Marshall, *!Kung Bushmen Hunting Equipment* [film] (Somerville, MA: Documentary Educational Resources, 1966); John Marshall, *N!owa T'ama: The Melon Tossing* [film] (Somerville, MA: Documentary Educational Resources, 1967); and John Marshall, *Bitter Melons* [film] (Somerville, MA: Documentary Educational Resources, 1971).

111. Gregory Bateson and Margaret Mead, *Balinese Character: A Photographic Analysis* (New York: New York Academy of Sciences, 1942).

Shooting and Viewing Video

How did I learn to shoot video? In 1985, I was still accustomed to viewing movies and television programs shot with stationary cameras, before which various actors would perform. After all, I was part of the first TV generation. Jean Renoir has perhaps the best description of this kind of filmmaking. In an interview with André Bazin, he states:

> The camera has become a sort of god. You have a camera, fixed on its tripod or crane, which is just like a heathen altar; about it are the high priests—the director, cameraman, assistants—who bring victims before the camera, like burnt offerings, and cast them into the flames. And the camera is there, immobile—or almost so— and when it does move it follows patterns ordained by the high priests, not by the victims. I don't want the movements of the actors to be determined by the camera, but the movements of the camera to be determined by the actor.[112]

To change the way I shot and viewed footage, I had to learn two things: to accept a less steady image and to move to the center of the action. Often, an insightful piece of video would be out of focus, badly lit, or shaky. My goal was to use the camera in such a way that the footage would best describe the topic I was exploring and express my view of that action. If that meant incorporating a piece of video that was badly lit, so be it.

A breakthrough in my videography occurred one afternoon when filmmaker (and Temple University professor) David Parry came to shoot with me at the Hennigan School. Parry moved with the camera into the center of the action without creating a disturbance. He held the camera in front of him, with both hands, and then moved it in and out of the center of activity. I was shocked. I was sure he would invade the personal space or "bubble" surrounding those he was videotaping. I had never dared move so close to the children as they worked. But the children were comfortable with Parry because he was comfortable with what he was doing. From that day on, my camera work changed; the camera moved with me and seemed to pull me into situations. When I participated in activities with the children,

---

112. André Bazin, "Interview with Jean Renoir," *Sight and Sound,* (1959).

the camera was turned on and was close to them. Eventually, I stopped thinking about the camera.

I also had to learn how to record sound. Powerful visual images could be rendered impotent without good sound. At the Hennigan, I chose a directional microphone, a Seinheizer ME 80, with a 4-foot cord. With the camera in my right arm and the mike in my left hand, I would approach a child, place the mike down on the table facing her, and then sit down. The directional mike also enabled me to shoot from a distance and still pick up the voices of my subjects. At Bayside Middle School, I stopped using an external mike because I found it limited my casual relationships with the children as we hung out in the hallways and classrooms. However, when I sat down with one or two students for a more serious interview, I either used a small directional mike or clipped a tiny Lavalière mike onto their clothing. (My Lavalière attaches to a piece of clothing and has a cord, so I only use it when we are sitting outside in one place, and when there is a wind. Wind in the in-camera mike has ruined more than one of my video interviews.)

I hold the camera close to my body: the larger VHS cameras on my right hip, the smaller ones either on my lap or pressed tightly into the center of my upper chest to increase stability of image. Early on I discovered that pointing the camera up gives the viewer the feeling of looking up to a child. To maintain eye contact during the conversation, I often videotape without looking through the viewfinder. Although I have a sense of what the peripheries look like (for cut-away shots and to inform me of what's going on around me), I am more concerned with what's going on at close range. I situate myself quite close to the center of the action in order to recreate for viewers a feeling of intimacy. I videotape an interaction for as long as it lasts, stepping back from time to time and panning with the camera in order to provide the context for a given scene. And I only videotape those who invite me into their worlds and those whose invitations I want to accept.

Annotation: The Hennigan teachers used to say, "Ricki, is something wrong today?" whenever I didn't have a camera nuzzled into my hip and resting affectionately on my right arm. I knew they had begun to see the camera as being attached to my body.

Becoming a Participant Recorder: Outsider's Privilege, or Price?

Was I different in the spring of 1993, when I first started visiting and videotaping at Bayside Middle School? Some things had changed with regard to how I conducted a video ethnography—better cameras, more experience, and more confidence in my method, but many things had not changed. I still liked to think of myself more as a participant recorder as than an observer.[113] I still preferred to participate as a member with a research project. With Keven Elder, Joe Grewal, Jordan Tinney, and other teachers who provided students with many differing viewpoints about the issues, we worked together to create a climate—a video culture as a way to conduct a socioscientific investigation. Many of the Bayside teachers were already deeply involved with forestry issues and with the economic, ecological, and social development of Vancouver Island. Each had relatives or friends whose livelihoods depended on tourism, fishing, or logging. Looking back, I find that the teachers and administration carried the project guiding students through a networked investigation of environmental and forestry management issues. I became a member of the culture, insider and outsider simultaneously.

In this second ethnography, I was more willing to construct the study according to my points of viewing. This time I could move in whatever direction I chose. However, unlike at the Hennigan, I did not have a large community of researchers with whom to exchange ideas. My only constant colleague was Ted Riecken from the University of Victoria, and he was often engaged in other projects.

At Bayside, the teachers did not expect me to provide computer training and maintenance. At the Hennigan School I always felt that the teachers' needs were greater than what I could handle. In retrospect, I now understand that university-school partnerships are always negotiated within a given set of boundaries, yet the agreements that are established are different. Bayside already had a computer-rich environment and an eager staff—a staff that prides itself on being open to researchers. The Bayside teachers do not expect that I will train them or maintain their equipment. We barter. When I get a large government grant, I pay a teacher to work with me and the students. When conferences are announced, I submit papers and arrange presentations that include Keven, the teachers, and the students. When they need an extra camera for a while, or a hard drive, or a scanner, I put the machine in the trunk of my car and go to the

---

113. See Ricki Goldman-Segall, *Learning Constellations: A Multimedia Ethnographic Research Tool for Exploring Children's Thinking*, Ph.D. diss. (Massachusetts Institute of Technology, 1990).

island. But these are the material aspects of the relationship. What we really exchange is mutual respect and a sense of adventure. Keven is the kind of vice-principal who wants to look around the corner even before he gets to the end of the block. He just can't pass anything up that will be good fun for the cultural life of the school.

As I mentioned in my description of Bayside in chapter 3, on my first day I mostly poked around to get the feel of the place, carrying my camera with me. The young people and teachers at Bayside quickly adapted to my video recording.

As a society, we are all more comfortable with the video camera in the 1990s than we were in the 1980s. We are used to seeing our images on monitors in department stores, in private homes, and even on computers. The tiny Hi8 camcorder I use has a liquid crystal display (LCD) monitor that sits on a brace attached to the body of the camera; instead of only aiming the monitor toward my viewing eyes, I often turn it toward the student I am videotaping so that she gets to see what I am recording. (In 1993, cameras did not have monitors built in, so I had to figure out a way of simulating this reflexivity.) This LCD monitor can become a distraction, so I only use it when I sense that there is a strong need to build on mutual trust. Using the monitor can give the person I am videotaping some degree of control over the images I make. To affirm my commitment to bringing the videomaking culture into the day-to-day lives of students, I often pass around the small Hi8 camcorder and let them videotape their own scenes. Most often they interview each other and videotape from a

Fieldnotes (May 1993): It's Friday afternoon in Joe's classroom; a few groups are working on collaborative projects, rushing to meet their deadlines; the class is relatively quiet as several young people are still gathering data in the library. The doors are open. The room is warm and comfortable. A few of the grade 8 girls have finished their assignment and are lazily working on homework, talking. I sit down at their table and before long Amber asks me for my camera. I pass it to her and she interviews me. The first question is whether I am married and the second is if I have any pets. Then she asks me how much money I make as a university professor. I stammer. If I avoid answering, why will she and the others want to talk candidly to me? Boom. I blurt it out. The interview continues. In a much more relaxed fashion we move into the kind of conversation that has "I know you" written all over it.

range of angles, including upside down. Sometimes they interview me, playfully reversing our roles and putting me in the hot seat.

Some teachers and students feel uncomfortable with the camera recording their movements and, especially, their voices, so I am careful not to push it in their faces. Kelli, a dramatic young person, loves being videotaped. She wants to become a movie star—among many other careers for which she is equally well suited. In fact, over the past few years, she has appeared on a local television adventure program televised across Canada. When I come to the school with my camera, she immediately begins to construct scenarios featuring herself as the main "actress." The school owns several older VHS camcorders (circa 1988), which students can check out from the library. When I visit the school, I notice that Kelli often has one of these heavy silver camera cases and a huge tripod in her hands. As an attempt to encourage more students to get the feel of the medium, I leave

Annotation: The video camera is not a good tool for conducting research with people who don't like being videotaped. This is an obvious and considerable limitation for ethnographers who believe they need to build portraits of a representative sampling of the cultures they study. However, I would contend that every ethnography is limited by the tools being used.

one of my small 8-mm camcorders in Joe's class, in case anyone has the urge to use it there or take it home for a weekend. (Sometimes I show them a few "video tricks," such as pans, cut-aways, pull focus, and other common rhetorical devices for shooting film or video.) In this way, the camera becomes one of the everyday tools in the classroom.

The Bayside students begin to think of innovative ways to use the camera and their computers. In one case, they produced "Welcome to Bayside Middle School," a multimedia project initiated by Joe and his assistant, Amanda Smith, describing life at the school. The students interview staff, administrators, teachers, and other students. They select chunks of video, digitize them, and put them into the HyperCard-based interface. In the Clayoquot Project, several groups of young people, mostly girls, conduct video interviews of classmates, their peers in other classes, and local people around Brentwood Bay about logging at Clayoquot Sound. They also videotape their interviews on the field trip we make to the town of Tofino in Clayoquot Sound. For weeks, they work on selecting their video chunks, making sure that each of their classmates is fairly represented and then digitizing the video onto the computer. "Being fair" is extremely important to them, and the girls are very concerned that one of the boys, who exerted pressure on them to put him in many scenes, might be overrepresented. In short, serious discussion about these kinds of issues occurs while they are carrying out their video-based studies.

Clearly, in my role as a video ethnographer at Bayside, I am not the traditional outsider, maintaining strict control over the tools of my trade. I don't sit with my notepad or camera, trying to gather data. My fieldnotes, as you have seen and will see from the excerpts in this book, are events contextualized by my interpretations. My method of video data collection focuses on participating in the culture in order to elicit and to create meanings—theirs and mine. The young people often do the shooting and their video data become part of the collective memories on their culture.[114] We make things and talk about them; we find new connections and new meanings; and we do this together.

Joseph Tobin, David Wu, and Dana Davidson, in their audiovisual ethnography of preschools in China, Japan, and the United States, wrote about how they elicited meanings from young preschoolers, yet they paid little attention to their roles as meaning-makers in charge of the audiovisuals. "Our research methods are unlike those used in most comparative research in early child education. We have not tested children.... Our focus instead has been on eliciting meanings."[115] My audiovisual ethnography is about co-construction; those I view use the same tools to view me and to view themselves. As I elicit meaning from others and from myself, so they elicit meaning from me and from themselves; in this way we build cultural artifacts as a community of inquiry. Images are reflected back and forth as our gazes meet. And in the end, we are all affected as our relationship grows. The camera becomes a tool capable of aiding our common memory of what has come before and what may come again.

In short, when I reflect on my relationship with the young people, I have to admit that I sometimes see myself as an aunt with a video camera—someone who is not always around, who is a bit indulgent and a good listener, and someone who doesn't have to worry about disciplining and judging. Although, being an adult and a professor, I am in a clear position of power, I try to acknowledge the accompanying privileges, and not misuse them in ways that would undermine anyone else's positioning. I share my authority to create a climate of co-authorship within the community of teachers and students. This is not an easy task, and I am not always successful.

---

114. One of the first visual ethnographies in which the informants use film and video to tell their cultural stories was conducted by Beryl L. Bellman and Bennatta Jules-Rosette in their pioneering projects, which they describe in their book *A Paradigm for Looking: Cross-Cultural Research with Visual Media* (Norwood, NJ: Ablex Publishing Corp., 1977).
115. Joseph J. Tobin, David Y. H. Wu, and Dana H. Davidson, *Preschool in Three Cultures* (New Haven: Yale University Press, 1989), 5.

Developing Technical Skills for Multiple Photographic Gazes

The gaze caught in a visual artifact, film, video, or painting can both feature the illustrator's views and situate power relations. For example, for decades art historians have interpreted paintings by analyzing the gaze of the persons depicted in them. Where is Mona Lisa looking? In what directions do the man, the woman, the dog look in a Gainsborough painting? What does this tell us about interpreting positions of power, privilege, and passion? A photograph in *National Geographic*, described by Catherine Lutz and Jane Collins, depicts the intersection of seven kinds of gazes: the photographer's, the magazine's, the magazine reader's, the non-Westerner's, the Westerner's, the academic's, and that of the person whose gaze is captured and transformed through instruments of reflection.[116] Imagine the video stream of images, with its potential for fluidity of movement and location. As video ethnographer, I am often instigator, creator, recorder, viewer, and producer of multiple gazes. This complexity is almost enough to discourage me from using the video camera. No matter how hard I try to enter into the culture of children, I am always an outsider.

Lutz and Collins maintain that presenting colonial attitudes as depicted in *National Geographic* serves a purpose—the images show us how people viewed other people in distant lands. They acknowledge that, regardless of the difficulty of locating the exact meaning of privileged gazes, there is much to learn about ourselves and others in this analysis. The challenge facing us now is to create a culture of visual literacy that is not naive with regard to either hidden or overt messages—the denoted and the connoted image—and to re-examine not only the photograph but the photographer's gaze.[117]

What does the video ethnographer need to learn in order to welcome the gazes of others on (and through) her work? To once again use myself as an example, I will describe the video skills that were critical to my developing a gaze that encourages others to analyze my texts. In the early stages of videotaping at the Hennigan, I thought of the camera as a device to examine subtle patterns, patterns that I had not been able to discern through the use of fieldnotes and audio tape recorders—such as Josh's hand slapping his knee

---

116. For a detailed description of seven kinds of gazes found in photographs, see Catherine A. Lutz and Jane L. Collins, *Reading National Geographic*, 187–216.
117. See Erving Goffman, *Gender Advertisements* (New York: Harper and Row, 1979); and Laura Mulvey, "Visual Pleasure and Narrative Cinema," in *Film Theory and*

every time he thinks of a new invention that changed the world. I also used the medium as a way to reflect, to view and review what I had experienced only hours earlier. Daily I would view my "rushes," examining both the content and the technique of my shooting. This instant self-instruction, combined with regular feedback from faculty, graduate students, and budding filmmakers, taught me how to see what was worth filming and what was not. It taught me how to invite the gaze of others. As I gained more expertise, I noticed how subtle changes in my movement around the room while I was videotaping helped me capture the flow of events, and edit "in my head." I learned how to think about the lighting, depth of field, pull-focus, composition, moving frames, and sound—all while interviewing a child. I learned to see the room from many diverse points of viewing. My research informed my video skills, and my video skills made me a better researcher, a researcher more capable of understanding that I was indeed encouraging a layering of multiple gazes through my photographic gaze.

Annotation: If you have ever watched the television program called *Law and Order*, you will have noticed that it uses a common rhetorical device known as the "pull focus." In a scene with two persons standing at different distances from the camera, the focus suddenly moves from person 1 to person 2, and the image of person 1 becomes soft or fuzzy. The filmmaker is directing your attention to person 2.

Temaner and Quinn point to a similar process in their making of the film, *Home For Life* (about a home for the elderly in Chicago):

> Filmmaking and research began to become one process.... We employed the shooting, the viewing of our footage, and the editing as methods of study. Even at this early stage, when we did do some shooting, we immediately edited the material to help us learn more about our subject and to help us decide on further shooting.[118]

Criticism: Introductory Readings, eds. G. Mast and M. Cohen (New York, Oxford University Press, 1985), 803–816. Roland Barthes writes about the *denoted* (analogon or marked message) and the *connoted* (or suggested) message of the press photograph. Earlier scholars interpreted press photographs as carrying only a one-to-one (denoted only) correspondence with the text they illustrated. Barthes connects the role of the reader to the reading of the press photograph, adding the connoted meaning. See "The Photographic Message," in *Image-Music-Text* (New York: The Noonday Press, 1977).

118. Gerald Temaner and Gordon Quinn, "Cinematic Social Inquiry," in *Principles of Visual Anthropology*, ed. P. Hockings (The Hague: Mouton, 1973), 57.

Developing a photographic gaze that includes others' gazes means first learning basic techniques of shooting while thinking about lighting, sound, color, shadow, emotion, content, and movement. Yes, these are things one can learn by reading a basic video technique book.[119] But developing a gaze for encouraging others' views also entails paying attention to things that, at first, seem to be insignificant, but which might become significant if you give them time to unfold.

Annotation: I also learned to expect that serendipitous events might occur when they were least expected. So, you might ask, does this mean I had to keep the camera on all the time? No. I learned to accept that many moments in life will live within me, not as images on video, but as peripheral visions that inform my contextual understanding of events and inform my videography.

Developing a photographic gaze that invites others to participate in viewing means learning how to see events from diverse points of viewing. In my own work, I not only change my physical location as I videotape, but I also imagine how my video might look from different angles and different people's points of viewing. (And I pass the camera around so that others can add their views.) I imagine diverse cameras capturing and creating the event from a range of angles and positions, with beams of light refracting and interacting with each other. Then I imagine a group of viewers watching through their interpretive lenses. It all becomes a meshing of viewpoints. Or, rather, points of viewing. This is not to say that I have resolved the problem of power. Yet I do attempt to break down the hierarchies of power by encouraging multiple gazing.

Accepting Performance

The last and most important issue I must address in describing how I became a video ethnographer is: How do we know that what young people tell us while they are being recorded is what they really think? Quite simply, we don't. We never completely know if "informants" are being sincere with us. Nevertheless, for 10 years now I have been asked this question.

---

119. For a hands-on instruction book on the language of filmmaking, see Daniel Arijon, *Grammar of the Film Language* (Los Angeles: Silman-James Press, 1976). Despite somewhat sexist drawings of young men and women posing in front of cameras—typical of the 1970s—the book manages to explain the basic procedures needed in learning the language of moving media forms.

My first response is that many young people (and some older ones, too!) seem to enjoy performing in front of the camera in much the same way that preschoolers love to dress up to try on new roles or identities. However, when videotaping is not accompanied by evaluation, testing, competition with peers, or time pressure, people do not perform for the camera as much as one might expect. The more they are exposed to being in the view of the camera, the less they are conscious of it.

However, this issue is more complex than saying that children become comfortable with the camera. The point is that our understanding is not sullied if they perform. After all, don't we all perform in different settings? And who is to say that schools and classrooms aren't environments that call for performance?

Annotation: How often I remember coming home from my elementary school in the north end of Winnipeg on a cold winter day, sitting in my black tunic and crisp white blouse on our purple art deco sofa, knees up to my chin, contemplating how different I was at school and at home. I don't know which of the two performances I thought "most like me." I was gregarious at school, always getting into trouble for talking too much in class. I could learn things quickly, so I always had to wait a long time for the lesson to finish. Sometimes I would lose my patience and feel that I just had to run, play, laugh, and talk. At home I was reserved and watched others closely; I was the good, obedient child. Looking back, I was discovering the social context of personality and how different parts of our personalities emerge when we are with new people in different places.

How can we think that schools are natural settings in which to observe young people? Not only are they social constructions whose purpose is to manage and enculturate the next generation, they are places where performances of gender, class, race, and economic status are played out at every turn of the head. And it doesn't change much as we get older and embark on our chosen careers. Each day, based on what we wear, what scent we put behind our ears, and how we perform the ritual of our jobs, we send messages to others.

Schools are full of performances, some of which are openly labeled and to which we are invited as individuals or groups. But many other

Annotation: We can all remember times when we were so immersed in what we were doing that there was little time to think about how we looked or acted. We were engaged with both mind and body. As we come to feel more comfortable in being ourselves, our many selves, we learn not to be so concerned about our performance. Some days we do the suit thing, some days we do the jeans thing. But wearing jeans is no less a performance than is wearing a suit. I remember a boyfriend from my late teens who teased my closest girlfriend about her outfits. In her wisdom, she looked him with a gleeful disdain and said, "And your jeans and leather jacket aren't an outfit?"

events in the life of a school are the result of the mixture of cultural performances. When the camera becomes part of the cultural performance, it makes overt that which was formerly covert. It opens up the multilog of social discourse, legitimizing performance as an acceptable way of being in the company of others.

One of my goals in studying the emergence of technological cultures in schools is to show how young people very quickly appropriate the camera, making it their own. Some direct the scene; others enjoy being directed. Those who are videotaped tend to become more animated than usual, more dramatic, more full of the stuff of life. Videotaping provides them with a way of responding to situations. Even Keven, the vice-principal at Bayside, performs for my camera. On our way into the Wickaninnish Center to see a wildlife film about tidal pools in rainforest areas, Keven waves his arms in a hugely exaggerated manner and starts talking to me in a funny little voice: "C'mon Ricki. Let's go into the Wickaninnish Center to see some movies." Did he think his comments would provide a good narrative context for my video about our trip to Clayoquot Sound? (They did. I used his performance in a digital video segment called *Walking Through a Rainforest.)*

When we introduce paints to children, new responses to the physical world of color and texture are elicited. In a similar way, children exposed to the video camera develop new expressive means of communication (even when the camera is not in their hands). The students I study often seem articulate and dramatic in front of the camera. The camera contributes to their expressiveness, and those who choose to perform seem to enjoy the performance. I have already mentioned that, in working with children, I view myself as an interested aunt. The camera helps me to encourage their playfulness and energy. So I don't mind when, at first, children jump in front of my lens. I expect it. I encourage them to see themselves, to videotape others, and to eventually construct serious projects—projects that encourage them to control the video and construct stories about who they were, who they are, and who they are becoming.

Conclusion

When I use video as my ethnographic partner, I ask fewer questions, wait longer for responses (several seconds at least), make fewer suggestions, and guide the discussion less than I do when I use an audio tape recorder or pen and paper. I find that the longer I wait, the more open both the students and I become about being in each other's company. The students sense that what we are doing is more mutual; we are both exploring where our relationship will go. I know that I can go back to the details of what was happening—not just what was said but what the person's eyes, mouth, hands, and shoulders were doing. This, along with knowing I can review the video at my leisure, takes away any anxiety I might otherwise feel in the midst of an engaging discussion. Without the camera, I would worry that I was "missing something."

Sitting quietly beside a student with the camera turned on creates an intimate space. At the Hennigan, I wanted to engage in a mutual sharing of experiences. At Bayside, where I spend most of my time in Joe and Jordan's classrooms, my shooting is more public. From time to time I actually "teach" a class of Jordan's, showing the students video rushes from our field trip to Clayoquot Sound. Then, as a community, we talk about our plans for the project. When I am interviewing at Bayside, I am also recording the day-to-day events that make up the school's life. Interviews seem to go better when we are sitting together on a rock or even on the pavement outside at recess than when we are in a closed room. We seem more open to and accepting of the range of our performances, more willing to share this range with each other, and less entangled in roles we never wanted to take on but felt obliged to, within the school walls.

When I videotaped at the Hennigan, I "hung out" more than I interviewed. I would meander up to a child in the computer pod and ask an open-ended question by way of commenting on the immediate situation: "Can I sit here and watch what you are doing today? Do you want to tell/show/talk about what you've been doing? That looks interesting; would you like to tell me about it? What have you been doing lately? Hi, what are you working on today? Your game has really changed; what have you been doing to it lately? What have you been working on since the last time we talked? I really like what you've done with your [canoe trip through the Amazon]. I really missed you this past week; where have you been?" These questions were not scripted; they were specific responses to specific situations. Only when I felt invited did I take the next step into a conversation. In contrast, at Bayside, after my hanging-around phase, I developed a set of questions that guided my interviews. I also made sure that I met regularly with all the young people in the class to check out what they experienced.

The central link in the complex puzzle of becoming a video ethnographer is to include those we videotape in the process so they can choreograph their own parts in any given performance. We need to provide them with tools to conduct their own studies, as Bellman and Jules-Rosette discovered.[120] And, even with this intimate form of participation in the methods of our inquiry, we will probably never know what a given event meant for them. What we see on videotape may be only what people wanted to show us at that particular time and place, but it is still worth making sense of others' actions. How else will we ever be able to build bridges between countries, cultures, races, and genders?

---

120. Beryl L. Bellman and Bennatta Jules-Rosette, op. cit.

Learning Constellations
Constellation Map
http://www.merlin.ubc.ca/tools/lc

Constellations 2.5
Star Entry
http://www.merlin.ubc.ca/tools/c25

The Global Forest
Opening Page
http://www.merlin.ubc.ca/projects/gf

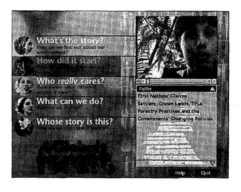

Web Constellations
Star Entry and Search Window
http://www.merlin.ubc.ca/tools/webConst

5
Designing Digital Learning and Research Environments

The "writable" text ... is plural and diffuse, an inexhaustible tissue or galaxy of signifiers, a seamless weave of codes and fragments of codes, through which the critic may cut his own errant path.

—Roland Barthes
On the Pleasure of the Text

Designing Tools

Would I have embarked on this journey to build digital research and learning tools to support both my work as an ethnographer and my thinking about ethnography had I known then what I know now about how difficult it is to make meaning from digital media texts? Probably. I am an eternal optimist, certain that with enough hard work and perseverance limitations can be overcome. It was in 1985 that I first ventured into this unknown world of interactivity and random access, knowing I would find the people and finances to bring the conceptual and actual models for these environments together. And to this day I am not sure if the learning and research environments I have designed are tools or ways of thinking about digital data analysis.

The questions I ask in the process of developing these tools face most digital ethnographers. Yet these same questions face the home Internet user with either a computer or a Web-linked television. How do we segment video, text, or sound "streams?" How do we save and use these media segments? How do we add our comments or notes to these segments? How do we tag them with thematic markers? How do we find them according to themes, participants, and/or authors? How do we build groupings to identify broader patterns? How do we work collaboratively at all phases?

Current applications for creating digital movies and information environments, such as Adobe Premiere or Macromedia Director, are superb tools for digital video construction, but do not answer these questions. Rather, my questions are addressed by tools to help users learn from what they find important and significant to them, even if, as Roland Barthes suggests, signifiers are always plural and diffuse. My goal has been to design a tool to enable researchers and learners alike to learn from each others' points of viewing, to facilitate participants' negotiation of different views, and to bring forth theory making that unfolds as collaboration grows.

For those of you who are new to the idea of reconfiguring digital video, text and sound, I invite you to travel with me as I tell you the story of my becoming a digital ethnographer, a story that also chronicles the dramatic changes that have occurred in video-based technologies in one short decade. For those who have been addressing these issues from your own knowledge domain, I invite you to partake in this discussion of ideas that I have developed, knowing that much of what I say now has been shaped by viewing the articles and tools you and others have produced. Together we can design better models of environments for learning from each other's views.

Star Notes and Learning Constellations

After a few short months "in the field" at the Hennigan School, I had collected stacks of videotapes, neatly (and not so neatly) labeled and arranged on my bookshelves. Even when I was careful to mark the tapes and write up notes about what I videotaped on a given day, I often had trouble locating a certain clip when I needed it. Linear editing helped me become familiar with my material, but I still had to find the tape, put it into the deck and watch it in its analog form. I would regularly edit 5- to 10-minute sequences to share with colleagues. And, as I mentioned earlier, these video sequences were the focus of my presentation to my colleagues about children's thinking. Familiarity with my video data was not the problem.

I knew what was there. I just could not find it fast enough, and when I did find it, I could only watch it as a linear analog sequence, a stream of video.

One of the first videodisk environments that I used was produced in 1978 and 1979 by the MIT Architectural Machine Group, a research community that was the precursor to the Media Lab. Inspired by a mock-up of the Entebbe Airport constructed in the Israeli desert and used to prepare for a hostage-freeing mission in 1973, the Arch Mach Group designed a walk through the town of Aspen, Colorado.[121] *The Aspen Movie Map* did not treat video sequences like the linear streams one sees in the movies or on television; video was thought of as information bytes, a story without an author. Sequences were not arranged by the person who edited them but were open to the navigational preferences of the user. In this simulated environment of walking down a street, one could choose whether to visit a local pub, go into a barber shop, or proceed

Annotation: The first random access video, text, and sound storage medium was a videodisk. One videodisk could store up to half an hour of analog video streams. A videodisk player played the video streams in the order they were pressed onto this silvery disk that looked very much like a 12 inch record. Hooking a videodisk player to the computer with cables created an environment that enabled users to segment the video into chunks by a simple system of "telling" the computer program the *in-point* (the beginning) and the *out-point* (the end) of the sequence one wanted to define. Various computer interfaces or programs could keep a log of the various segments.

to the next intersection. One could also change the seasons or alter the time, seeing a building as it was photographed years earlier. Another demonstration project developed at the lab taught the user about cars from the perspective of an auto mechanic. As the mechanic would talk about the motor, for example, related links would appear on the computer screen. Users could choose their own learning pathways. The idea of the auto mechanic as guide was a clever one, giving the user a sense of "being there." In the more fully developed application called *New Orleans in Transition*, created by Glorianna Davenport, users could choose multiple pathways through a dense 3-hour documentary movie about the architectural redevelopment of New Orleans.

---

121. In Stuart Brand's *The Media Lab: Inventing the Future at MIT* (New York: Viking Press, 1987), he notes that the first prototype for the *Aspen Movie Map* was a term project produced by an undergraduate student, Peter Clay, who went scooting about a building in a wheelchair holding a movie camera. The town of Aspen was chosen as the site for its charisma, its size, and its manageability.

These early interactive video environments served as models for my thinking about how I could organize my research data. I needed to segment and mark video segments, linking them to other segments. Reluctant as I was to "open" my data to others and give up the control I had had in my linear editing, I could also see a more inclusive way of thinking about research. Yes, I was concerned that others would segment their own chunks from my chunks. I also worried about how to keep the "integrity" of my "story" intact. And I wondered what would happen to the role of the ethnographer.

Fieldnotes (September 1987): At IRIS, interactive hypermedia environments are used for supplementing course work. Several professors from different disciplines have worked with the interface designers to use this medium in a way which integrates the technology with the curriculum. The terminals are located in an open space in the basement of an ordinary-looking building on campus. Students sit in rows at terminals. The course work ranges from history to English literature to biology. The most densely designed content focuses on English Literature. A student can choose a given poet or writer and then follow various paths established by the professor and the designer.

On a visit to meet with George Landow and his colleagues at the Institute for Research in Information and Scholarship (IRIS) at Brown University in 1987, I tried out their hypertext environment for teaching English literature courses.[122] A student could learn about Shakespeare, for example, by choosing any number of nodes (highlighted words) in the electronic document. What became so powerful as a model for thinking about hypertextuality was not only the interface, which was still primitive, but Landow's groundbreaking way of connecting poststructural theories of knowledge and hypertext.

> The very idea of hypertextuality seems to have taken form at approximately the same time that poststructuralism developed, but their points of convergence have a closer relation than that of mere contingency, for both grew out of dissatisfaction with the related phenomena of the printed book and hierarchical thought.[123]

122. Nicole Yankelovich, Norman Meyrowitz, and Andries van Dam, "Reading and Writing the Electronic Book," *IEEE Computer 18*, no. 10 (1985), 15–30; see also Nicole Yankelovich, Bernard J. Hann, Norman K. Meyrowitz, and Steven M. Drucker, "Intermedia: The Concept and the Construction of a Seamless Information Environment," *IEEE Computer 21*, no. 1 (1988): 81-96.

123. George P. Landow, "What's a Critic to Do? Critical Theory in the Age of Hypertext," in *Hyper/Text/Theory*, 1. An intriguing aspect of Landow's work is his belief in providing students with the *context* of the subject matter. To further explore postmodern political

Unlike Landow and many of his colleagues in the mid-1980s, I was less interested in instructional environments in which students could learn course material and more interested in constructionist environments in which people could build interpretations of their data. I was also more interested in process: the technique of making meanings and finding patterns from, for example, the extensive video data that continued to pile up on my shelves. And I wanted to find a way to share this process with others. What my colleagues at Brown had provided were hypermediated ways of accessing course content. (One sees this instructionist enthusiasm returning these days as university professors and classroom teachers busily plan their courses for *instruction* rather than *construction* on the Web.)

To explain this difference, I describe the nature of my talks with Glorianna Davenport over the last decade. Davenport is a media artist who has a deep grounding in cinematography. Her vision is to create seamless stories that respond to a viewer's preferences automatically and intelligently. Her cinematic sensitivity addresses audience interaction without losing the storyteller's narrative flow. Describing digital cinematic "primitives," Davenport has broken down the elements of digital language for viewing reconfigurable digital data.[124] In short, she creates audience excitement in the documentary genre by translating a medium that once seemed flat and fixed into one that is fluid and "elastic," to use her word. She and her research team have embedded complex database structures into interfaces designed over the last decade; to the user they seem hidden, yet they are just slightly below the surface. Viewers partake in the sensual emergence of a story that continues to unfold through their choices.

From her interactive cinematographic works, *New Orleans in Transition* and *Elastic Charles*, to her most recent exploration with her research team about the Big Dig (Boston's redevelopment of an underground highway through the downtown core), Davenport keeps her eye on a presentation target rather than a representation environment.[125] In one of her most recent projects with

---

theory and hypertext, see Charles Ess, "The Political Computer: Hypertext, Democracy, and Habermas," in *Hyper/Text/Theory*, ed. G. P. Landow (Baltimore: Johns Hopkins University Press, 1994), 225–267.

124. Glorianna Davenport, Thomas Aguierre Smith, and Natalio Pincever, "Cinematic Primitives for Multimedia," *IEEE Computer Graphics and Applications* (1991): 67-74.

125. Glorianna Davenport, "New Orleans in Transition, 1983–86: The Interactive Delivery of a Cinematic Case Study," *The International Congress for Design and Planning Theory Proceedings* (1987): 1–7; Glorianna Davenport and Hans Peter Brondmo, "Creating

graduate student Natasha Tsarkova, Davenport shows how her interactive system for storytelling conducts intelligent searches as the viewer continues to navigate through the environment. In Tsarkova's documentary digital video story of a visit to Cafe Vittoria, a traditional Italian coffee bar in the North End of Boston, a collage of video images moves from a shadowy background to the foreground as the viewer makes simple choices.[126] A story unfolds without the database being seen. Another graduate student, Kevin Brooks, developed Agent Stories—"a story design and presentation environment for nonlinear, multiple point-of-view cinematic stories."[127] In yet another website and accompanying CD-ROM environment about the life of Jerome Wiesner, the intellectual founder of the Media Lab and a past president of MIT, the interface looks like the inner wall of the Media Lab, also known as the Wiesner Building.[128] The wall, designed by artist Kenneth Noland, is covered in gray square tiles with linear strips painted in bright colors. Davenport's interface uses a photograph of that wall as the interface background. Wiesner appears as a young man in the top left tile. Moving across and down, as we read text, Wiesner's life and career unfold. The Davenport signature on this work is the way in which making one choice subtly moves the viewer into the next series of choices. The shadowy image of Wiesner in a window suddenly becomes a stronger, clearer image, and other images fade with the click. Database searches and retrievals are handled by complex algorithms that lie underneath the surface, yet seem open to all.

As a researcher, I was (and still am) interested in the presentation of a story, but I am more interested in making the opaque transparent. Even in those earlier years, I was interested in building a tool to segment, categorize, annotate, and cluster video data. Less interested in the cinematic experience, I was captivated by the construct of elements that would lead one to create an aesthetic understanding. Thus, from my initial concern with how to find a video clip from piles of videotapes, a deeper issue emerged. How do we build environments in which users can deconstruct video streams into chunks, then

---

and Viewing the Elastic Charles Hypermedia Journal," *Hypertext II Conference Proceedings* (1989): 1-6.

126. Natasha Tsarkova, *The North End Chronicles* [digital film] (Cambridge: MIT Media Lab, 1996).

127. Kevin Brooks, "Do Story Agents Use Rocking Chairs? The Theory and Implementation of One Model for Computational Narrative," eds. W. Hall and T. D. C. Little, *Proceedings of Multimedia '96*, the Association of Computing Machinery (1996): 317-328.

128. See <http://ic.www.media.mit.edu/JBW>.

code or mark these video streams with thematic tags and build clusters? How do we open up a database of tags and markers to others so they can see the tags and add their ways of understanding the data? How do we make database engines visible and easy to manipulate? How do we design tools to layer people's views enabling stories to emerge in many different forms? These were among the many questions I was struggling to answer in this next phase of my journey as a digital ethnographer.

Arranging Chunks for Linear and Nonlinear Delivery

At this phase of the project, I was joined by Brazilian filmmaker Vivian Clara Orni-Mester, who was interested in the selection and editing of video for videodisk environments. Our first problem was to compare the process of editing for creating linear *stories* to that used in editing nonlinear stories. I use the term *story* because the data needed to be organized in a manner which made descriptive and narrative sense.

Conventions for constructing digital video stories have not yet been established. Some designers opt for sectioning off an existing linear piece into bite-size chunks. Others organize a linear piece for easy subdividing at a later date (as was done in the American Broadcasting Corporation's videodisk called *The Holy Land*). However, when a piece that was edited for linear presentation is segmented, the beginnings and endings of the cuts can be problematic. Another problem is that the context is usually destroyed. Furthermore, a short or long segment which worked well in the linear story may not stand on its own in the nonlinear story.

In deciding how to edit for videodisk environments, we designed (with the assistance of graduate student Hans Peter Brondmo) a HyperCard application called Star Notes for making decisions about how to select relevant scenes; how to segment video sequences; how *big* the segments needs to be in order to communicate the message; and what segments go well with other segments, and for what purposes.

Selecting Video Segments

Orni-Mester and I first reviewed about 80 hours of relevant video data. Each viewing brought us to a new understanding of what the children meant when they did or said certain things. Through several stages of reviewing and selecting video with many colleagues, we were able to choose 10 hours of video footage from which to make the final selections for the videodisks.

HyperCard, an Apple application for the Macintosh computer, was released in the fall of 1987. The different segments of video data could be described on a "card"—a window on the computer monitor which resembled a filing card. We thought of each card as a *chunk* of information, one segment of video. Cards were arranged in "stacks" according to categories from a keyword box. When one called up a stack, each card in the stack appeared and was replaced by the next card in the stack. Searches were carried out easily as each word in a field was an object to be found and displayed. Magdaline Lampert and Deborah Lowenberg Ball define this process in the following way:

> Hypertext is a representation of multiple and flexible links between discrete pieces of data which allows users to navigate among multiple paths through a network of chunks of information and to build and store their own links. When the data to be linked include video, audio, and graphic as well as textual information, the representation is called multimedia.[129]

On each card in Star Notes there was a space for the following information about a chunk of video data: the name of the scene, a description of the scene, the source tape on which the chunk can be found, and the date the video was shot. Each card also contained a list of categories, or keywords; stacks of cards in the same category were instantly accessible by clicking on the name of the keyword.

With Star Notes, we subdivided the video data into discrete units. By describing each scene, we manipulated the information of each card as a separate entity. Categories emerged which reflected our interpretations of the footage. While we were categorizing, no predetermined set of keywords existed. We would watch the video and then decide on the keywords according to the content. The themes which emerged

---

129. Magdalene Lampert and Deborah Lowenberg Ball, "Using Hypermedia Technology to Support a New Pedagogy of Teacher Education," unpublished paper (East Lansing: Michigan State University, 1990), 5.

were: Inventing, Imagination, Girl/Boy Talk, Storytelling, Lying and Punishment, Discipline, Reflecting on Oneself or Others, Teaching/ Learning, Gestures, Cooperative Learning, Curriculum, Independent Play, Space, and Reflections. These thematic keywords were organized into stacks, or groups of cards, to compare and contrast the data. For example, all the cards with "Inventing" as a keyword were grouped together, both in the computer and in hard copy. Not only were cards grouped into stacks, but stacks were grouped within stacks and searches were done throughout the stacks to link various subgroups. As we were linking and comparing the text data, unexpected connections began to occur. For example, Andrew's story about a boy traveling from planet to planet could be cross-referenced with data from his teacher, Linda Moriarty, teaching Logo commands in a class project on the planets during their study of the constellations. Did Andrew get his idea from her project?

Keyword stacks were grouped together by arranging them into 30-minute videodisk chapters. By combining the notion of thick description with themes, we were able to chunk the video more precisely. We selected video chunks which we thought would thicken the description.

Orni-Mester and I struggled to decide whether the chunks should make sense if viewed linearly, from beginning to end. After all, why not take advantage of both linearity and nonlinearity? An idea emerged—each videodisk could function as a chapter. However, the user—unlike someone reading a chapter in a book—would have the advantage of being able to move to a related theme, find out more about each person, search for recurrences of a word or phrase, and, most importantly, keep track of what she wanted to save along the way so that it could be grouped together as a cluster. In short, in deciding how to select and arrange video segments so that we could make the best use of videodisk real estate, we paid closer attention to the notion of themes and thick description.

There was a story-like order to the whole body of six videodisks: Videodisk One was the introduction and overview; Videodisk Two was an indepth portrait of one child, Josh, at home and at school; Videodisk Three followed the "Invention" and "Imagination" themes in the work of the children using with Logo and LEGOLogo™; Videodisk Four was a close look at Andrew's storytelling and his efforts to distinguish between fantasy and reality; Videodisk Five was a description of Mindy's girl/boy talk and the children's views on punishment, lying, and interpersonal aspects of the learning environment; Videodisk Six was the end, a closure to the videodisk set, with a variety of people talking about the relationship between education, technology, and humanity.

Looked at as a whole, the set of six videodisks reflected diversity. The children's stories, as we understood from the original footage, guided each videodisk separately, but our themes and thick description established the constraints within which we negotiated the videodisk real estate. Each of the six videodisks can be thought of as a novella—the set of six as a visual book.

Learning Constellations

The purpose of building Learning Constellations was to create a tool for connecting videodisks with computers for my analysis of video data. However, the environment was also conceived as one wherein my observations and interpretations of children would be shared. To build the interface for Learning Constellations, David Greschler, a HyperCard programmer and developer, joined our design team.

One of the unique aspects of Learning Constellations was that each card could be thought of as a *star* and the combining of stars as the building of thematic *constellations*. I chose the name Learning Constellations because stars appear to group together differently from different perspectives in the universe. The linking of one set of *stars* to another is dependent on where one is located at a given moment. The fact that we draw conclusions from what we are able to see and grasp from these different perspectives makes stars and constellations not only a good metaphor for thinking about how we learn, but also a helpful model for designing ethnographic tools where different users can explore a range of ideas from many points of viewing.

When one entered Learning Constellations, several introductory cards appeared explaining how to think about units or stars of discrete chunks of video and text. The Galaxy Map acted as the main artery through which all navigation occurred. One could begin the exploration by watching my 15-minute video (transferred to videodisk) called *The Growth of a Culture*. Another option was to click on the Dissertation domain from the Galaxy Map and read my textual analysis. Special video icons took the user to the actual video footage relating to that chunk of text. These "video notes" were represented by an icon resembling a video camera.

Another domain was the Videodisk Table of Star Chunks. This table of contents provided the user with the actual breakdown of the chunks so that she could skim through the topics and make choices. Clicking on a selected line brought one to the Video Star card on the computer screen and to the corresponding video on the monitor. Arriving at the selected video chunk, one could read the transcript; find the background information; search according to person, topic, or word throughout the system; and "grab" a chunk to create a constellation with other video chunks.

The most important feature of a research tool was the ability to make annotations and keep track of these annotations. Two types of annotations were possible in this system. When the "Write" button was clicked, the user could make a regular *note* or a *footnote*. When a word or phrase in the text field was clicked, a new field for writing footnotes appeared. A pencil icon was permanently embedded in the regular text once the note was created.

Analyzing Data in a Videodisk Environment: Case Studies

How does the digital ethnographer move from tagging and grouping data to analyzing data? And how does one construct individual case studies from linked chunks of video data? The next phase moves from the period of using Learning Constellations as a research tool for analysis to that of writing case studies. This phase can be thought of as a time of deconstruction leading to reconstruction. The most basic multimedia tool, the search function, proved to be a powerful organizing tool. Searching for a word, a person, or a topic through the whole body of research data led to new connections. Less dramatic were the daily uses of the "Topic Search" button.

The best example of a surprising search which led to a "discovery" was when I followed the topic "How Things Happen/Work." In the first chunk of video, Josh is telling me what he would buy if he were a millionaire. He would get "all the Buddy Holly records ever made" for his dad, "a big house and a maid to clean it" for his mother, and so forth. When I asked him what he would buy for himself, without hesitation, he told me:

Josh: There's this store in the Dedham Mall and it's called The Enchanted Forest. It's a store and everything in the store is stuffed animals. They're like, minks, and everything; and they're stuffed animals; and there's, like, a giant one, like, as big as this car, and they have, like, they have a string hung across the thing and *it doesn't need power. It doesn't need power.* And this little guy is on his unicycle and it's a little bear. This little stuffed animal bear and it goes back and forth. *It doesn't need any power*, it just, like, put it [on] one side and it keeps on rolling. *[It] won't stop unless you stop it. You have to get it started but it won't stop!*

Before using this digital video analysis tool, this chunk was a cute anecdotal comment about a young boy's fantasy rather than a clue connecting it to his fascination with the source of energy. However, using Learning Constellations to link this chunk to other chunks of video made me realize the pervasiveness of his thinking style in various domains.

The smooth slow-motion feature was also indispensable. When Linda Moriarty, Josh and Andrew's teacher, describes Josh in one video segment and Andrew in another, her hands move differently as she speaks of each child. Furthermore, they connote different meanings. Using the slow motion feature of Learning Constellations makes the contrast more evident. When she is describing John, she moves her arms in upward, circular motions; when describing Andrew, she moves them from side to side, erratically and in a confused fashion. Another example is when Mindy tells me about Josh and Joe while I videotape her in her classroom. During this conversation, there are several interruptions. The slowed-down video shows her responses to a classmate, her teacher, another classmate, and me, the interviewer. In slow motion, we can see how she never loses track of her conversation, no matter how many times she is interrupted. Particularly helpful is the fact that the sound is cut off while the video moves slowly or fast. Without sound, the focus is on the gestures.

One could ask why slowing down the movement is important for researchers studying human behavior. One response would be that facial imaging, a topic under investigation by computer cognition researchers, relies on understanding the meaning of gestures.[130] Turning the focus to gestures links what one says with what one means.

The Emergence of Video Data Analysis Tools

As the first version of Learning Constellations was being completed in the late 1980s, other relevant work in the development of tools for chunking, linking, and annotating video data was emerging in the research community. Beverly Harrison and Ronald Baecker from the University of Toronto pointed out the difference between notation systems for representing material from videotapes—such as the Heath Notation System—and video analysis systems for controlling the video, coding it in some way, and then having some additional tools to help in the analysis.[131] This second group included: GALATEA, a graphic system for analyzing and marking up video of biological phenomenon; the GroupAnalyser, which displayed animated diagrams; EVA for both online real time coding and off-time more detailed coding; U-Test designed as a usability testing system for real time online coding, and Virtual VCR, which provides a system of tagging and making short comments.[132]

Jeremy Roschelle from the Institute for Research in Learning (IRL) and Randall Trigg from Xerox PARC designed an annotation system in the late 1980s called CVideo.[133] CVideo was prototyped by Roschelle and released as a commercial package in 1992. With CVideo, a researcher could keep a running log of analog video by marking "in" and "out" points and being able to locate previously logged video. CVideo also enabled researchers to add

---

130. See Paul Eckman, *Darwin and Facial Expression: A Century of Research in Review* (New York: Academic Press, 1973); Nancy Burson, Richard Carling, and David Kramlich, *Composites* (New York: Morrow Press, 1986); and Terry Landau, *About Faces: The Evolution of the Human Face* (New York: Anchor Books, 1989).

131. Beverly Harrison and Ronald Baecker, "Designing Video Annotation and Analysis Systems," *Proceedings of CHI '92* (1992), 157–166; Christian Heath, *Body Movement and Speech in Medicine Interaction*, (Cambridge, England: Cambridge University Press, 1986).

132. Michael J. Potel, Richard E. Sayre, and Steven A. MacKay, "Graphics Input Tools for Interactive Motion Analysis," *Computer Graphics and Image Processing 14* (1980): 1–24; Marcial Losada and Shaul Markovitz, "*GroupAnalyzer*, A System for Dynamic Analysis of Group Interaction," *Proceedings of the 23rd Annual Hawaii International Conference on System Sciences* (1990), 127–133; Wendy Mackay, "EVA: An Experimental Video Annotator for Symbolic Analysis of Video Data," *SIGCHI Bulletin 21*, no. 2 (1989): 68–71; Susan Kennedy, "Using Video in the BNR Utility Lab," *SIGCHI Bulletin 21*, no. 2 (1989): 92–95; Bill Buxton and Thomas Moran, "EuroPARC's Integrated Interactive Intermedia Facility (iiif): Early Experiences," *Proceedings of the International Federation for Information Processing* (1990), 11–30.

133. Jeremy Roschelle, Roy Pea, and Randy Trigg, "VideoNoter: A Tool for Exploratory Video Analysis," *IRL Technical Report*, no. IRL 90-0021.

both transcripts and annotations. One could easily find a location on the video and scan the video by using a movable bar. CVideo did not link chunks of video together into groupings; it kept a linear record of video data for further analysis at a later date. CVideo could control video from Hi8/VHS video sources and videodisk players, a feature also to be found in VANNA.

VANNA was the Video ANNotation and Analysis Tool prototyped and designed by Harrison and Baecker. Not available commercially, it was a tool for coding and annotating video. In its most portable configuration, a video camcorder with an external mini-monitor could be hooked up to a Mac PowerBook using the playback on the video camera. Harrison built input devices ranging from the finger on a touch screen to a digital stylus. Its most interesting feature was that it supported real-time annotation and coding of data. It also had a system of annotations that could be added later. VANNA was designed using a series of human user tests, including brainstorming sessions, with many versions occurring over a short time. A later application that grew out of VANNA, TIMELINES, was a time-based annotation system for the researcher who wants to add time markers and tag the video while viewing.

More recently, other text-based qualitative data analysis tools have added support for video data analysis. Two of these are MacSHAPA and NUD•IST. MacSHAPA is a spreadsheet database which allows you to track variables (columns across the spreadsheet) across time (rows of the spreadsheet). It has built-in support for VCR control, and can import VCR timecodes. NUD•IST, designed for text analysis, allows researchers to organize pieces of data into a hierarchy of categories. It supports the use of many file formats, including digital video, and it can control a VCR using CVideo.

From Learning Constellations to Constellations

My original goal in designing Learning Constellations was to create a multimedia research environment which maintained the integrity of the original source material. In 1987, the last thing I wanted was to encourage others to change my video chunks. The Hennigan School video data were "sacred" to me; I felt about them as the cinematographer or author feels about her story elements. She does not want her images or text edited, or, worse, rearranged, by someone else. After all, an author infuses meaning within a text by carefully placing each word or image beside another, and this meaning can be lost if texts can be reassembled by any reader. Can you imagine the visual artist giving us the pieces of her work and saying, "Here, *you* do the construction of the painting?"

Along the way, I recognized that inviting others into the conversation was precisely the way to look at issues surrounding the validity—*validus*, or strength—of ethnographic conclusions. Encouraging the participation of others, both those who are being studied and those who are reading and viewing the content, could bring about new groupings, or constellations, of significant data to deepen the description. Maybe I would lose control over the final product and weaken *my* story, but it might just be worth the chance. For the next 5 years, I worked with Monika Marcovici and Lawrence Halff, the two central designers in MERLin, who built prototypes of a generic, collaborative tool to enable researchers to work together in digital video data analysis.[134]

Inspired by our predecessors and

Annotation: Most people would be reluctant to break apart a work of art in order to build their own artifact from the remaining pieces. Imagine tearing up the Mona Lisa, for example, to create your own representation. No, I am not suggesting that we destroy an existing work of art, but I do question the boundaries that separate us from learning lessons from those who have come before us. I question an intellectual framework which does not encourage us to build novel creations in collaboration with those who inspire us. In most cases, we are discouraged from putting pieces together in a unique way in order to create meaning for ourselves. When the image of a famous painting is used in a commercially sold puzzle, for example, the pieces have to go back together in the same configuration. From the time of our childhood, we are taught to follow patterns that others have delineated for us, rather than use existing artifacts as building blocks to make new constructions. This paradigm changes dramatically in the light of digital technologies. We now have computer applications that let us manipulate a digitized reproduction of the Mona Lisa to make our own electronic rendition. Not only can we change aspects of a reproduction of the image (as did Michael Duchamps, the deconstructionist who put a moustache on Mona) we can break the whole into components and create something quite unlike the original. In a sense, we now have tools with which to understand what the early modern artists knew already—that tearing and pasting pieces into a collage is a new way of looking at what we thought we knew. It is our interpretation that becomes the work of art.[135]

colleagues but recognizing a different mission, we blurred the boundaries between database and presentation tool. We wanted to develop a prototype for a tool that could be used not only by other ethnographers using

---

134. Lawrence Halff, *De/Composing Constellations: Reflections on the Development of a Collaborative, Multimedia Ethnographic Research Tool*, M.A. thesis (University of British Columbia, 1996). This document can be found at the MERLin website. <http://www.merlin.ubc.ca/publications/decompose>.

135. Ricki Goldman-Segall, "Deconstructing the Humpty Dumpty Myth," in *Contextual Media*, eds. E. Barrett and M. Redmond (Cambridge, MA: MIT Press, 1995), 27.

digital video, but also by researchers and users across domains. As you will see, our mission proved harder to carry out than it initially seemed. Yet looking back, we did construct working prototypes which encourage a way of thinking about video data, as well as a way of sharing perspectives to layer views.

The metamorphosis of Learning Constellations into Constellations in 1992 included developing a tool to handle digital data stored as QuickTime™ movies. Although colleagues of mine were designing tools for analog video logging and annotation, I decided to focus on digital data for two reasons. First, I knew that within a few years, digital data would start being easily shared between distributed locations on individual desktop computers. Even before the Internet, it seemed obvious that collaborative distributed technologies would become the standard.[136] The second reason I chose to invest my research efforts in digital data, rather than video from videotape, was that I was no longer worried about logging every video sequence. In my first ethnography, at the Hennigan School, I treated every video clip, every sequence, as if it were sacred. When I started the ethnographic study at Bayside Middle School, I could more easily identify what I wanted to analyze before digitizing. I would sit at my Hi8 EVO 9300 video editing machine, carefully selecting "in" and "out" (start and end) points from the video. Because the Hi8 videotapes were time-coded, the editing deck could later locate the selected segments and copy them onto a blank Hi8 tape inserted into the record deck. I would then convert the analog signal from output from my edited tape by the video editing machine into a digital video file, using a Macintosh equipped with a Radius VideoVision Studio board and Adobe Premier.

How could I make the right choice of segments to digitize? Making selections is always an important phase when working as an ethnographer: deciding what to keep and what to throw away is a difficult process for all of us, regardless of our respective fields of research. The temptation is to keep everything, to cherish, and to make holy, because we possess a recording of past experiences. Sometimes one wants to find gem in the rock and sometimes to keep the rock just as it is. Digitizing video allows

---

136. Visits to Xerox PARC in the mid- to late 1980s convinced me that collaborative computer tools would easily handle digital video data for ethnographic investigations. See Lucy Suchman, *Plans and Situated Actions* (New York: Cambridge University Press, 1987); and Austin Henderson, "Video and Design," *SIGCHI Bulletin 21*, no. 2 (1989): 104-107.

both. I can keep everything on videotapes (which tend to gather layers of dust as they sit on my shelves), and I can select and digitize moments. I make these choices based on the criteria of the project on which I am working at a given time. And because I have learned how to recognize patterns both in the data and in my own life, I can "measure" what might become important to me. In short, I no longer feel so obliged as I once did to attach themes to each chunk of data in order to build my constellations. I select, then do my tagging according to criteria I have established. But how would I store these video chunks?

By 1993, the CD-ROM had become the preferred storage medium for video data. Storing digital video on a CD-ROM was a breakthrough technology for a person who had piles of videotapes and a budget which did not allow for unlimited storage on a computer hard drive. I could view the video I was collecting at Bayside Middle School, make selections using my video editing machine, and then digitize the segments onto the computer. When I had enough data for a CD-ROM, I could "press" a CD-ROM, using a CD-ROM burner. Thus, the next version of Constellations was designed for CD-ROMs.

Our idea was to enable different authors to pool their data and create common databases. Different users could chunk their data by creating stars from video, text and sound files. They could add their themes and notes, having complete access to others' stars, without being able to change the actual data. For example, if I am looking at a star created by my colleague, I can add my thematic markers under my name. I can also create a new star using the same digital video file; and using a digital video control tool, set new "in" and "out" points to create a chunk from one portion of that file. The digital video file on the CD-ROM remains intact. When I want to resegment this video using Constellations for the

Lawrence Halff on Constellations: In the new version of Constellations, all of the primary program functions can be accessed from one window which is divided into four quadrants. The top left-hand quadrant, the entry information quadrant, displays information about the currently displayed star: its name, who created it, when it was created and last modified, what kind of data is attached to it, what themes have been assigned to it, and the ways in which it is connected to other entries. The top right-hand quadrant, the data display quadrant, is where the data found in the attached file are displayed. The bottom right-hand quadrant, the database access quadrant, is where the database users (authors) and themes are listed so users can search the database. The lower left-hand quadrant, the entry list quadrant, is where the results of searches are displayed as lists of entries. The inspiration for this new design came from prototypes developed by UBC graduate student Scott Flinn on a NEXT computer, using that operating system's interface standards.

purpose of data analysis, I can set new "in" and "out" points only within that particular file.

Our breakthrough in this version of Constellations was in rethinking our approach to layering. Not only could we layer by grouping stars into constellations and visually juxtaposing the chunks of data; now we could also use a *significance measure* with themes associated with a star, constellation, or note. Until this time, various users could access the same database entries and add themes, notations, and transcripts; but they could not easily see how different themes were rated by colleagues analyzing the same data.[137]

The significance measure is the feature in Constellations designed to rate the relative significance of a certain topic or participant to a particular entry. Constellations allows users to define specific themes within two categories (which happen to be especially useful to ethnographers): Topics, concepts important in the research being conducted, and Participants, people appearing in the data. These themes are shared throughout the database so that a theme can be assigned to any entry in the database. When a theme is applied to a specific entry, it can be assigned a numerical rating between 1 and 10.

Lawrence Halff on Constellations: When a particular theme is assigned to an entry, a colored vertical scale with a sliding button appears, and the user can move the sliding button up and down the scale, assigning a level of significance to that theme. In the information quadrant of the Constellations window, themes are listed by significance in descending order, the most highly rated theme appearing at the top. When you click on a theme, the scale appears and you can see the rating assigned to that theme. Selecting a user's name from the pull-down menu above the themes, you can view that user's themes and ratings. When you choose to look at a different user's themes, her list of themes and ratings replace the ones currently shown. You can also view a chart with different users' ratings of all of the themes assigned to this entry in a pop-up window.

These numbers can "mean" whatever a community of researchers decide they should mean. The significance measure allows you to see what themes or what pieces of information are most important to various users.

Suppose one community interested in a particular research area decides that they want to analyze a common database of video segments using a common set of themes. Each researcher could use the significance measure

---

137. Ricki Goldman-Segall, "Interpreting Video Data: Introducing a Significance Measure to Layer Description," *Journal for Educational Multimedia and Hypermedia* 2, no. 3 (1993): 261–282.

to rate how important they think a each theme is to each piece of video. If the project is similar to the one I conducted with young people, a group of researchers may be analyzing a segment of video where a teen is discussing how her parents help her with her school projects, for instance. One researcher specializing in how children learn might assign a high rating to the topic "collaborative learning." Another researcher interested in family relations might instead assign a high rating to the theme "parental involvement."

After layering a star with themes and ratings, each user could search the database for those entries to which a particular theme has been applied and given a particular rating. For example, the researcher interested in family relations could search the database to find all of the clips where that particular topic was important. By using a combination of browsing and different kinds of searches, researchers looking at the same pieces of data could compare layerings, exploring each other's different points of viewing. In this way, layering complements the building of constellations by facilitating the researcher's exploration of the ways in which she and her colleagues intentionally or unintentionally group data. Thus, a community of researchers can transform a simple database into a rich, layered analysis by having the different users add thematic topics and measures.

Lawrence Halff on Constellations: To perform a database search in Constellations, you select a theme from the lists in the database access quadrant, enter a range of ratings in the fields below the theme lists and choose the "Find" menu option. Constellations will then list all of the entries which have been assigned that theme with a rating within the specified range in the Entry List quadrant. If you select both an author and a theme in the database access quadrant, Constellations will list all of the entries where the specified author has assigned the specified theme and rated it within the specified range of ratings.

This kind of layering data through sharing perspectives, using a tool for rating information, is an introduction to more sophisticated tools that, in the near future, will more "intelligently"—or at least automatically—be able to compare similarities and differences according to topics. At the present stage, however, the layering of significance is an interpretive approach (more than a numerical one) wherein the researcher can view multiple frameworks and perspectives. It is not meant to replace a conversation, but rather to act as a pointer for discussion among colleagues. Nor is it meant to quantify the personal views that different users have. The purpose of the numerical coding is to alert researchers to possible patterns.

The Global Forest CD-ROM: Back to Content

> Imagine you are blazing a trail without a compass—where will you end up? You'll probably do a random walk, but if you don't start out with a particular goal, I suppose that doesn't really matter ... and if it is a nice forest you'll enjoy the scenery.... I suppose that describes my career. [138]

In the summer of 1995 I was facing the following hurdle: How could we present the large collection of materials on young people's thinking about Clayoquot Sound? I was facing the final phase of the study of young people at Bayside Middle School and I wanted to use digital media to tell two stories: one about young people's thinking, and the other about how we researched this temperate rainforest. What I envisioned at the time was a CD-ROM-based application that would eventually hook up to the Internet so that viewers in any geographical location could learn about Clayoquot Sound from the ideas of young people from Bayside, and add data about their own local environmental issues.

The Global Forest was completed in September of 1995. Although still in prototype form, it contains a rich, comprehensive collection of information dealing with this complex social, political, and ecological issue. The information is organized using an application developed in Oracle Media Objects to facilitate dynamic data entry for collaborative explorations of ecological research.

This time, we were less interested in how to present "raw data" for viewers to cluster information in their journeys through the material. The content needed a presentation front-end where people could first learn about Clayoquot Sound—from the young people's ideas, from articles from newspapers, and from interviews with a host of knowledgeable experts— and then add their own data about local issues.

What drives our work in MERLin is designing and creating tools to encourage educators and designers to think about learning as a layering and webbing of ideas. The more intricate the webbing of connections becomes, the greater the understanding of the complexity of issues that can eventually lead to pattern recognition and invention.

---

138. Excerpted from a recording of Jerome Wiesner, former MIT president. To hear Wiesner, visit Glorianna Davenport's tribute to him at <http://ic.www.media.mit.edu/JBW>.

Our goal is to develop tools with which to visualize those patterns from the messiness of layered webs.

To design this interface (given limited funds, no distribution resources, and three years of video, text, and sound data), we selected material that provided an in-depth description of our journey. Our research team approached this challenge by first reviewing the footage we had gathered to identify themes.[139]

Clayoquot Project Study at the Bayside Middle School

I had visited the school site approximately twice a month for two or three days per visit, shooting video and making textual notations on my PowerBook. By keeping my computer on and my files open I made these text reflections available to teachers, young people, and parents. When the data were gathered (and while they were being gathered), chunks were selected that best exemplified the approach used by the young people in designing their projects. These data were digitized and made accessible to collaborative data analysis by myself and colleagues. At this stage, I looked for themes to gain a picture of the broader issues. I often built digital vignettes portraying the young people's thinking. I used Constellations to collect and combine chunks into clusters, building the foundations for these vignettes.

Let me step back a bit to explain that the project emerged from a community of inquiry that included researchers from the University of Victoria, headed by Ted Riecken, the University of British Columbia and school staff interested in the use of technologies in the classroom (see chapter 3). Planning meetings with teachers and the vice-principal took place in 1992 and 1993; implementation meetings occurred throughout the project, mainly through email and in and around the regular class schedule. Lawrence Halff, my research assistant throughout the study, spent most of his time working with the young people to solve technical problems. However, he also conducted interviews, spent time with kids on the field trips, and suggested many theories about how to think about young people's construction of their sexual identities.

---

139. The team was comprised of Lawrence Halff, designer and programmer; Will Pritchard, visual designer; Avner Segall and Aaron Willinsky, text researchers and writers; and Ricki Goldman-Segall, videographer, digital video editor, and project director.

Both girls and boys built portfolios about the issues, using both primary and secondary sources. Text-based information came from the Ministry of Forestry, logging companies, environmental groups, WWW servers, and the usual resources in encyclopedias and school textbooks in the library. However, these young people also had first-hand experiences from which to draw their understandings. We went on field trips, talking to people in the towns of Tofino and Ucluelet (situated in the heart of Clayoquot Sound). We slept in sleeping bags on the school gym floor at the only school in Tofino, and met the local kids—playing basketball with them. We videotaped interviews with locals, attended special lectures from experts in related fields, and visited scientists working in Clayoquot Sound.

Fieldnotes (March 1993): Kelli got hit in the nose with a ball playing baseball and we rushed her to the hospital in my car. Her nose was broken. It was difficult to see her in pain. As she once said to Jan who was videotaping us, "Ricki and I are going to sole-to-sole," after she and I had discovered we wore the same size Birkenstock sandals by trying each other's style of sandal. This first year has been the year of establishing bonds within the culture of young people. Of letting them know that I was interested not just in my research project, but in their lives as young people in their school culture.

Back in Brentwood Bay, visitors to the school provided a range of up-to-date information about such issues as First Nations rights.[140] Leading environmentalists such as Vicky Husband from the Sierra Club and Valerie Langer from the Friends of Clayoquot Sound also spoke to the young people, explaining the potential dangers facing the planet as a result of clearcut logging methods. Logging companies took us on trips to local sites, showing us their attempts to reforest the land. We learned about tree farming and harvesting. In the meantime, the young people built multimedia representations, using HyperCard and HyperStudio, as they delved deeper into the web of discourse surrounding the dispute at Clayoquot Sound.

In short, the young people investigated issues from as many perspectives as possible, using all available recorded media; discussed these issues in class on a semi-regular basis as part of their science classes; visited the site conducting interviews using video, tape, pen and paper, and portable

---

140. The First Nations (the name indigenous people in Canada have chosen) were not recognized by the British Crown and their explorers. David Cohen, Dean of the Faculty of Law at the University of Victory, explained the meaning of Crown Lands—lands claimed by the British Crown when no civilization inhabited a place; Tree Farm Licenses; and the commons. He encouraged us to consider ourselves members of the commons and, moreover, to understand that it is the peoples of British Columbia who lease lands to logging companies.

computers; assembled the text, sound and video data; conducted school surveys about attitudes and ideas for change; used experts from various locations in British Columbia and elsewhere; and became resource persons for others interested in the rainforest issue in BC. At the same time, we coordinated the methodological approach for analyzing the data about the process. Young people were interviewed and events recorded. We developed a relational approach to reporting our findings, involving the student research team.

Young people analyzed the video data we collected from these videotaped interviews and field trips. They were given copies of the videotapes to take home and watch on their VCRs. We asked them to select a few minutes that best conveyed the topic they were focusing on. However, that is *not* what they did. The young people chose video that best reflected the highlights of the field trip as they saw them! Wading into the low, rolling waves at Cox Bay was interesting to them, and so that is what they selected. Another favorite event was the scene they called the "Bear Scare." Jordan, their teacher, told them how bears like to live in the empty spaces that are caused by trees growing on nurse logs. (As the nurse log disintegrates from its use as the source of sustenance for the growing cedar, a huge hole is left at the base of the tree.) Then he encouraged a few of the girls to go explore the mossy hole. As they entered to have their picture taken, he ran around the tree and came into it from behind, growling like a bear. We all screamed in shock. An odd story to be the pinnacle of the year. But there it is—young people constructing their own icons for describing events.

Young people were shown how to digitize movies using a range of tools, including Adobe Premiere. Three of the girls seemed to take this task the most seriously. They first logged all the data onto logging sheets they had designed, and named specific chunks. Newspaper clippings, photographs from the field trip, and maps were scanned into the computer. Electronic journals were also entered as part of the database.

My analysis of the video and text data occurred throughout the investigation. Categories were constantly developing. Interviews with individuals or groups took place in the classroom or out on the school playground, when the moment was right for videotaping. In the previous year, I "hung around" more, and got to know the school and the children through a range of activities including baseball games and other school events. In the next year, my interviews included 10 questions addressing their views of the project and their learning.

Bayside Interview Questions:
1. Would you like to tell me about your Clayoquot Sound project?
2. Which aspects of the project do you find most interesting/boring? Why?
3. Does the project relate to your life? How?
4. Does this make it easier or harder for you to study science? Why?
5. What do you think we should do with the material we are gathering?
6. Do you think others would be interested in our study? Why?
7. What changes would you like to see in how people learn science?
8. How would you evaluate your ability to study science? Why?
9. Have you ever thought about a career in science?
10. What do you want to ask me about my role in this project?

The study was conducted as a community of inquiry. We did not try to find solutions to the Clayoquot Sound dispute. Rather, we examined it and used it as a "tool-to-think-with," as Papert would say. We turned it around in our hands and on our computer screens, looking for ways in which to make sense of our experiences with this "object." What we found was that it was our relationship with an object, how we turned it into a subject of interest for us all, that kept our interest levels high.

With videotapes collected over 3 years, we set out to find the overriding themes that would determine the structure of our CD-ROM. Along with the video, the young people and our team had been collecting articles from three newspapers, Victoria's *Times Colonist*, the *Vancouver Sun*, and the *Globe and Mail*, and from a host of newsletters and brochures from groups with differing views. We decided on these frames for the CD-ROM:

What's the story? How do we find out about our environment?
How did it start? How do we learn from our past?
Who really cares? How do we value different points of viewing?
What can we do? How do we work towards change?
Whose story is this? How do we critique the media?

Thus, the conceptual rationale for *The Global Forest* was to create a model for thinking about global, project-based learning. Content-rich electronic learning environments enable learners to enter into a large collection of relatively organized information and then branch off to build paths of thinking about these data and the data they gather in their local areas. They help learners understand issues from many points of viewing. In the Constellations metaphor, users build stars and then put them together into constellations. In *The Global Forest* metaphor, users enter into a virtual green space, choosing existing trails and then *pathways*. Taking a path, the user can either follow the *markers* established by the design team or start a new journey. Starting a new journey means that the user can log onto the system, identifying her geographical location, and then add her paths and markers.

Searching a database that continues to grow and change as each user adds her paths and markers is similar to the process of using Constellations. When a user attaches a chunk of data to a marker on a pathway, the chunk is displayed with fields for attaching related themes and people. Fields also show who the author is, when the data were collected or constructed, what geographical location the data describes, who created this marker, and when this marker was created.

The Global Forest: What is a marker, you might be asking? On a hiking trail, markers are brightly colored strips of plastic tied onto branches, marking a path. In our database, a marker can be any chunk of data that the computer has access to. It can be a video, text, or sound chunk that "lives" anywhere on the hard-drive, a connected server, or a URL site on the Internet. When the marker appears, it displays the data without moving the chunk from its place. *The Global Forest* simply points to that chunk of data and displays it.

(After all, user Clara could be in New York City adding a chunk of video data that a colleague shot while in Brazil several months ago.) In this way, the database begins to be open to users regardless of geographical location—precisely realizing the potential of the Internet.

In many ways, Constellations and *The Global Forest* are similar in both conceptual and practical models. Both are constructionist in design. Although *The Global Forest* provides established pathways with markers already intact, learners are encouraged to travel off the beaten paths and add their own paths and markers for the next user. Both have search engines based on themes entered into the database as users add markers or stars.

Perhaps you will ask: What happened to the notion of coding the same chunks of data from other people's points of viewing? Because there is no significance measure in *The Global Forest*, the best way to compare analyses is to ask several users to add the same piece of data to the database and then compare the topics they attached to the markers they created. But one needs to remember that *The Global Forest* was not designed to "replace" Constellations. Instead, we wanted to create a rich, content-based environment filled with many existing links so that the user could create new ones as she used the program. We also wanted to establish a *way of thinking* about distributed, project-based learning on the Internet. We designed the CD-ROM as a prototype that we could further develop with a software company, and also use as a teaching metaphor so that others could see the potential of working on projects in this way.

The Global Forest contains a rich, comprehensive collection of information designed to facilitate dynamic data entry so that future development can enable the trading of information over the Internet. This open-ended approach to developing multimedia educational environments supports the understanding developed by the young people at Bayside in the course of their research—that learning is about being involved with issues that are personally relevant.

Tools and Situated Learning

Tools for thinking about research and learning have once again changed as global networking has become possible on our desktop computers. The Internet has stretched the bounds of the personal computer, enabling learners and researchers alike to speak to each other and reach across curricular borders that once defined education. Within the short history of computational tools for learning, conceptual models have changed. Once we thought that tools could be used as simple instructional aids. The original computational learning tools were designed to help students with rote memorization tasks. One important change was the move to instructional tools with which teachers could better illustrate what they were teaching; the computer became the best blackboard the classroom ever had! Teachers could more easily demonstrate simulations of events in order to better teach chemistry, physics, and even English literature. A move away from didactic practices happened in many places simultaneously. (See chapter 2, pp. 49–53.) Constructionism, Seymour Papert's rewording based on Jean Piaget's theory of Constructivism, became the buzzword of the 1980s. In fact, many of the most diehard instructionalists became constructionist proponents, praising the computer as a tool with which to empower young people to create artifacts and representations that result from their own personal experiences.

Running parallel to the theory of Constructionism and with similar roots in Grounded Theory (theorizing from data to theory) was a movement that gained momentum with the appearance of an article by Jean

---

141. Jean Lave, "Cognitive Consequences of Traditional Apprenticeship Training in West Africa," *Anthropology and Education Quarterly 8* (1977): 177–80.

Lave.[141] The approach became known as Situated Learning. Those of us who were engaged in designing learning environments understood the need for situating learning in real-life controversies and problems. It seemed obvious that if we wanted to make learning dynamic for young people, we would need to include them in the research process. The line between research and learning would have to become more permeable. Learning and research would have to walk hand in hand into the next millennium if we were going to use computers in convivial ways, as Ivan Illich had recommended in the 1970s.[142] We would have to think simultaneously about global issues and local knowledge, while changing classroom learning into more project-based learning, where students could become global ethnographers, studying the social and cultural life that ties our curriculum together.

Educators using the Internet are beginning to seriously apply project-based learning that reaches across different domains. By project-based learning, I mean using a theme, such as an endangered rainforest, as a window to explore a range of other topics. For example, it has become common knowledge that one cannot be a good biologist without understanding the ways in which biology and social realities interact. We used to say that "no man [sic] is an island;" now we can say, no field of inquiry is an island. We cannot learn about the lives of chimpanzees without looking at our cultural and social practices. We cannot explore a rainforest by looking at one species, or even at the interactions of many. The future of rainforests has become a global issue that touches on the economic and community practices of those who have used the forests' resources for thousands of years. In other words, all of us are implicated by our day-to-day actions, such as reading a book made from trees—such as this book, for example.

Turning our schools into places where real-life problems are looked at in an interdisciplinary way, using emerging technologies, is not easy, but it may be the way to instill the enthusiasm that is so sadly lacking. At a recent gathering of the 1996 National Academy of Education, a panel of distinguished educators addressed a controversial article stating that the claim by situated theorists that there is no knowledge transfer between tasks is highly

---

142. Ivan Illich, *Tools for Conviviality* (New York: Marion Boyars, 1973).
143. The participants John Bransford, Allan Collins, James G. Greeno, Lauren Resnick, and Ann Brown (who acted as chair) were responding to a provocative article by John Anderson, Lynne M. Reder, and Herbert A. Simon, "Situated Learning and Education," *Educational Researcher 25*, no. 4 (1996): 5–11.

exaggerated.[143] Ann Brown, chairing this discussion, asked: "How tightly bound does the transfer have to be for us to call it transfer?" What is knowledge transfer? Can we ever know how one learning experience enhances another? How do we know when a direct transfer, or what is often referred to as "cognitive residue," occurs? James Greeno suggested that eventually we come to understand how things occur. "Transfer" might just be the wrong word. Perhaps knowledge is a more obtuse construct that informs in ways not directly known to us, but which come to be known to us through our experiences. Maybe we need to think more incrementally about how we construct and deconstruct our understanding of the world. As Allan Collins ironically suggested, "The road to transfer is multiple contexts and abstractions; and abstractions need to be grounded so that they apply." And as John Bransford simply asked about the results of situated learning environments: "The question is, how does my experience help me learn something else?"

Maybe the purpose of engaging in research is not only to inform others of what one has "discovered" in the research process, but to learn about one's subject and how it connects to related subjects. For example, designing research tools, I not only learned about the young people I focused my video lens on, but also about my own thinking as a digital ethnographer. Through my experiences, I have opened a window into thinking about research as a learning activity. Such research has become a place in which to construct views of complex interwoven moments recorded on a videotape, digitized on my computer, stored on a CD-ROM, analyzed using Constellations, and presented in *The Global Forest*. Moreover, the research tools I have prototyped and tried out in my own research process have become learning tools. The bifurcation that usually exists between what is research and what is learning has blurred.

Where are we heading in the design of video-based tools for research and learning? The Internet has certainly made the flow of information easier. It is remarkable that anyone with a computer, a modem, and some free software has the tools to log onto millions of websites with information from all over the world. In fact, as I write this, the distribution of technologies for connecting television to the World Wide Web, Web-TV, has already begun. The simplest use of this technology may be a profound example when examined more closely. A mother places the pictures she took at the birth of her child on her website; and family members, wherever they live, read the birth announcement, see photos shot at the birth, and watch the video of the baby's first meeting with Mom and Dad. Everyone sends their greetings and a family discussion ensues about the baby's name after the new parents ask for input. Should she be named after the father's grandmother or the mother's great grandmother? A cousin puts up some photos of the great grandmother, born in Istanbul, on her website. A sister finds some home movies of a holiday dinner with the father's grandmother, transfers the film stock to video, and places a clip on her website. The ongoing conversation shifts its focus to other, related issues—the sharing of memories and family stories, immigration, politics, family feuds, and festive dinners. The issues become webbed and interwoven. *The Connected Family*, the name of Seymour Papert's most recent book, is not only a metaphor for the Internet; it is an inevitable result of our connection with others in domains where private and public merge.[144]

But why don't we extend that family, as Papert has suggested, to include those members who share common concerns—those who enter into a discussion because a topic is important to them? Not only do they respond to others' issues, but they add their ideas to the communal pot. They begin to find connections between their own issues and others'. They build new ways of thinking about what they are viewing and discussing because what they are engaged in is constantly permutating and taking on new shapes. And the media forms they use to express their ideas are not only words, but images—moving images. Now, think about this kind of community building in light of conducting research or explorative learning. Think about how collaborative research is, finally, not a vision for the future, but an activity that is within our reach.

Multimedia and digital ethnography have now arrived at a time and place where the ideas of Geraldine Gay of Cornell University and Mark Horney of the University of Oregon are becoming interesting to anyone browsing digital data. Both researchers, well versed in ethnographic theorizing, have produced thoughtful models for organizing digital

---

144. Seymour Papert, *The Connected Family* (New York: Longstreet Publishers, 1996).
145. Geraldine Gay, "Issues in Accessing and Constructing Multimedia Documents," in *Contextual Media: Multimedia and Interpretation*, eds. E. Barrett and M. Redmond (Cambridge, MA: MIT Press, 1995), 175–189; Mark A. Horney and Deborah Healey, "Hypertext and Database Tools for Qualitative Research" (paper presented at the 1991 Annual Meeting of the American Educational Research Association).

data.[145] Gay's research team, concerned with making meaning from large quantities of data, took the simple spreadsheet template and reinvented it into a sophisticated tool for logging and annotating video data; Horney reconceptualized links as "threads" and developed a visual way to illustrate the threads. The emergent patterns easily identified major themes in the data set.

Ideas in MERLin have developed around metaphorical models—stars; constellations and galaxies; and forests, paths, and markers. Our stellar metaphor went from the small chunk to the larger grouping, whereas the forest metaphor went from the larger grouping, the forest, to the smaller, the marker. What we are looking for in our forthcoming designs are more generic tools with which the user can decide whether to work from the idea down to the detail or from the detail to the larger idea or theory—or decide to do a little of both. However, the principle of layering and working collaboratively to build multiple points of viewing is still guiding our design decisions.

Web Constellations Meets *Points of Viewing Children's Thinking*

Most recently, we have been working on ways to think about tools for online annotation and digital video analysis at our website. To establish a foundation for this work, we decided to build our website around the notion of features, in the sense of a movie feature. For our first "feature," we took *The Global Forest* and built a linear narrative, with links to video stories, based on the CD-ROM's introductory slide show.[146] This way, a visitor to our site can "enter a rainforest to find a variety of life forms, growing and changing with the peoples who have lived there for thousands of years." The visitor can choose to view video or hear audio segments from the young people, a spokesperson from the Friends of Clayoquot Sound, a foreman from a logging company, or a university professor who is also a member of a First Nations band. The story line is meant to provide the context for a conversation about the issues. It situates the conflict. It is also meant to interest the viewer in exploring the links we have provided to other organizations working on these issues, such as organizations that are trying to turn

---

146. See <http://www.merlin.ubc.ca/projects/gf>.

Clayoquot Sound into an international park site protected from tree harvesting. And it is meant to stimulate discussion about how to teach science and social studies in middle schools.

The most recent feature story at the MERLin website is about this book. The reader can go to the website, view video, and enter into a conversation with other readers, researchers, and members of our original research community. Web Constellations is the first server-side, Web-based database system designed to enable a community of researchers to catalog, describe, and meaningfully organize data accessible on the Web.

Lawrence Halff on Web Constellations: The user can access this database system using any browser which supports Javascript 1.1 or better. Like Constellations, the underlying metaphor for Web Constellations is stars and constellations. Unlike Constellations, researchers in dispersed locations can use Web Constellations to access the same database and collaboratively analyze that set of data. Stars and constellations can be tagged with keywords and researchers can engage in dialog about particular stars and constellations using the annotation discussion system.

Our central ambition is to conduct online data analysis among a community of interested visitors. Yes, there are many problems to solve: some are ethical; some technical; and some fundamentally ideological. Nevertheless, I have always believed that technologies must be used to push the bounds of our humanity in the early stages of their development if they are not to be used destructively. The history of science and technology is filled with examples of how good inventions are used for the wrong purposes. Designing tools for data analysis may not seem like an important issue to those who are providing food for hungry people, campaigning for human rights, or working for world peace. But little steps—enabling us to get to know each other better and build commensurable cultures willing to share a range of meanings with others—may help us overcome the hurdles we face when trying to solve important problems.

I don't think we can talk about tools for communication without talking about why we want to communicate. When people listen to each other and understand how each of them sees and makes sense of the world, then changes can happen. We can sit down together, even if only at a virtual cafe, and discuss issues that we see differently. We may not change our views, but we may learn to accept that our views are only one important piece of an ever-expanding puzzle, a story never to be completed but always seeking completion, a journey that can only occur when we place our stories beside those of others with quite different stories to tell.

Any attempt to weave a historical whole out of a random walk must be dismissed as insufficient. Nonetheless, the very act of constructing a hyper-portrait indicates the pressing need to better understand how an individual's contribution can affect the broader population's pursuit of personal dignity and political well-being. The technology allows us to publish an unfinished portrait which will expand and evolve as we add stories and as our audience engages in dialog with it and with each other.[147]

To take a walk through an online collaborative research environment and become part of our community of digital ethnographers, visit <http://www.pointsofviewing.com>. After all, we are all on a random walk through the forest, blazing new trails and finding links to a common path—the search to expand our knowledge and humanity.

---

147. Glorianna Davenport, <http://ic.www.media.mit.edu/JBW>.

part III

storytelling

The filmmaker limits himself to that which occurs naturally and spontaneously in front of his camera. The richness of human behavior and the propensity of people to talk about their affairs, past and present, are what allow this method of inquiry to succeed.

—David MacDougall,
"Beyond Observational Cinema"

The Other Side of the Double Helix: Children's Views

In the following chapters I present portraits of girls and boys in computer-rich learning environments. Their stories demonstrate our need as adults to celebrate diversity and similarity among and between children. I have composed and presented these portraits of children because I sense a crisis looming in front of us, a crisis of technological illiteracy that I believe we can overcome as a society if we simply listen carefully to the stories that young people tell us about their understanding. Although we introduce innovative programs in an attempt to reach students, we do little to find out about *how they view their own thinking.* Instead, we apply more and more antidotes and theoretical solutions from above. How many more "educational experiments" will we impose on our schools without listening to how children view their learning?

The issues that first motivated me to construct these narrative portraits include my deep curiosity about why girls (and women) do not possess a greater role in contributing to the social and scientific decisions that affect the well-being of our planet. Why are adolescent girls finding themselves at risk from anorexia nervosa instead of gaining inner strength from the freedom this generation of women has attained? Why do young African-American, Latino, and other minority boys fall through the economic and social cracks instead of building, as the movie suggests, their *Hoop Dreams?* Why do privileged children and adults often lack empathy with those who are not privileged? And why do young children faced with poverty, hunger, homelessness, and disease receive little material and psychological support to change their situations? In my work, I look for patterns in the thinking of children. Patterns that point to how we might begin to address these problems.

I continually ask myself how we can begin to untangle the mess we have created so that good things can begin to happen for all children and young people. Is becoming a village the next step, as Hilary Rodham Clinton suggests in *It Takes a Village?*[148] My suggestion is that our first step is to listen to how girls and boys make sense of their worlds as they enter the digital world. And, if we are sincere about our interest in making changes in

---

148. Hillary Rodham Clinton, *It Takes a Village: And Other Lessons Children Teach Us* (New York: Simon and Schuster, 1996).

our schools, we need to get a handle on the challenges they are prepared to overcome and how they understand the world as it unfolds online and in real time.

These portraits are based on an analysis of digitized moments on video that will open a discussion about how children, as epistemologists in their own right, make sense of their digital, home, and school worlds. One of my recommendations, described more fully in chapter 10, is that children be encouraged to "cross-dress" epistemologically and culturally. If what we are striving for is multiculturalism and the creation of a global village, then young people need to be able to try on each other's ways of understanding the world and to reach beyond their own limits. But before they can do this, children must feel secure in knowing that the position from which they start is situated and legitimated.

How do I tell these stories and invite you and others to find common threads that will help us address the obstacles that young women and men face? Traditionally, the tension created by an author leads the reader to want to find out the author's answer. We are all dramatic readers solving mysteries, formulating hypotheses, or recognizing personal issues as we voraciously read ourselves into texts. We want to try on new personae, alternative ways of thinking, and interesting intrigues to encounter and resolve. Given this tendency for you to seek my answer, how do I hold myself back so you can find your own? How do I captivate your imagination without filling in all the blanks and giving you a comforting sense of closure? Will you want to read these stories if I tell you that my purpose in writing them is to elicit a concern for children and not to give answers? Will you want to enter into a conversation with others, electronically or otherwise, in an attempt to find new ways of thinking about the issues that haunt our educational systems, rather than relying on my conclusions?

These portraits do not represent a taxonomy of ways of thinking in computer cultures. Nor do the young people represent "icons" or "archetypes" showing the full range of epistemological or cultural diversity. What they say and how they say it extend far beyond my conceptualizations. Because I have grown to care deeply about them, I tend to overlook their shortcomings. I don't see them when they are hanging out with their buddies in the mall or at parties. I don't see them when they are in trouble. I have only been invited to one of the children's homes by his parents, so I do not see them when there are dishes to be done, errands to run, and rooms to be neatened. Furthermore, what I see is only one small slice of the diversity of what can be seen "out there" in our schools. This slice is what I want to share with you, a slice that represents these children's actions in their socialized, intellectual worlds as they make sense of electronic media—the space that lives beside the spaces we call schools.

As borders between school subject areas begin to overlap, students who have an opportunity to try on diverse ways of thinking may be better equipped to meet the challenges facing the 21st century. The "Jills-of-all-skills" and "Jacks-of-all-trades" will move seamlessly from person to person, from task to task, and from theory to theory, building on the ideas and constructions of others and creating worlds for us all. This ability to navigate and to link parts into new wholes is not just a trivial skill aided by a computer culture; it is a prerequisite for meeting challenges in the collaborative and distributed learning work environments of the future.

6 Minding Machines

How can a disk hold information? How can it hold little words? Like, in the 1800s, things weren't as easy as they are now—cars; we have so many advanced new things—cars, video cameras, VCRs. Even computers. If you think about the Logo we do, FD [the command for moving the cursor forward] has to be a procedure somewhere, right? And the things you put in a procedure have to be a procedure, right? And it just goes back to electronic pulses and microchips!

—Josh

Dreaming Up Our Future

I meet Josh at the Hennigan School on a day when the fourth-grade teacher, Joanne Ronkin, is using carrots as a prop to help the children learn how to describe objects. The clock on the wall. Artwork on walls. Overhead florescent lights, forbidding the shadows cast by other light sources. Formica tables pressed together in a large rectangle. The visual impression is one of brightness, color, and organization. Joanne stands, with the comfortable demeanor of an experienced teacher, in front of the tables around which the children are scattered. Joanne's hot pink shirt and black corduroy pants are as striking as the wave of silver-gray in her black hair. A long chain holding a handful of keys hangs around her neck, clanging whenever she moves. Her presence is felt, heard, visceral.

Carrots are strewn on the tables, and Joanne reads to the class. Each young person has written a description of a carrot on an index card, and the task in which the children are keenly and good-humoredly engaged, is to match the description with the carrot.

> **Joanne:** The first thing we need to do is check and see which of these carrots is ten inches long. And that will eliminate all the others. So, Tiffany, would you measure at this table; Latoyah, would you measure at the circular table; and Josh, would you check these carrots over here? Ten inches! This person was very specific in his description. And that's what you need to identify the carrot. This carrot has black marks at the top. So, how many people think it's this one?

Joanne holds up one carrot, and the children murmur, "No" and "Maybe." She holds up another, and the children again murmur, "No" and "Maybe." When she holds up the third one, the children, in unison, call out, "Yes!"

> **Joanne:** Whose carrot is this?
>
> **Josh:** It's mine.
>
> **Joanne:** Is this your carrot?
>
> **Josh:** That's my carrot!
>
> **Joanne:** Excellent! Excellent description! Great carrot!

Josh is sitting on a desk at the back of the room. He has pale white skin; a thin, lanky body; light brown, straight hair; and alert, twinkling green eyes. He squeezes his knees tightly with both hands while Joanne praises him for his excellent description. Then, for the first time, he glances furtively into my camera while pushing the sleeve of his shirt up to his elbows in a nonchalant yet self-conscious gesture.

This is the first time I videotape Josh. His glance expresses both curiosity about my presence and a degree of discomfort with being the focus of my video recording.

Josh calls out to his classmates, "Did you see the little engravement?" Joanne asks if he wants to point it out to everyone, so Josh jumps from his place and excitedly walks toward her as she holds the carrot lengthwise between her hands.

Joanne: Is the engraving at the top or the bottom of the carrot?

Josh: At the bottom.

Joanne: That's the only thing I would have added to your description, but otherwise it was—

Josh: Wait a minute, hold on! This isn't my carrot!

Joanne: That's not his carrot!

Josh gets flustered. The more flustered he gets, the more the other children tease him for not knowing his carrot. I suspect that the laughing has nothing to do with the carrot.

Josh: It's not? Hold on—

Joanne: Wait a minute—

A child: (off camera, in a teasing voice) I thought you knew your carrot, Josh!

Joanne: Josh insisted he knew his carrot. (The children laugh while Josh looks at the carrot and at the other carrots on the table.)

Josh: My carrot's not here!

Joanne: We have to call the FBI. I tell you what, check in this bag and see if someone else claimed your carrot.

From this time on, Josh often asks me, "Can I see the carrot video?" I respond by trying to set up a time to do this, eventually realizing that the question is his way of getting my attention. This marks the beginning of our many conversations over the following 2 years.

http://www.pointsofviewing.com/157

Thinking About Moving Things

Josh has many interests, both in and out of school. At 11 years old, he is especially curious about why and how objects move. Whatever the circumstance, Josh asks what causes things to move, where the beginning of an action is located, and how inventors invent new things.

> **Josh:** The first invention must have been [thought of by] a real real smart person. Like, it's amazing how many things we have, and how many things we do. It's so amazing that we can have a car! Only the top auto mechanics know how a car works. All I know is there's a pedal and it moves. I don't know what happens, how everything moves. All I know is that there is a fan belt and a fan. D'you know how a car works? It's amazing that you can make a car move with just energy, not even energy; a liquid can make things move.

When Josh's parents invite me to visit their home, Josh and Annie, his sister, take me on a tour of the house. Josh's room is filled with posters that express both the cuddly side and the mechanical side of his eleven-year-old consciousness. A poster of a mother possum with her babies on her back, another with a mother polar bear and her cub climbing big rocks, and yet another of a motorcyclist decked out in full leather attire hang on the wall facing his bunk-beds. However, none of these are as special to Josh as are his beloved sports car posters, especially his latest acquisition, the black Lamborghini poster. "This is awesome. Check it out, Ricki!" he says as he unfurls the poster for me to videotape.

Josh also has a soft red Lamborghini stuffed car—a teddy bear Lamborghini! As he walks around the house, he holds it close to his body, clutching it with his left arm and caressing it as though it were a beloved pillow or blanket. Cars are Josh's special objects—objects-to-think-with, to dream with, and to invent with. Most of his Logo games have cars as their central objects, and he spends a great deal of time thinking about "how someone could dream them up." Dreaming them up means inventing—a perfect expression for a child whose thinking about inventions is just as connected to imagination as to notions of mechanical structure.

Josh: Some things you can just dream up. Like when someone made an invention like a car. It probably came from the bicycle. They thought about a wheel. They thought about everything. To think about something [new], you have to think about every detail.

Annotation: Where is there time in the busy school day for schmoozing, "dreaming up" new things, and figuring out all the details needed to complete a working project? Uninterrupted collaborative work time gives children the chance to learn the language of working in teams but, you may ask, where is there time in the eight blocks of the school day for uninterrupted collaboration?

Josh is convinced that simple things, like bikes, lead to complex things, like cars. Josh's theory is similar to modern-day scientific thinking—all life moves from simple to more complex arrangements. He believes that someone first thought about a wheel, then came up with the idea of a bike, and then, finally, the car was invented.

Thinking About Gears

Building with gears is a large part of the Headlight culture at the Hennigan School. Using LEGO™ bricks, wheels, gears, and other movable parts, children build the things they want to build. Through building things, children learn to talk about how they think about how things work. As Papert has written:

> We understand "constructionism" as including, but going beyond, what Piaget would call "constructivism." The word with the v expresses the theory that knowledge is built by the learner, not supplied by the teacher. The word with the n expresses the further idea that this happens especially felicitously when the learner is engaged in the construction of something external or at least sharable ... a sand castle, a machine, a computer program, a book. This leads us to a model using a cycle

http://www.pointsofviewing.com/159

of internalization of what is outside, then externalization of what is inside and so on.[149]

If the deeper levels of thinking underlying constructionism are rooted in anything from Papert's past, it is most likely his childhood fascination with gears (which he found provocative while playing underneath his parents' cars). Gears were part of his "natural landscape [and were] embedded in the culture around [him]."[150] They were objects he could turn in his hands while thinking about the laws that governed their behavior.

> I became adept at turning wheels in my head and at making chains of cause and effect.... I found particular pleasure in such systems as a differential gear, which does not follow a simple linear chain of causality since the motion in the transmission shaft can be distributed in many different ways to the two wheels depending on what resistance they encounter. I remember quite vividly my excitement at discovering that a system could be lawful and comprehensible without being rigidly deterministic.[151]

Josh also uses gears as tools for thinking. He hopes that if he can understand how gears work, then he will be able to understand how someone can "dream something up." When he talks about bicycle gears, he offers an explanation that includes a sophisticated notion of power.

> **Josh:** Gears on bikes are amazing! I don't know how anyone could dream that up. It's just the littler the circle you make, the faster you can go. And it goes lighter and lighter or harder and harder if you want. Like, in one pedal, if you have like a 12-speed bike, when you put it on the 12th gear, it just goes!

For Josh, one "pedal" means one full rotation. Understanding his use of "lighter and lighter or harder and harder" is more problematic. Does lighter

---

149. Seymour Papert, "Introduction," in *Constructionist Learning*, eds. I. Harel and S. Papert (Cambridge, MA: MIT Media Lab Publication, 1990), 3.
150. Seymour Papert, *Mindstorms: Children, Computers and Powerful Ideas* (New York: Basic Books, 1980), 11.
151. Ibid., vi.

mean easier? What does lighter mean when one is riding in the 12th gear? Does he understand the basic premise that the easiest thing to do is to use whatever gear is appropriate to the situation at hand?

> **Josh:** One pedal! If you do one circle, it will go twice as far than if you're in the first gear. Like, if you're in the first gear and you take a pedal, you only go one pedal. You have to keep on pedaling. But, if you're in 12th gear, you take one pedal and you'd go five feet! It's just easier to do it.

It seems that lighter and harder refer to the force needed to pedal. He focuses on the person-power required to move the system while pedaling.

> **Josh:** Like, when people [first] made bikes—they wouldn't make it so you just have the pedal attached to the bike. They have to make it so, when it could move, there'd be a chain in the back pulling the back wheel and the front wheel. And it wouldn't be just on the front wheel—like one up here and one back there and when you pedaled, it just moved the front wheel. That would hardly work.

Josh presents his ideas about gears in a historical context. Mechanical geniuses knew that directly driven wheels would not turn as fast as chain-linked wheels. In his description of the theory of mechanical advantage, he understands the trade-offs between gear size and distance traveled per pedal.

Josh's ability to think through and verbalize how gears work does not come without experience with bikes. Josh loves cycling. As long as the ground isn't covered with snow, coming home from school means getting on his bike to visit his neighborhood friends. His mother, a teacher, encourages him to explore complex ideas; his three older siblings expose him to conversations about related issues; and his dad, a house painter, works with his hands to change and improve physical spaces. Moreover,

http://www.pointsofviewing.com/161

through grades 4 and 5, Josh worked intensely with LEGO™ bricks and gears, consulting with MIT researchers who always enjoyed talking about how things work.

Thinking About LEGOLogo™ Inventions

Building objects with LEGO™ bricks and using Logo as the interface for sending commands to them was a common experience for Josh and his classmates. Josh learns about the transfer of energy from one object to another by connecting an object—such as a car—to a wire that is connected to an interface box, and then writing a range of commands for moving it. He experiences the meaning of sending messages and causing actions. But more than observing simple cause and effect relationships, he is making things move according to his own design. He plays with LEGO™ "intelligent bricks" in a totally choice-driven manner.[153]

Annotation: In the spring of 1996 I ask Steve Ocko what he is doing that is different from what he did with young people at the Hennigan 10 years ago. He tells me that these days he works more closely with young people to enable them to *deconstruct* sophisticated robotic "creatures." He believes that knowledge is best constructed by breaking apart a robust working model and learning about the parts. This seems to corroborate Nira Granott's doctoral research at the Media Lab, in which she worked with adult students as they tried to make sense of complex mechanical creatures.[152]

Using LEGO bricks attached to a Logo interface, Josh follows no traditional curriculum; there are no rules, no grades, and no expectations. From the beginning, Josh approaches LEGO workshops with excitement. At first, he builds what most children start off building—cars (presumably Lamborghinis and Porsches). Within weeks, however, he builds more imaginative cre-

---

152. Nira Granott, *Microdevelopment of Co-construction of Knowledge During Problem-Solving: Puzzled Minds, Weird Creatures, and Wuggles*, Ph.D. diss. (Massachusetts Institute of Technology, 1993). For her more recent description on the similarity between learning and development, see Nira Granott, "We Learn, Therefore We Develop: Learning Versus Development or Developing Learning?" in *Adult Learning and Development: Perspectives from Educational Psychology*, eds. M. C. Smith and T. Pourchot (Mahwah, NJ: Lawrence Erlbaum Associates, in press).

153. Intelligent LEGO™ Bricks have tiny micro-processors hardwired into them. Fred Martin, Steve Ocko, and Mitchel Resnick, researchers with the Learning and Epistemology Group at the MIT Media Lab, designed and built these robotic objects with the sponsorship of LEGO™ Corporation.

ations of moving things, such as a room in which a person is being propelled out of bed. He calls this contraption his *Alarm Clock Bed*. Josh explains that getting out of bed in the morning is usually difficult. As a precaution against his falling asleep again, the little LEGO person is ejected from his bed and propelled onto a conveyer belt, which takes him into the bathroom. Not a bad device for those of us who are bleary-eyed on waking.

Another of Josh's inventions is equally imaginative. I watch him fooling around with a LEGO motor, pretending it is an electric shaver and rubbing his 11-year-old face—not finding any whiskers to remove. I videotape the entire sequence of his moving from playful fooling around to invention. He pretends to shave his face with this motor while scrounging through a large bucket of multicolored bricks. With characteristic puttering, Josh puts a wheel on the bottom of the motor and holds it from its wire, allowing it to touch the table. The thing contorts in strange and unpredictable ways. When I ask Josh what he is doing, he tells me he's making an electronic breakdancer. He then proceeds to build a discotheque from the bricks for his breakdancer, adding quite a sophisticated assortment of strobe lights that are set off every time his dancer drops into the discotheque. Then, he explains the disco lights.

> **Josh:** See, I just made a light here. Like, there are these little blocks and he goes down [and] there is a wheel spinning on the motor; and all he does, when he goes down, is go wild.

Curiously, Josh never changes his electronic breakdancer into a recognizable person. The breakdancer remains a motor and a wheel. Other children I know would try to make their objects more person-like. But Josh is interested in what the object can do, in its performance, rather than in what it is.

http://www.pointsofviewing.com/163

Logo Inventions:
Making a Computer Game Called *Obstacle Mania*

Josh's work with programming has the same imaginative flair as his work with creating objects. He redesigns the car game he and Thomas, his best friend, started a school term earlier, building a rather sophisticated computer game called *Obstacle Mania*. In *Obstacle Mania*, the computer screen is divided into two sections by a lime-green line that has a small opening. The user can control the direction of the car cursor by pressing the L or the R key on the keyboard. L turns the car 15 degrees to the left, then moves it 5 steps forward; R turns it 15 degrees to the right, then moves it 5 steps forward. The goal of the game is to get your car through the obstacles. As Josh explains to me, "The only way you die is if your very middle hits. Watch the

Fieldnotes (November 1986): Josh's Logo creations all contain explosions, fires, take-offs, or ejections from one place to another. Objects change composition, transform, and become new objects of discovery. He uses his created computer environments to think about the nature of moving things—why and how energy is transformed from one thing to another to produce more powerful effects. Cycles and bicycles and gears and wheels—changing energies.

screen, watch the screen!! See, my bumper can hit; anything can hit except the very middle. Only the very middle can make it die."

Josh makes it sound as if it is very hard to die in his game. Speaking from experience, I found it very easy to die in his game—the car exploding in vivid colors on the monitor before my eyes. Josh thought that I was not a good player, and maybe he had a point.

Thinking About Movement and the Transfer of Energy

One sunny spring day Josh and I sit talking on a hill outside the school. He speaks candidly not only about gears and cars, but also about the nature of energy. Our conversation never strays very far from his favorite subject, moving things.

As cited in the opening lines of this chapter, Josh examines the process of energy transfer from one object to another. While explaining how programming procedures in Logo work, or how information is stored on a disk, his body movements increase, expressing his amazement. He sits squatted with his left arm on his left knee. With his right hand, he squeezes the watch band on his left wrist and flicks his fingers against his skin. He looks directly into my eyes, eyebrows raised. Then he moves his eyes away from me, toward the open field.

> **Josh:** How can a disk hold information? How can it hold little words? Like, in the 1800s, things weren't as easy as they are now—cars; we have so many advanced new things—cars, video cameras, VCRs. It's amazing how people.... Even computers. If you think about the Logo we do, FD [the command for moving the cursor forward] has to be a procedure somewhere, right? And the things you put in a procedure has to be a procedure, right? And it just goes back to electronic pulses and microchips!

Josh tries to understand just what was happening at each step, "pushing the beginning back further and further," as another MIT researcher, Mitchel Resnick, wrote in an annotation using Learning Constellations. Josh takes his own theory to the level of the ridiculous in order to make it clear to me just why the process of storing information electronically is so amazing:

> **Josh:** You'd have to meet a genius who knew how a little electronic pulse traveled through computers, hit the microchip and it changed something around, and a word pops up. You press something [on a keyboard] and a letter comes. Now, how could they do that? I mean, you press a key and a letter comes.
>
> **Ricki:** Are there any books which might help you find the answers?
>
> **Josh:** Well, it would be impossible to explain. An electronic pulse comes and it holds the information. How does an electronic pulse hold information? I mean, do you just stuff a word in it? How can an electronic pulse hold it, go into a microchip and travel around a lot and pop up on a screen? Amazing!!

http://www.pointsofviewing.com/165

Josh introduces another element into his theory about energy here: Information is converted to pulses of energy that are somehow held or stored in microchips or, as he explains later, on CDs or computer disks. In Josh's thinking, energy and information (like motion and particles) are almost interchangeable. Consider how he connects movement and information:

Ricki: What other kinds of things do you think about, Josh?

Josh: Mostly things that move. Like, how does a muscle move? Even if it is a muscle and it has strength and everything, how does it move? How does a disk contain information? How can it hold little words? Whoever came up with a disk is amazing! What about CDs—a laser reads these things. You can put it on the ground, step on it, and it won't do anything. The only way you can break it is if you split it in half or something. And it's amazing—a laser goes down onto a piece of metal and it makes sounds, makes music. A tape, a slip of paper, cellophane—it makes music. Isn't that amazing? If you look at cellophane, it's amazing that it can hold music. Even records, it's not like, I used to think that it was carved into it and when the needle went over it, it scratched out the sound. But how does it scratch out: "Ahhhh"? You can't. Like, how does a laser read off a CD? It's so amazing!.

Josh is fascinated with the cause of movement—energy. What is curious to me is how, after locating the source of energy within a particular object, he focuses on its release and on what it can do when it acts on that object. A laser reads the disk and music is created. A needle goes over the grooves in a record and sounds are heard. "Amazing!"

Annotation: Uri Leron, a mathematics education scholar from the Technion in Israel, believes that "Josh needs to locate the source of energy in a place." Certainly Josh's sense of wonder about how cellophane, records, CDs, and disks "hold" information supports Leron's analysis.

Transfer of energy is not limited to mechanical objects in Josh's scheme of things; he shows an equal fascination with the speed of a fastball thrown by Boston Red Sox pitcher Roger Clemens:

Ricki: What else do you think about, Josh?

Josh: Roger Clemens. Like, Roger Clemens can throw a fastball, like, 95 miles an hour. Now the fastest person that ever ran, ran about 15 miles an hour. And you can throw something 95 miles an hour. In just 60 minutes it would go 95 miles if it didn't, like, run out of power. That's how fast some people can throw.

Josh tries to understand how an object thrown by a person can go faster than the person himself; something happens to the ball that gives it the power to do that, but what? How? Josh's sense of wonder over the transfer of energy is apparent whether we are speaking about baseballs, computers, CDs, records, or tape decks. He simply uses whatever is in his environment in order to think about how things move and how energy is changed.

Thinking about Resistance, Recursion, and Perpetual Motion

Josh also thinks a lot about resistance and recursion, although those are not his terms. He tells me what he would buy if he had lots of money—the "if I were a millionaire" scenario. After listing all the presents he would give others, he said that he would buy a toy store in the Dedham Mall called *The Enchanted Forest*. His favorite toy in this store is a little stuffed bear that travels back and forth along a large string.

> **Josh:** Ricki, it doesn't need power. It doesn't need power. This little bear is on his unicycle. This little stuffed animal bear. And it goes back and forth. It doesn't need any power. Put it on one side and it keeps on rolling. Won't stop unless you stop it. You have to get it started, but it won't stop!

Josh provides a new twist to his understanding of moving objects while fantasizing about owning a toy store. This highlights just how pervasive his concern with energy is; he thinks about mechanical processes not only in the context of what we traditionally call *science*, but also when choos-

http://www.pointsofviewing.com/167

ing a toy. He tries to understand how the toy keeps rolling without stopping. He expects it to stop, as a bicycle will eventually stop when he stops pedaling, because he is familiar with resistance to moving objects: You get something started and it runs out of energy. But this toy bear keeps going until you stop it.

Josh is confronting several problems simultaneously: perpetual motion, resistance, recursion, and how a little effort can lead to a big result. The toy bear doesn't require much energy to get it started, but it keeps on going until it is stopped. The use of recursion in computer programming works the same way: you write a procedure so that the action repeats itself, and the object you make keeps moving. Josh uses recursive commands in his programming of the car game, *Obstacle Mania*, without too much trouble. What he may have realized, consciously or unconsciously, is that a seemingly small effort causes much movement in his objects.

Designing and Building Computer Games

One morning at the Hennigan, Josh is working alongside his regular computer partner, Thomas, who, as usual, is determined to keep Josh engaged in conversation. Thomas, unlike Josh, would rather play a game rather than design or to program one. However, like Josh, he is both verbal and a high achiever. He has short, dark brown, wavy hair and wears rectangular tortoise-shell glasses with thick lenses. His dark eyes, round face, and smooth light skin glow almost mischievously when he speaks. (He looks like the kind of intellectual child who would get beaten up after school by the tough guys, and, sadly enough, this is the case. Thomas related, in an ironic voice, how the school bully picks on him. But he has learned to develop strategies for getting even with Chester and seems to get some pleasure in finding clever ways of getting around difficult situations.)

When I ask Thomas and Josh why they so frequently make games while working at the computer, Josh answers me by saying, "Games are the best thing.... It's not just like seeing something or making a picture, which is boring." Then Thomas moves the conversation in a slightly different direction: "Of all the things on computers, making the game is the boringest thing. But actually playing the game might be the funnest thing. That's what's bad about our games. If you wanna play, you gotta make it!"

For Thomas, the fun is in controlling the game, not in making it. And as far as he is concerned, control is achieved not by creating, but by manipulating. Thomas is bored when he has to build something before he gets to play with it. He hates having to watch someone else play without being able to join in. "It's better when somebody else makes it so you can move it, than when you just get to watch."

Josh sits motionless, eyes glued to the computer. Mumbling, he says "Say, like, I just made it, and it's hard to, like, find the keys. And so, you have to—" (and here he pauses for several seconds). Yes, he is in his own world. So I turn to Thomas and ask him whether making a game takes away from the excitement of playing it. After all, wouldn't he know the tricks pertinent to beating the game? "No, cause you could do it differently. Say, maybe go around that way, maybe go around that way, maybe go through a hole in the middle, next time you play." Thomas and Josh build their car game so that each time they play it, they can play it differently. But I still question their answers. It seems to me that authors of games infuse their predispositions into their constructions. They know the rules and structures hardwired into the game. Even if this doesn't limit their possible moves, it must influence the surprises that a game has to offer. Maybe Josh and Thomas are saying that actually playing something that works, that is your own product, is satisfaction enough.

Josh finally breaks his computer-centered gaze and looks up at me, saying, "Ricki, making it makes you feel like you achieved something. Just playing it doesn't." The real challenge for Josh is in the constructing, the creating, the building. The constructionist, Josh, thinks of the parts that make up the whole; the instructionist, Thomas, thinks of the utility of the results, the playing of the game. The source of Josh's creativity is his preoccupation with questioning and his dedication to details. The source of Thomas's creativity is his ability to manipulate the inventions of others for his own entertainment. For Josh, achievement is linked to creating the game; for Thomas, manipulating and controlling the cards that are dealt out to him, as the saying goes, and developing a strategy for making them

http://www.pointsofviewing.com/169

work in his favor, is challenge enough—especially if the cards are dealt by Chester, the school bully!

Computer Buddies: The Hedgehog and the Fox

Having a friend with whom to talk about important strategies, plans, and maybe even philosophical issues while working on a joint project is important for people, both young and old—especially for people like Thomas, who are focused outwardly. However, enabling the growth of friendships between children while they work together within the school is no small accomplishment.

Often Josh is immersed in his programming and it is Thomas who has to initiate contact and establish a relationship.

> **Thomas:** Josh, what do you like better, Josh, making a game or playing it?
>
> **Josh:** Well, making it makes you feel like you achieved something. Just playing it doesn't make you feel—
>
> **Thomas:** Well, after you've made it and then play it, doesn't that make you feel like you've achieved something else; you've made a game that works?
>
> **Josh:** Yeah.
>
> **Thomas:** I mean, like, I could make a game that doesn't work and wouldn't feel like I achieved something.

Thomas is clearly more interested in making meaning about the things he and Josh create on the computer. More focused on human interactions than Josh, Thomas checks out what Josh thinks, asks him his opinion, and then usually decides to go along with him. Josh, more caught up in his own thoughts, is not interested in engaging in conversation about his creations while he is busy making them. He *is* interested in reflecting on inventions, but only *after* he has invented them.

---

154. Isaiah Berlin, *The Hedgehog and the Fox: An Essay of Tolstoy's View of History* (London: Weidenfeld and Nicolson, 1953).

What both Thomas and Josh seem to recognize is that a relationship with someone who sees the world differently can be of mutual benefit. When Josh notices that a dog Thomas designs in Logo looks more like "a telephone receiver" than a dog, he teases Thomas about it. They banter back and forth, Josh casually leaning on his chair and pointing at the monitor until Thomas makes the dog look more like a dog. They seem to enjoy the banter and negotiating that lead to the end product. But who can tell whether Thomas is offended by Josh's authoritative and convincing manner? Who can tell if Josh has any notion that Thomas might be offended?

The Hedgehog and the Fox: In the making of electronic artifacts, I have witnessed *hedgehogs and foxes*, to use a comparison that Isaiah Berlin makes much of.[154] Some young people enjoy conversations with others while they are in the midst of creating their artifacts. They scamper from person to person learning how others are making sense of tasks. The conversation seems to take them to some new way of thinking about what they are doing. They enjoy the tangential aspect of moving with the flow of the external world as they internalize what's happening around them. They are less focused on completing a perfect vision of what they had "seen" in their mind's eye when they started designing. Sometimes we think these types are superficial but they have an inner focus on gathering ideas and opinions that roots them in action. On the other side, hedgehogs do not want to engage in "conversation" about what they make until their artifact is completed according to their original vision. They see the object in their head so clearly that any distraction by tangential comments is disruptive to their creative flow. I have worked with many programmers, both young and old, and have found variations on the same pattern—foxes work best in conversation and hedgehogs only reappear once the project is complete and ready. Artists at work, both of them.

Two boys working side by side for over 4 months building versions of the same computer game; this is what I observe and record with my camera. Although they both work on it, the computer game carries a different meaning for each boy. Thomas makes games, even though he finds it boring; he cavalierly says, "If ya wanna play them, ya gotta make them." Josh, on the other hand, makes games because it gives him a feeling of accomplishment.

Thinking back, I now reflect on how differently children make meaning for themselves, even when they seem to be engaged in the same act.[155] How simple it is to categorize most boys as *hard* programmers; how unfor-

http://www.pointsofviewing.com/171

tunate it is that we often don't see the boys, like Thomas, who are negotiational and who seek out conversations rather than elegant solutions. In any case, children such as Josh and Thomas, who work together to construct artifacts for thinking about their thinking, can begin, over time, to try on each other's ways of knowing (just as we adults learn new ways of thinking from our friends and co-workers). Could it be that what is now emerging is neither fox nor hedgehog but the "avatar,"[156] a being who mixes human ways of knowing with those of our computer agents. Certainly the intellectual metaphors for understanding our relationships with others (and with machines) are changing.

Knowing, Learning, and Teaching

Sitting on a hilltop overlooking the school playground, I ask Josh whether there should be a curriculum for teaching Logo. It would be a "punishment" if there were a curriculum in Logo, he says, because it is important for children to pursue their own the ideas—especially in Logo.

> **Josh:** You see, no one thinks it's fun, if you're drawing something and you want to do something else, and they're making you draw something that you don't want to do. And if you have another idea. It would be like punishment for the kids who really don't like it.

Punishment, for Josh, is not being able to do what he wants to do—a far cry from the punishment many children receive at school and home. If Josh wants to follow through on his work, to develop his project or to finish his drawing, and his teachers do not let him do it, then he is being

---

155. In chapter 4, I try to understand how the same action often has quite a different meaning for the observer than it does for the person being observed. Moreover, different observers obviously interpret what appears to be the same action quite differently. Gilbert Ryle's *Collected Papers* and Clifford Geertz's *Interpretation of Cultures* both deal with the complexity of understanding intention.

156. For theoretical analyses with case studies of young people exploring the world of Multiple-User Domains (MUDs), see Sherry Turkle, *Life on the Screen: Identity in the Age of the Internet* (New York: Simon and Schuster, 1995); and Amy S. Bruckman, *Moose Crossing: Construction, Community, and Learning in a Networked Virtual World for Kids*, Ph.D. diss. (Massachusetts Institute of Technology, 1997).

punished. Adults often punish children (or each other) by restricting their leisure-time activities. No wonder Josh feels punished when someone takes away his freedom to express himself in his self-directed work activities.

Josh also believes that "only teachers who don't know what they're talking about have to use curriculum; they don't have anything else to teach without it." And teachers who do not want to use a curriculum shouldn't have to. Josh's ideal school would ensure that for half the year, children would be able to do whatever they wanted. As he says, "if you want the teacher to help you with ideas and everything, then you can ask her." According to Josh's educational theory, teachers should not coerce children into doing things they don't want to do; they should help children when asked; and, most important, they should let children follow through on their ideas.

> **Josh:** A teacher should make things [so] that if you didn't want to do them, you didn't have to and you could just draw something. But if you did want to, you could. That's the way it should be. Because if you come up with an idea, and you really want to do it, you should be able to do it. If she gives you something and you can't think of anything on your own, and you just want to [do what she gave you], then you can! That should be it: You should be able to do what you want, but do what she gives you if you want to.

Playing devil's advocate, I ask Josh what happens to children who do not have any ideas for self-directed projects. He looks at me briefly, with disdain, and says: "Ricki, all kids have ideas. Even if you are a kid that comes off a [housing] project or something—which it doesn't really matter." If you are a child from a housing project, "you'd probably make two kids fighting, or something, cause that's what you see, that's everyday life." He pauses for a second, then says, "You get imagination just from facts that you see, things that you see." (I find these statements both enlightening and troubling. That Josh has a theory of knowledge, however

http://www.pointsofviewing.com/173

contradictory epistemologically, at 11 years old is remarkable. That he thinks housing projects are places where people fight is disturbing.)

Josh believes there is an external reality from which we derive our thoughts. We imagine something new when we are inspired by external realities.

> **Josh:** Well, people, like, get ideas but they have to get it from something. You see a rock, you might think of something carved out of it, or something. But you could never know if there were no rocks. You never think of rock, unless you were trying to think of something new. If you were trying to think of a new substance or something. Most imagination is—you see a car and an airplane, and you put them together in a picture.

Empiricism in Josh's thinking begins to mix with rationalism when he says, "you might never think of rock, unless you were trying to think of something new." Although seeing the rock might give you the idea to carve something on it, Josh acknowledges that what you do to the rock is determined to some degree by internal human factors that may have nothing to do with the rock itself. This may be why Josh plays with the notion that if a person tries to think of something new, then something other than objective reality must be at play. Reflecting on his own imaginative processes, Josh understands knowledge as the act of putting known things together in a unique way. The unknown is revealed to the learner by the interplay of experience and contemplation, building points of viewing.

Thinking about Teaching

Josh is not only an inventor but also a teacher, a person who loves to explain how things work. One day, he tells me how *Repeat* in Logo helps him build a square. (His rhythmic way of describing his code sounds poetic.)

> If you want to make a square without saying
> FD 5, RT 90, FD 5, RT 90, FD 5, RT 90, FD 5, RT 90,
> you can say,
> Repeat 4 [FD 50 RT 90].
> So, it's gonna do this 4 times;

It'll do it 4; it'll do it:
FD 50 RT 90,
FD 50 RT 90,
FD 50 RT 90,
FD 50 RT 90,
and it'll obviously make a square.

Obviously. Examining this scenario, I find that Josh employs three teaching techniques. First, his use of body movements infuses his explanation with vitality. Each time he mentions the turtle cursor making a turn and moving, he holds his left hand in front of the monitor and bends it backwards, following the movement of the turtle. Second, to explain how the square is made, he actually makes it. He shows me the code and demonstrates how it works. When he says the word "obviously," he hits the Enter key and the square instantaneously appears. Third, when I ask him what a procedure is, instead of defining the nature of a procedure, he shows me how to make one. For Josh, understanding things means understanding how they work.

Thinking about Neon Lights and Video Cameras

When Josh talks about imagination, he claims that its role in our lives is to create new things, such as, cars, video cameras, VCRs, computers, and compact disks. His mind revels in the technological advances made in the last hundred years. He ponders how inventors came up with the idea of neon lights. Josh emphasizes the role of the creator, rather than the existence of "facts that you see."

> **Josh:** Inventors think real hard and they use things that people have already come up with. Like the light bulb. People thought of it real hard and they came up with neon. Not neon, but, y'know, those lights that light up and are in different shape, to light up

http://www.pointsofviewing.com/175

signs and everything. They just thought about the light bulb and they just put it in things. And like when they made video cameras, like you're shooting me with now. When they made them, they probably thought about cameras. You take a picture, each second, if you put them together, you make a video, a scene happening. That's how somebody discovered it!

As he describes these inventions his body language changes. His hands move; his face becomes more animated. He moves from a squatting position to sitting up on one knee. He turns his body toward the camera when he refers to the making of video cameras, pointing directly at it. Josh understands the making of the moving image—that individual pictures with a small difference in movement placed one after the other and viewed quickly give the impression of movement. Animation. In fact, Josh has watched his sister, Annie, create non-computer animation. And he is most likely influenced by the fact that I am videotaping him as he talks. Given his exposure to the culture of movie-making, Josh's thinking about the moving image is not surprising. Yet it is interesting to see how he integrates videomaking into how he thinks about the inventive process. People who thought about movie cameras first had to think about how placing a still image "one second" apart, as he says, would yield the impression of movement. "Now how did they do that?" he asks. How indeed, Josh!

In closing, I reflect one final time on conversation we had on the hill, when Josh casually commented, "FD has to be a procedure somewhere, right? And the things you put in a procedure has to be a procedure, right? And it just goes back to electronic pulses and microchips!" Josh, as thinker, has what I would call an epistemologically metaphysical and historical attitude about the world. He is always looking for the meaning of events and for causes-what is the essence of this experience, and how did it happen? He traces the route of electronic pulses through microchips in order to find the source of the energy flow that enables words to pop up on the screen when one pushes a key.

Josh is an inventor who is not only building new technological devices for his own pleasure, but also rethinking the nature of energy according to emerging epistemological frameworks. Thinkers and philosophical tinkerers, those who putter with ideas and tools, need to have the time and space to contribute to humanity in their own ways. They need to be able to make connections and try out their contraptions. Who can predict how Josh and his school friend Thomas will affect the world as they grow to understand the hidden power and responsibility of the tools we use for construction?

> **Josh:** You know what's even more amazing, Ricki? Nuclear things! An atom bomb could be as big as that rock right there. And you'd drop it on this country, it would blow up half this country. That little thing! Well, it's little compared to half this country. It could blow up half this country if it were an atom bomb! That little bit might just take up just the amount of space I'm sitting on and it would blow up half this country. It's scary!! If people never came up with nuclear things, they wouldn't have atom bombs.

7 Image-ining Our Selves

Like, when you make a picture in Logo, you're not sure how it's gonna come out; you're not sure it's gonna come out like you want it to come out, and if it doesn't, you kinda like it. Yeah, and you sort of say, "it's a new invention!"

—Mindy

Inventions and Making Girls

A space exists between the lives of those I observe and the lives of those to whom I speak through using words on this page. The space between the observed and the audience is occupied not only by the tools of recording, but also by the author. When I describe the lives of girls in schools, I cannot help but see my life and the lives of the girls I knew in school. I often think about those years of transition from girl to young woman, both in school and out. Perhaps that is why I have struggled in telling this story. I wrote and rewrote this chapter more times than I want to think about. It is an awesome task to represent girls by telling the story of any one girl or group of girls. But this story is not only about Mindy and girls like her; it is also my story about watching clouds race by as I sat in my chair behind my desk wondering and daydreaming. And yet this story is not mine, because it also lives in the writing of the story, that magical process that weaves its own story as the writing progresses. And it is now your story.

Even before reproductive hormones kick in, children are fascinated with their images and with the images they create of themselves. They write their names in the sand, or with different colored pens; they write their names over and over again on paper. They draw pictures of themselves in fantasy homes with famous people surrounding them. They become instant fashion designers, script writers, and architects of their various personae. It is tempting to attribute this adolescent obsession to the media's representation of the (female) body as an object of desire. But what I am referring to is not the saturation of our culture with brainwashing media images of "techno-babes," anorexic catwalk models, and sexless Barbie dolls, but rather the desire in us all to recreate and remake ourselves in our own image, to become our own creators, to transcend the work of our biological parents. We want more than a better eye, hand, or brain—we want to reinvent our selves and to open the possibility of a range of virtual partnerships with technological artifacts made by others.

Scientist and artist have this common desire to create themselves. Each builds representations to invent new paths for self and others. Each believes that her artifact is the one which best describes her world at that moment in time and maybe, just maybe, can be an inspirational creation for others. However, even if the artifact a young person makes does not enlighten or inspire others, it often gives her a deeper understanding of her own life, opening new doors. The activity of the image-ination can be a wondrous adventure.

Where does this fundamental desire to replicate the self and to make an image of the self come from? Does it spring from the desire to have children, which essentialists would have us believe is an inborn trait present in all women—in short, the biological imperative to give life to others who are like us? Perhaps it is social construction; we are both inspired and brainwashed by our cultures to create, procreate, and recreate. Deborah Britzman does not accept essentialist notions that claim the female mission

---

157. Deborah Britzman, "Gender and Multicultural Education," in *Gender and Education, Part 1*, eds. S. K. Biklin and D. Pollard (Chicago: University of Chicago Press, 1993), 40.
158. Ibid., 33.
159. Deborah Britzman, "Anne Frank, Anna Freud and the Question of Pedagogy" in *Lost Subjects, Contested Objects: Toward a Psychoanalytical Inquiry of Learning* (Albany, NY: SUNY Press, in press).

is to ensure that society values the inherently nurturing voice of women. She recommends that any discourse on gender include the study of race, sexuality, and class. Thus, gender identity, for Britzman, is full of the "tensions, volatility, and slipperiness of identity."[157] As an ex-Marxist turned Freudian (neo-Anna-Freudian?), she turns her lens inward and outward simultaneously, asking us to question our interpretations of our selves by coming to understand the ways in which our gendered selves have been constrained by external structures: "The point is to question the stable and limiting ways gender is perceived, understood and policed and to address the power relations that shape the ways gender becomes lived as a relation of domination and subordination."[158] Britzman claims that learning is painful, full of inner tension and unresolved ambiguity. Her recent work on Anna Freud and Anne Frank addresses the pain suffered by girls growing up in an unfair world, where there is a good chance that they will suffer from discrimination and subjugation.[159] Anna and Ann are treated as icons that exemplify the tensions of the inner soul as it searches for reparation for the horrific pain of life under tyranny.

Although I will address the creation of self from the eyes of an 11-year-old African-American girl (and, of course, from the eyes as a 40-something Jewish woman who has spent a lifetime in schools and universities), I am not excluding the male contribution to acts of creation and creativity. Rather, I bring into focus a less popular way of looking at inventive thinking—a way that is concerned with making self-images, a way that can connect the romantic fantasies of an 11-year-old girl with her intellectual life.

I struggle with Mindy's fascination with romantic love, re/creation, and recreation. But then I have to ask myself whether my interest in the making of creative digital video artifacts emerged from my adolescent passion to doodle pictures of girls in glamorous clothing. In junior high school, I was the fashion editor for our school newspaper; at 14, I had a subscription to *Seventeen Magazine*. So I shouldn't be surprised at the following exchange between myself and Mindy: "What do you like about playing?"

http://www.pointsofviewing.com/181

I ask. She confides that she loves playing games and "making girls—on paper, on computer, on cardboard, on anything, chalkboard!" Mindy's beloved Logo project is a graphic illustration of a girl with a bright yellow triangle for a skirt. She whispers conspiratorially, "I like playing and discoverin' stuff."

Annotation: What might happen to girls if they could be encouraged to build on their interest in "making girls"? What might happen if they could use this interest in understanding human relationships within the curriculum? Learning modules on insects, explorers, and the planets may not hold as much excitement for the budding young woman as a module set in more socially contextualized dramas—for example, examining the lives of individuals, of family members, and of cultures and societies, or exploring the tenuous relationship between the world of humans and the world of plants and animals.

Mindy paints her nails bright red, although the polish is usually cracked along the edges. On regular school days, she wears her off-white satin dress, white lace stockings, and white dress shoes. Does Mindy choose to wear this dress to school or is she expected to look "pretty" in order to please her family? Are they clothes that were bought for going out, for a family celebration? Are they her only good clothes?

In our spiraling conversations, Mindy has a rhythmic way of engaging me. Maybe it's her big dark eyes grabbing my glance when I pan a room with my camera. Maybe it's her gestures—her winks, her shrugs, her hand arrogantly resting on her hip (signaling intrigue, joy, anger, frustration, sadness, embarrassment). Or maybe it is simply her outgoing nature that makes it so easy to spend time with her. Whatever her combination of sophisticated interpersonal skills, Mindy inspires hope. She shares her stories, not needing objects to reflect on the nature of life. Her own life and her stories are the stuff of her inventions.[160]

One cold February morning, Mindy and I sit on the orange-carpeted floor of the computer pod outside her classroom. She leans to one side, her head tilted and gently resting on her shoulder. The mood is calm, in spite of the excitement and chatter of 25 children working at their computers within yards of our conversation. Out of the blue, Mindy turns to me and describes her husband-to-be.

> **Mindy:** If I get married this is what I want my husband to be: I want him to be helpful, loving, and I want him to be understanding. Like,

---

160. Mindy is, however, interested in having her own room, reminding me of Virginia Woolfe's *A Room of One's Own* (Toronto: McClellan and Stewart, 1929).

if I date someone else, he won't get all huffy and puffy. And, if he dates someone else, it's OK by me.

I am quite surprised when Mindy comes up with her theory of open marriage. Mindy has just returned from a 3-week trip to Haiti, where she attended her father's wedding to his second wife. She lives with her mother and visits her father. When she first tells me about their arrangement, she says confidently, "I go over to my father's house every weekend. Well, every other, every next weekend;" and then, under her breath, she adds, "once in a while."

One of her brothers is dating "an older girl who wants to marry him." Mindy does not think her brother should marry "a girl who is older than the boy." When I tell her that my husband is younger than I am, she giggles her self-conscious giggle and changes the subject. (I sense that my sharing details of my life with her is confusing, and she doesn't quite know what to do with the information.) Then, with the conviction of a Virgina Woolfe, she tells me about the room she will have in her father's new home: "I'm getting my own room within my house too."

Annotation: Having a room of her own is as wonderful an image for Mindy as dreaming about owning a Lamborghini is for Josh. Her room is a place to have talks with her girlfriends, have sleep-overs, and be alone. Being alone is something Mindy only experiences when she is being punished.

In her fantasy room, she imagines a computer and a television. "When I look at the TV, it's like a deep spell or something." Her favorite television character is Chrissy, whom she sees on reruns of *Three's Company*, which ran in the 1970s and early 1980s.

Mindy: I'm not lazy [about doing my homework], but—

Ricki: You'd rather do something else?

Mindy: When I take one glance at the TV, I just—it hypnotizes me.

Ricki: Mmm, you love television!

Mindy: Yup!

Ricki: What are your favorite programs?

Mindy: Well, when I was, like, last year, I liked *Laverne and Shirley*; that was my favorite one. And uhmm [now, I like] *Three's Company*. I like Chrissy's personality. Yeah, the way she laughs, it's so funny. And I like *Different Strokes, Silver Spoons*, oh, and *Gimme a Break*.

Three's Company is a situation comedy about two women and one man who share an apartment. Chrissy (played by Suzanne Sommers) is portrayed as the stereotypical good-natured "ditzy blonde" who is constantly wiggling out of sexually compromising situations. Being naive and sensitive, she continually needs the protection of her housemates—Janet, a sensible young woman, and Jack, a heterosexual man pretending to be gay so that their landlord will agree to his living with two women. The program pivots around the taboo of an unmarried heterosexual male living with two unmarried heterosexual females. Although it does not surprise me that Mindy chooses a young female as her favorite television character, it seems peculiar, at first, that she would select a stereotypical, whimsical, White character such as Chrissy! (More than 40 years after the 1954 Brown vs Board of Education Supreme Court case, in which Black children choosing White dolls was one of the more persuasive arguments against segregation, Mindy's preference reminds us that the racial issues that shaped that famous case are still with us.) I ask myself where her African-American role models are. Then I wonder whether she would want to identify with an African-American woman whom she might not see as powerful. On the other hand, the lead character from *Gimme a Break* is Nell Carter, a powerful Black woman! As Britzman put it, one has to ask the race and class questions within the same breath.

Whatever her reason, Mindy is captivated by the power that Chrissy seems to have, in spite of Chrissy always needing help from her roommates. After all, she has fun and yet keeps her naiveté, and even her virginity, intact. Mindy, through Chrissy's persona, can be adventurous and sexy, all the while holding steadfastly to the social mores of mainstream culture—a different kind of power for a young woman who is caught in the gender play of day-to-day life.

Mindy is especially attached to her make-believe girls and to her dreams of having a sister and of becoming a teenager. She "loves" writing procedures in Logo, she tells me. Her procedures are graphic representations that, when assembled, become computer drawings of girls. For Mindy, this is the ultimate invention, because mystery and serendipity are always part of the process of creation. Quite differently from Josh, Mindy draws creative energy from her social relationships—often using her dramatic language tones and exaggerated body movements to tease, goad, and get the attention of others she spends time with. However, she is also building from within. Epistemologically, she creates from an inner *attitude* that connects the history of her life with the stories of others' lives. And in the process, she is content if the product she makes, the image of a girl in her Logo program, does not match her original conception. Flexing her imagination in order to meet the world of social constructions around her is satisfaction enough.

> **Mindy:** Like, when you make a picture in Logo, you're not sure how it's gonna come out; you're not sure it's gonna come out like you want it to come out, and if it doesn't, you kinda like it. Yeah, and you sort of say—it's a new invention!

For Mindy, a new invention means a new way of looking at what she has done or what she already knows. Perhaps a new way of thinking about what she has done. The end product does not have to match perfectly with what she has in her mind while she is programming. Instead, she is open to the possibility of a new creation. Mindy becomes very animated when showing me one of the girls she has "invented." She places her hands in front of the computer monitor as if to hide the surprise. Then I am told to close my eyes. Embracing the computer with both arms while munching on a wad of pink gum, she singsongs an invitation for me to see her work.

http://www.pointsofviewing.com/185

Mindy: Wanna see it? Close your eyes first. OK, I'll turn it on. Here it goes. This is what I have so far. [A graphic drawing of a girl appears on the monitor] See, I'm making the hair on the shapes page and the other foot on the shapes page. I made this on the shapes page [she points to part of the girl]; and I'm going to make the lips on the shapes page; and the hair and the hands and the feet.

Women, knowing they might become mothers, never question their ability to make girls (and boys). Our dolls are our first babies, and we are guided by adults to nurture those younger than ourselves. The culture of the female child and her dolls is as powerful and inculcated as that of the male child, and the toy soldiers and guns with which boys are expected to become engaged. Not surprisingly, boys are often stimulated by toys which offer the irresistible power of detachment and girls are domesticated by toys which can provide the comfort of attachment. In spite of the fact that many parents encourage their children of both sexes to explore a range of gendered activities, we see boys, even those with feminist parents, choosing guns and toys of destruction. Do children merely replicate the pattern of male as hunter-warrior and female as earth mother nurturer? Is the object a transitional obsession, as Freud would have us believe—a fetish around which to gather our images? Or can the object provide a sociocultural window into a thinking process, a way to think about thoughts and about the lives we live? Maybe the girls that girls make are indeed epistemological inventions, subjects rather than objects-to-think-with, as Mindy suggests. As Leslie Miller, Melissa Chaika, and Laura Groppe have so simply stated in their research on girls' software preferences:

Using girls' imaginations and learning styles as the starting point, rather than expecting girls to be accommodated by male-produced and accepted games is the next step in providing alternatives that may ultimately lead to re-capturing girls' interests in computing and its associated professional opportunities.[161]

---

161. Leslie Miller, Melissa Chaika, and Laura Groppe, "Girls' Preferences in Software Design: Insight from a Focus Group," *Interpersonal Computing and Technology: An Electronic Journal for the 21st Century.* This article may be found at <http://www.helsinki.fi/science/optek/1996/n2/miller.txt>.

Thinking About Relationships

Scoring high on aptitude tests, Mindy is a student in Joanne Ronkin's grade 4 advanced-work class. She sits poised and ready, her gaze moving sharply from one person to the next at any sign of movement. Her eyes rarely rest, although she is not overly active. She never moves fast; even her dancing is slower than the other children's.

In one of our many conversations during independent work periods, Mindy talks comfortably with me while simultaneously responding to a number of other events in the room: her teacher's homework announcement, a discussion between Josh and Thomas about their computer program, and some skirmishes among other kids in her immediate vicinity. She observes these events quite effortlessly, while maintaining our videotaped conversation.

My video camera is placed on a table beside me, quite close to her, while we talk. In the foreground of the frame is Mindy, in her off-white satin dress, the white line of a bra strap showing on her shoulder; in the background are Tammy and Moses at their respective desks. We discuss boys, stories, and computers. She enjoys telling me about her relationship with Josh and Thomas. She tells me how she engages Thomas in conversations in order to provoke and tease Josh.

While Mindy and I talk in the busy classroom, Moses, an African-American boy, jumps into the camera's view and, looking right into the lens, blurts out in a teasing voice: "Ricki, Mindy lives in a housing project!" Moses, painfully anxious for me to have him at the center of every frame, tries to get my attention whenever I walk into the room or the computer pod. Mindy, surprisingly, remains calm and does not respond to Moses. How does she remain calm as another child puts her down by telling me she is poorer than he is? Is Deborah Britzman right? Do gender, class, and race have to be seen within the hegemony of the classroom?

I have examined this segment of video many times, trying to understand how Mindy remains so calm while a classmate uses her poverty as a

weapon against her. Mindy, a good observer of human nature, does not seem to take Moses too seriously. Moses is someone Mindy would call a "troublemaker." Another possibility is that Mindy is more focused on being appreciated by me than she is on being interrupted by Moses. She continues talking about Josh and Thomas as if nothing at all has happened. They always talk in class, she says, and want to do the opposite of what their teacher requests them to do. When comparing herself to Josh and Thomas as they make objects on the computer, she points out that they can do things she can't, like "making things moooove." But, while impressed with what they can do, she is very happy with her own work— making images of girls! For Mindy, being technologically literate is being able to do what she needs to do: Create and invent images of herself.

Then Mindy suddenly loses her composure and shows disapproval at being interrupted by Moses. She turns her whole body around in her chair and stares nastily at him. Instantly, her composure returns and she tells me about her work on the computer, once again by comparing it to Thomas and Josh's. "In the computer they make sounds. But I just like making pictures and writing procedures. Yeah, I love writing procedures. Yup, cause it's like I'm inventing something." This time she uses the word "just," which indicates to me that she thinks her work is not as creative as theirs. I reflect on a videotaped incident involving Mindy, Josh, and Thomas. Mindy is teasing Josh by making fun of his grasshopper-shaped Logo figure. With her hair held up in a big red plastic clip, she leans over the side of her chair and says, "Thomas is magnificent." Her fingers move rhythmically with every word. She concludes with her dark brown eyes rolling up toward the ceiling.

Josh, to Mindy: Thomas is magnificent?

Mindy, to Josh: I don't like you! You just want me to like you, but you're too ugly, and you have a hard head, with your Pinnochio nose.

Mindy, to Ricki: Thomas is the one who taught Josh everything he knows.

Josh, to Thomas: C'mon, I taught Thomas everything. C'mon, Thomas, admit it. Thomas, just say it. Who taught you how to do the airport? Who did most of the airport? (Thomas continues working, paying no attention to either of them.)

Mindy, to Ricki: Josh wanted Thomas to help him do the grasshopper.

Josh, to Mindy and Ricki: Oooo, ooo, it was the best file he ever did. And I did most of it!

Mindy, unlike anyone else I observe who has contact with Josh, knows how to ruffle his feathers. She recognizes that Josh probably does not realize the extent to which Thomas or anyone else in his immediate surroundings contributes to their common projects. Mindy not only observes their working relationship, but, in wanting to be included, is willing to tease Josh to get his attention, attract him away from his work, and get him to acknowledge her contribution.

> **Fieldnotes (December 1986):** In spite of all the hours I have observed the three young people in the computer pods, neither Josh nor Thomas have paid much attention to Mindy while they work on exploding cars and airplanes in their computer programs. The boys ignore her, provoking her even more. When she teases them, they pay attention to her teasing and seem to enjoy it. Sound familiar?

When I ask her if she has any stories to share with me, she takes out a pile of unbound, crumpled papers from her desk and begins to tell me about something she has written. Ten or more pages are strewn around her desk. The main character is a girl named Princess Alice. The story is called *Alice and the Unknown Rabbit*. It is ostensibly about finding a wife for a king whose queen has died, but actually entails finding a prince for Alice (interesting, considering her father's new marriage and her own concern with finding boyfriends). The story also seems to build on *Alice in Wonderland* and *Sleeping Beauty*.

Mindy: *Alice and the Unknown Rabbit*, written by me, pictures by me. [Dedicated] to my friend, Reshiah, my friend Clea, and my father.... The first chapter is on page 2. It's called, "The Day the Queen Died." Sad! [Mindy pouts with a touch of a smile and lifts her eyes.]

Ricki: Why is it sad?

Mindy: Because she was so young [Squints her face in a question]. I think Alice was about eleven. Yeah [confidently], she was eleven. Alice, her mother was the queen that died. And then, her father has to get a new queen. To do all the chores.

Tammy: A queen doesn't do chores!

[Mindy looks around at Tammy as if to say, "It's my story, don't bother me!"]

Tammy: Never mind.

Mindy: Then the witch—

(Tammy interrupts again and Mindy gives her a strong but humorous look of disapproval.)

Mindy: Then on chapter 12, "The Witch." Then on chapter 18 is "The Rabbit and the Prince." See, that's what I like, friends.

[Moses is muttering and complaining in the background. Mindy ignores him.]

Mindy: That's how she met the prince and they got married. The 20th chapter is "The Happy Marriage."

Mindy's story raises many questions directly relating to her own complex family life. How does a young girl respond to a situation in which the old queen is no longer around and the king still needs a woman "to do the chores?" How does she come to terms with a father who is looking for a young queen? What does she understand about the roles of men and women in relationships, especially when they get "all huffy and puffy" with each other over dating others? And how does she find a prince when there are witches and other obstacles with which to contend?

Mindy is busy trying to make sense of her life, whether having a casual conversation with me on the floor, sitting at the computer, or

---

162. Joan Skolnick, "A Rare Commodity," in *Gender Tales: Tensions in the Schools*, eds. J. S. Kleinfeld and S. Yerian (New York: St. Martin's Press, 1995), 12–18.

thinking about stories. She uses whatever technologies are around: computer as word processor or computer as graphic illustrator. Her family problems overpower the demands of the school curriculum, and she recognizes the need for help from older girls. She tells me that she wants a big sister so she can go to her with her problems. In a spontaneous act of wanting to relate warmly, I offer to be her sister, but I do not meet her requirements.

Kindly, Mindy tells me she means a younger sister, so that she can give advice. Having gently rejected my offer, she returns to her reason for wanting an older sister; she wants another female with whom to work out issues related to her sexuality. Then, with both resignation and confidence in her voice, she decides that she can give herself advice. "I just ask myself, what should I do? And then I just do it." Being the only female child in a one-parent household (consisting of herself, her mother, and her four brothers), Mindy is used to giving herself advice and, no doubt, sees her brothers as needing support and guidance as well. Our conversation moves in circles.

Annotation: I recognize that being a "sister" within the African-American culture means someone of your own kind. In a case study reported by Joan Skolnick, Lisa, a teacher, is first courted by a group of girls until they "sabotage" her classes claiming that she is more lenient to the boys—a common complaint of girl students regardless of race, color or ethnicity.[162] Although the girls seem to want the closeness with a teacher who has shared stories about her difficult adolescence in a White school in the 1970s, these girls are reluctant to trust her.

> **Mindy:** I really want a sister.
>
> **Ricki:** I'll be your sister!
>
> **Mindy:** (giggling) A baby sister! So, when she gets older, if she's having boy problems
>
> **Ricki:** She can come to you?
>
> **Mindy:** Yep! Well, actually, I want a big sister, so I can come to her with boy problems.

http://www.pointsofviewing.com/191

Ricki: What kind of boy problems would you want to talk about if you had a big sister?

Mindy: Well, like troublemakers! And the boys I like.

Ricki: Do you need some advice?

Mindy: Yeah!

Ricki: About the boys you like?

Mindy: Yeah. Well, actually I can get my own advice. I just ask myself what should I do, and then I just do it.

Ricki: Does that work for you?

Mindy: Yeah. [A long pause here.] And it turns out to be that the boy that I like, likes me. Almost every time; all the time.

Ricki: So, do you have someone you really like now?

Mindy: Yeah. His name is James. Actually I have three [boyfriends].

Ricki: Three?

Mindy: Three. James, Henry, and Jimmy. And that's all. They're cute. Nice personalities.

How, then, do those of us who are in positions of "authority" form meaningful relationships with our students?[163] How do we create an atmosphere of deep respect and caring without imposing intimacy? How do we learn to imagine ourselves as unequal partners whose responsibility it is to elicit information about their worlds for their own benefit and not ours? How do we help them make the connections they need to become integral members of convivial and caring cultures?

Mindy and I delve more deeply into her desire for boyfriends and her image of marriage. Cautiously, I ask her:

---

163. For another example of the complexity of adult-student relationships, see Samuel Wineburg, "When Good Intentions are Not Enough," in *Gender Tales: Tensions in the Schools*, eds. J. S. Kleinfeld and S. Yerian (New York, St. Martin's Press, 1995), 161–164.
164. Michelle Fine and Pat Macpherson, "Over Dinner: Feminism and Adolescent Female Bodies," in *Gender and Education*, ed. S. Knopp Biklin (Chicago: University of Chicago Press, 1993), 126–154.

Ricki: How will you know who to marry?

Mindy: I'll try a couple of dates. Until I really know him. Yeah, like, if I ask him to baby-sit, see how he reacts on the children; see if he's going to be coming back. See if he's OK when he comes back.

Ricki: If he keeps his word?

Mindy: Yeah. Honesty.

Ricki: So, that's an important thing [for you]?

[She nods her head.]

Interestingly, Mindy's view of marriage concerns finding a man who will treat (her?) children well. Does she mean that the person she marries may not be the father of her children? Or does she want to test out a prospective husband by seeing how he treats other people's children? There seems to be a decoupling of functions, in that the man who impregnates a woman is not always the one who stays with her and her children. Another of Mindy's concerns is that her prospective spouse be one who will "come back" and is "OK" when he comes back. What does OK mean? Does it mean he's kind to the children and to his wife? Has he been sick? What does it mean to Mindy? And what vision does Mindy have carved out for herself?

In Michelle Fine and Pat Macpherson's dinner chats with 4 adolescent African-American women, 2 of them from relatively impoverished backgrounds and 2 from privileged backgrounds, the young women seem to echo Mindy's views.[164] When Fine asks them about their future, Shermika describes her distrust of men. "I imagine bein' in my own home in my name. And then get married. So my husband can get out of my house." Sophie agrees that having a house is very important, so that she "won't end up like one of those battered women we were talkin' about." All four

http://www.pointsofviewing.com/193

want to be free from the domination of men. What Fine and Macpherson conclude, in agreement with bell hooks and others, is that a White upper-middle-class version of feminism does not always (and not often) translate across color, class, and age boundaries.[165] Fine and Macpherson feel "abandoned" as they watch the young women drive off with their quite different sense of feminism. "We thought we were concerned with their safety. Four young women in a car could meet dangers just outside the borders of Michelle's block."[166] Then they realize that "our abandonment was metaphoric and political. These four women were weaving the next generation of feminist politics, which meant, in part, leaving us."[167]

Passing and Failing

Notorious for not getting her homework done, Mindy often sits in an empty classroom while the other children are in the computer pods. She is rather stoic about her punishment and never complains. She tells me she has not done her homework, so she has to stay in the classroom and finish it. Knowing this consequence of her actions does not deter Mindy from going to parties or watching television even when she has homework. She knows there's a price to pay for not following the rules. "I went to Haiti for 21 days, and my teacher got maaaaad!" Her eyes roll and her whole face moves softly with her eyes, emphatically explaining why her teacher got angry with her. "I missed out on all my work. She told me to start working this term, the third term, so I'll be caught up on that; and I don't want to be kept back."

> **Ricki:** What does being "kept back" mean?
>
> **Mindy:** You have to stay in the same grade.
>
> **Ricki:** Oh, you mean fail?
>
> **Mindy:** Yeah.

---

165. bell hooks, *Yearning: Race, Gender, and Cultural Politics* (Boston, MA: South End Press, 1990).
166. Michelle Fine and Pat Macpherson, "Over Dinner: Feminism and Adolescent Female Bodies," 151.
167. Ibid., 151.

Ricki: That would be a drag!

Mindy: Yeah, I know! So, I have two report cards more to improve, and I'm going to improve.

Mindy's eyes open very wide and her face becomes resolute. Although we are both sitting on the floor and she is not much shorter than I am, she looks up at me sadly. Mindy seems genuinely upset that she might be "kept back." After all, she knows she is in the advanced-work class because she is smart! I pursue the issue: "So, what are the chances of your failing?" "Well—ummmm, sort of." A curtain comes down between us. Whatever common space we have shared over months of talking has temporarily vanished. She tries to lighten the issue, using her singing voice so that I will not detect how upset she is. Clumsily, I continue asking her questions, hoping to return to the previous space we shared. She throws me a naughty smirk and "sings:"

Mindy: Let's put it this way, I had seven F's and seven D's, and three A's, the rest B's and S's.

Ricki: What were your A's in?

Mindy: I forgot. I just took a glance at my report card. And my mother got it and she signed it and gave it to my teacher. And my mother's gonna be here on Open House and they're gonna talk!

Knowing Mindy prefers being with other people and watching television to doing homework, I present the following scenario for her to react to:

Ricki: Well, let's say you came to school and hadn't done any of your homework, because you had decided that you wanted to watch TV all night, and *somebody* asks you, "Why didn't you do your homework?"

http://www.pointsofviewing.com/195

Mindy: Why didn't I do my homework? Well, I would tell the truth. But some people would say, "Well, I don't have any homework. My teacher was absent so we had a substitute."

What I mean by *somebody* is her teacher. What she means is her mother or father! So, I ask again,

Ricki: And what would you tell your teacher the next day?

Mindy: I'd tell her that—the other person would tell her that she left it at home. See, when I look at the TV, it's like, a deep spell or something.

Ricki: You become mesmerized?

Mindy: Yeah. And then the show's over and I say, "Do I have homework?" and I say, "Yeah." And I go, "Oh, no! I'm gonna get in big trouble." The next day, I go to my teacher and tell her I forgot to do my homework, and Teacher goes, and there's a field trip coming up, "I'm just going to forget about your going on the field trip, or forget about your giving you a grade." That's what she really does.

Ricki: Do you think that's fair?

Mindy: Well, yeah! I mean, if you're gonna forget about your homework, well then she can forget about, like, what's important to you.

Ricki: Sometimes it might be worth taking the risk and telling the truth?

Mindy: Yeah! Like, you wanted to go to the party and you have to do your homework before you go to the party. You have tons of homework, and then you tell your mother you don't have any homework, so she lets you go to the party. Sometimes you feel all guilty and you come back and tell her, "I had homework, I'm sorry, but I just had to go to that party, it was real important to me."

Ricki: So how do you make these decisions about what's most important? Will it bother you if you're going to fail this [school] year?

> **Mindy:** Yeah!! [she nods] Cause I dream of being a teenager! Like, in the eighth grade. I always dream of that. Every dream I have, I'm a teenager, like, 17, 18, or 19 years old. And I go on dates. And I dream of a prom. Like, when I go to high school, am I gonna have dances or proms. I always dream of that. And when I grow up, I want to be famous.

Mindy's views are a challenge for me. I often worry that my cultural filters are so strong that I will not see Mindy as clearly as I need to. Yet when I do see her, I am reassured. The flow of her words and gestures calms me. However, to compensate for my sensitivity to my cultural preferences, I sometimes sharpen the focus of my camera and my attention too closely on the beautiful, the positive, without fully catching the ruses she employs with me. Yes, there is a level of deception in her sincerity. She talks about "another person" who might not tell the truth—a person who would lie to their parents or to their teachers. Would she lie to me? And why would she not?

Reflections on the Video of Mindy

When I left Israel to study with Seymour Papert, I was committed to proving that girls, and especially those from non-mainstream cultures, could do as well as or better than White boys on the computer. What I did not understand about my own objective was that I was applying a White male standard of what doing well in science, mathematics, or history means. Imagine my delight when I started videotaping Kathy, a very quick-minded, mathematically inclined 10-year-old African-American girl who was a hot programmer, more concerned with her programming than with boys or clothes—although her favorite topic was food! Often, as I videotaped her, she would be so engaged in working out a computer bug (or problem in her code) that she did not even notice my sitting down beside her. When

http://www.pointsofviewing.com/197

we spoke, she used jive inflections, which seemed to direct the movements of my camera. There were moments when the sound of her voice made my camera dance with glee.

The problem I have been struggling with for over a decade is not how to understand the Kathys of the world, but rather how to get a handle on the thinking of a girl like Mindy. Mindy is mostly interested in thinking about boys (and drawing girls), and as a result, is not doing very well in school, in spite of a high aptitude for learning. It has taken me a long time to realize that what is happening to Mindy, and what has been happening for generations to many girls as they approach puberty, is that they "drop out" of being smart—they feign behavior that will help them achieve the approval of males and older females at the expense of their intellectual needs.

However, the problem is not so black and white. Out of the ashes of what seems like burned-up time spent "making girls," many of us find paths into the re-creation of selves. We reinvent our selves over and over again, until we find a core that can glow in many knowledge domains.

Working with the video data on Mindy has taught me compassion instead of anger, which was my earlier, more "activist" response to female subjugation through gender-role stereotyping. Instead of trying to remake Mindy into a male scientist or to prove that she and other girls can be as good as boys in the sciences, I have begun to look at alternative learning experiences for both girls and boys, so that their ways of making sense of the cultures they create can be integrated into the curriculum in respectful ways. How do educators bring children's popular cultures into their day-to-day lives in schools? How do educators find links between generations of thinking?

More and more, I see the value of diversely gendered voices in working out very complicated human dramas. I define gender as a kaleidoscope of colorful interpretations of selves that include variations of choices. Surely this kaleidoscope is evident in the transgender dress codes of the young: earrings, nail polish, and bleached blonde hair for boys, and tattooing for girls. Their quest, it seems to me, is to find ways to stretch the boundaries. As educators, we need to think about what is inside the curriculum and what is outside it in order to facilitate various permutations that will enable young people to flex their gender choices. As frightening as this sounds, these permutations could be the source of great productivity and creativity. Opening our interpretations to others' views, to others' points of viewing the world, will help bridge the gaps between self and other, between sacred and profane, between "high" culture and "low" culture.

As we flex, our interpretations of what it means to conduct scientific investigations or social inquiry will change. We will begin to make connections between the dramas of our lives and the intellectual interpretations we use to address them. We will see how making discoveries can include discovering how to remake our selves through our own constructions. Constructionism, as a theory, can include recreating oneself, not only building objects-to-think-with in Logo or LEGO.

Some may contend that these human dramas are not the stuff of scientific investigation. However, until we begin to accept the potential knowledge gleaned from the interpersonal skills of persons whose main focus is the lives of human beings in relation to the world around them, we will never begin to restore the fundamental balance between the disparate categories we call humanities and sciences.

In thinking about Mindy's dreams, aspirations, and fantasies, I challenge us to consider how a girl's love for "making girls" can become an essential ingredient in the growth of social studies and even of science. As Bateson points out:

> Building and sustaining the settings in which individuals can grow and unfold ... is not only the task of parents and teachers, but the basis of management and political leadership—and simple friendship.[168]

---

168. Mary Catherine Bateson, *Composing a Life*, 56.

8 Connecting Points of Viewing

If you feel strongly about something, I think you should go for it and try to find out about it, and do things to help and do what you believe in.

—Mia

Social Activism

Mia is an earnest teenager with a pale, freckled face and long curly red hair, older and more sagacious than her fourteen years. When we talk, we discuss important issues that affect our planet. We talk about rainforests and the quality of air that my generation is leaving hers. She has neither time for nor interest in chatting or hanging out. She is a young person with a mission—to make this a healthier planet for all.

> **Mia:** To start saving our forests now we have to stop doing so much clearcutting. I think selective logging is a really good way of logging, but I realize that it would cost a lot more money to get it started and maintain it. But I'd much rather have to pay more money than to just destroy our world.

I meet Mia in the fall of 1993, the first year of the Clayoquot Sound project at Bayside Middle School. In that first year of the project, we lay the foundation for a content-based technology investigation, not using video and multimedia to the extent that we will in the following year. However, we used pen, paper, word processing, and a variety of visual resources (such as videos on rainforests and pamphlets produced by the various stakeholders) as constructionist tools. Our constructionist approach is evident in how we bring the range of ideas into our culture, by discussing the issues and designing portfolios. Moreover, we begin to brainstorm as a community of inquiry on what we would need to design a CD-ROM about our investigation. Mia is one of the students who becomes an ardent contributor to this design phase. For several months in that first year, she and her classmates actively gather newspaper clippings and other resource materials for their study on temperate rainforests.

When I first conceived of the Clayoquot Sound project, I thought it might be a good platform for providing less traditional science-type students with opportunities to build connections between science and their lives. I hoped young people like Mia would find a welcoming intellectual climate in which to see how people's interests are intimately linked to the study of science and social science issues. Inspired by Evelyn Fox Keller's description of scientist Barbara McClinock, I wanted to help young people make a connection between their lives and the organisms they study.[169] And indeed, we met many of our goals. Her end-of-term project consists of more than 50 pages (organized by topics) of well documented summaries of the articles she has gathered. Illustrations of clearcut forests are spread throughout. Diagrams, maps, and graphs lend credibility to her arguments. When I ask her about her project, she says:

---

169. Evelyn Fox Keller, *A Feeling for the Organism: The Life and Work of Barbara McClintock* (San Francisco: W. H. Freeman, 1983).

170. Arlene McLaren and Jim Gaskell, "Gender as an Issue in School Science," in *Gender In/forms Curriculum: From Enrichment to Transformation*, eds. J. Gaskell and J. Willinsky (New York: Teachers College Press, 1995), 136–156; Kori Inkpen, Maria Klawe, J. Lawry, Kamran Sedighian, S. Leroux, Rena Upitis, Ann Anderson, and Mutindi Ndunda, "'We Have Never-Forgetful Flowers in Our Garden': Girls' Responses to Electronic Games," *Journal of Computers in Mathematics and Science Teaching 13*, no. 4 (1994): 383–403; Robin Kay, "An Analysis of Methods Used to Examine Gender Differences in Computer-related Behavior," *Journal of Educational Computing Research 8*, no. 3 (1992): 277–290; Leslie Francis, "The Relationship Between Computer Related Attitudes and Gender Stereotyping of Computer Use," *Computers and Education 22*, no. 4 (1994): 283–291; Jane Gaskell and Arlene

Mia: I've been writing up my opinion on each of the issues.

Ricki: And the issues you've identified are?

Mia: Wildlife, environment, jobs, the economy, publicity, protesters, fish and rivers, systems of logging, old-growth forests, the government's decisions, forest practices code, and our future. And I've written on 8 of them so far, and I have two more to do and then I am going to gather a whole bunch of photographs on wildlife from magazines and I'm going to cut out newspaper articles and get some quotes.

As we talk, she tells me about how she came to understand these complex issues and about her own learning process. She says, "Well, I've researched and I've heard a lot of opinions; I've heard a lot of videos and I've read a lot of books on logging; and all the information I've gathered and just kind of stored in my brain." I ask her how she learns best. For Mia, learning is connected with feeling strongly about something. "When you feel so strongly about something you remember it and you try to learn about it." For example, when she watches a video in class about something that is uninteresting to her, she doesn't listen. "But I feel very strongly about logging, so I listen and I remember more when I want to know about it." Mia, like many people, learns best when the topic is something about which she feels passionate. "If it's something that interests you or is important to you, you'll learn more than if you don't really care for it at all." (I notice how she uses the less personal "you," rather than talking about herself.)

Another reason I chose to initiate a study about a temperate rainforest with adolescent girls and boys in a middle school is that the research literature seems to converge on the idea that learning about the sciences in middle schools does not bring girls into a steady stream of achievement, leading to careers in the sciences.[170] Girls and many boys, I might add. Some of the girls and boys I talked with told me that they are not good at science. Some think scientists wear white lab coats and kill little creatures

http://www.pointsofviewing.com/203

or make magic by mixing chemicals together. They don't conceive of a scientist working in the field studying natural phenomena or living among other creatures and life forms. Science is an activity that is carried out in a smelly lab by people who do not act or talk the way they talk, they tell me. Even when watching *Voyage to the Mimi* and the *National Geographic* videotapes, they do not always make a connection between these videos and their science courses because they do not get to do what the people in the videos do! They work with their textbooks and take notes on what others do. In a few experimental settings, young people work with creative teachers on team-based projects, collecting data and sharing it with scientists in the field.[171]

Mia, who had just finished a 6-month study of Clayoquot Sound involving biodiversity and ecological survival, did not quite realize that she had conducted a socioscientific inquiry. When I asked her if she thought that studying the Sound might affect her future career choices, she answered slowly and methodically, seriously reflecting on the question.

Mia: Yeah, I think so.... I know I'd never go into something with logging or something like that. And I kinda, right now, wouldn't mind being, like, a reporter or a journalist.

Ricki: What about a scientist?

Mia: I don't know. Science is interesting, but sometimes I don't understand it.

McLaren, *Women and Education: A Canadian Perspective* (Calgary, Alberta: Detselig, 1987), 21–29; Also see <http://scienceweb.dao.nrc.ca/can/women/wuseful.html> for a description of the advancement of women in science and technology with links to projects at Canadian institutions; <http://www.awis.org> for information on the Association for Women in Science; and <http://wwwcset.oit.osshe.edu/mmteam1/twist/page7.html> for viewing TWIST, Teen Women in Science and Technology, whose goal is to "provide female high school students with the opportunity to explore career opportunities in engineering technologies and to broaden their career options by encouraging academic preparation in math and science courses during high school."

171. The Collaborative Visualization Project (Co-Vis), a National Science Foundation project established by Roy Pea, enabled young people to learn about science by conducting science as scientists do. See <http://www.covis.nwu.edu>. See D. N. Gordin, Daniel C. Edelson, Louis M. Gomez, E. M. Lento, and Roy D. Pea, "Student Conference on Global Warming: A Collaborative Networked-Supported Ecologically Hierarchic Geosciences Curriculum," *Proceedings of the Fifth American Meteorological Society Education Symposium* (1996).

Ricki: But you understood it with Clayoquot, right?

Mia: Yeah, yeah, I understood the science of Clayoquot! And so maybe something in ecology or something. I haven't decided yet.

Ricki: So that idea has opened up to you as a possibility?

Mia: Yeah, yeah, I think so, because the more knowledge you have about something, the easier it will be to get interested or get into that kind of thing. So, I haven't really thought about [being a scientist], but maybe now I will.

Mia clearly sees herself as maker of meaning, an activist researching, gathering, and sorting through materials. She is continually filtering, rethinking her position, and making new connections. She continually considers her ways of viewing the data. Her goal is to inform others and to make changes. She is dedicated to the notion that, if you share what you learn with others, they will change their minds, and social transformation may occur. She believes that if people only know enough about the issues, they will choose to do what is best.

Mia: If you believe in something and even if you just do a little thing towards it, you feel better about yourself. Like, even if you recycle paper or even little things, they make you feel better. And instead of just sitting around and talking about it, go out and do something about it. I think one of the things you can do is learn more about it and if you learn more about it, you can inform others about it and share your opinions with others, and maybe they'll feel the same way and all together as a group you can go and try to save something.

This notion of action as a social construction matches Mia's way of thinking about the world of ideas. It's not only people who are connected through

http://www.pointsofviewing.com/205

social action, but also ideas. Mia sees connections among issues that many other people might put into separate boxes. She "ties together" complex issues because she can see how each of them "has a lot to do with" the others. At one point I ask her what she means by tying things together.

> **Mia:** Well, if you take the issues of fish in the rivers and how they're dying, it has a lot to do with how the fishing industry is losing money, and that has a lot to do with the economy. Cause people are going to lose jobs in the fishing industry if the fishing goes. And that has also a lot to do with the jobs and because the salmon are dying because the streams are getting polluted. And that has a lot to do with the environment. The environment, I think, is the main issue because if there wasn't the problem of the environment, the littler issues, or the issues that kinda go off of that, wouldn't exist. If our environment wasn't in great danger, our future wouldn't be in danger. If the present was good and well managed right now.

Annotation: Mia's concern for the environment reminds me of how worried I was about the possibility of a nuclear attack when I was in elementary school. By junior high school I was more worried about starvation in Biafra and other countries. Unfortunately, the only time we ever discussed any of these issues in school was during our ten minutes a day of "current events."

One of the things that Mia researched was how clearcut logging affects salmon streams. The topsoil and logging debris fill the streams, changing the balance of nutrients to the extent that salmon reproduction is seriously affected.

Connecting and Pulling Apart

Mia sees the relationships among various issues, especially those which "technology" has helped create. After all, clearcutting is a technologically advanced way of "harvesting and managing" our forests. Mia not only looks for the connections between technologies and our need for forest products; she searches for causes and solutions. When I ask her to explain how our future on this planet might be affected by clearcutting, she talks about ecological management. Previous governments and forest companies "decided instead of taking it slow and saving parts of the forest, that they could just take them now. I don't think they were thinking too much ahead in the future when they started all this, and now we have to get into a good system instead of staying with the bad." She offers selective logging as an alternative to clearcutting. Selective logging would not be as harmful to wildlife, because only selected trees would be logged and thus, the forests would remain viable both for wildlife and for their own regeneration. For Mia, reforestation after the clearcutting of trees is not the best solution (although it is better than leaving the land barren), because "the wildlife might not be able to walk, like, around underneath, and the trees might not grow back in the same manner, and streams by the clearcut might dry up because they're exposed to direct sunlight." Once again, she starts by examining one issue and then immediately links it with others.

Why is Mia able to make these connections? I cannot claim that this is a result of her working with multimedia technologies. After all, in the first year, the young people had only begun to become familiar with videotaping and digital media. However, computer technologies, with their capacity to forge links among discrete knowledge segments, will surely provide a person like Mia with tools with which to illustrate and develop her ideas. By studying Clayoquot Sound, Mia has connected what she is studying with her future goals. She is deeply committed to environmental conservation. Her fear is that the world she will inherit will not be one that can support life. "I've read in magazines how they're just cutting down our rainforests and they're gonna be gone in 50 years if they keep going at this rate; and it scares me because I know that we need trees to breathe." What a heavy load Mia must feel every day! "Ricki, this is probably the most important thing that's going on for me in school right now."

Annotation: I invited Mia to present her views about the Clayoquot Project to an audience of international education and multimedia specialists at the 1994 *World Conference on Multimedia and Hypermedia* in Vancouver. She explained why it is crucial to learn about science by focusing on an issue that is rooted in immediate concerns. Effortlessly, and without prepared notes, she articulated her views. When it was over, I asked her what it was like speaking in front of over 100 people. She told me that she thought it was important for her to develop these skills at a young age so that, when she is older, she will be able to address large groups and know how to share information that will bring about changes.

http://www.pointsofviewing.com/207

When I first start coming to Joe Grewal's grade 7 classes, Mia makes no attempt to be videotaped, unlike some of the other students. Our relationship buds slowly, carefully. She usually sits near the back of the room, focused on her work, without being distracted by either classmates or visitors. She moves slowly. Even her face is rather motionless, with an open gaze that could mean either intense concentration or a particularly intriguing daydream. It is only when I approach her that she responds, that she begins to open up. And she does not open up in order to get to know me or to play with or for the camera. She wants to tell me about her concerns, about her project.

> **Mia:** I've heard a lot about Clayoquot Sound before and I've seen a lot of videos and I knew a lot of what's going on with logging and stuff like that. And I feel very strongly about saving the trees and being able to breathe and still being able to log in more productive ways, like selective logging. So I kind of understand what's going on. I collected a lot of information from videos, and a lot of it, I just kind of took what I knew already.

She speaks her mind without fear, not looking for approval from either her peers, her teachers, or me. As I listen to her talking about logging practices at Clayoquot Sound, I am struck by the monotony of her intonation. Although she is passionate about saving the forests and sees herself as an activist, her voice is slow to show excitement or enthusiasm. She reaches out to me with her ideas. Hers is the voice of an observer, a recorder, and a researcher. She is a young woman with a mission to understand and to communicate what she knows in the hope that the world will become a better place for her generation and the generations to come.

Our only breakdown in communication occurs at the end of that school year. Throughout the first year of studying Clayoquot Sound, the students ask me if we will be going there on a field trip. Of course we are planning on going, but, as it happens, the school year is coming to an end and we cannot raise the funds for the buses. The trip is canceled. My visits to the school that June are painful. The students keep asking me when we are going. They are fully primed, with over six months of research under their belts, and, one must remember, they are adolescents; they find it difficult to delay gratification for very long. All I can say is that we will do our best to arrange a trip in the early fall. The only problem is that they will be in high school by then. I give them my word that we will have them join the next group of students, the incoming 7th-grade students who will be conducting the next phase of the study with an increased use of video and multimedia tools. As it turns out, we go on the field trip the following October with one incoming 7th-grade class but do not include Mia's group. With controlled fury, Mia writes letters to me, the school administration, and the school board. We have broken our contract and disappointed her community. After dedicating long and hard hours to an extracurricular project, they will not visit Clayoquot Sound as a group. She writes from her membership in her community of students and directs her attack as follows: Learning should be in context, and so, by not going on the field trip, her class has missed the totality of the learning experience. As a researcher and as a person who tries to keep her word, I am confronted with not having been able to do what I promised. In retrospect, I can look back and see how the events were probably beyond my control. But then I also realize that planning the trip for that first group of student investigators should have taken a higher priority.

I have begun to see the power of social activism, not only in solving the problem of clearcut logging at Clayoquot Sound or planning the use of emerging media technologies as tools for thinking, but in reminding people of their promises.

Making Media: Seeing Ourselves and Others

> **Nicole:** I think that the media is really important because without the media we wouldn't know what is really going on.... Like they could put ideas into our heads or take opinions out.

Nicole understands the significance of the media's role in shaping how she thinks. The usual lament of media educators is that students do

http://www.pointsofviewing.com/209

not recognize the extent of media influence.[172] These theorists want teachers to lessen the media's influence on children by making them aware of the rhetorical devices embedded in the structure of media forms—inoculating kids against the influence of the media. Too few theorists take the extra step of acknowledging that students are media makers in their own right.

Nicole, a 13-year-old girl at Bayside Middle School, says that the media puts ideas in our heads and take opinions out. (This is interesting: ideas are put in, while opinions, our interpretations of these ideas, are taken out.) A superficial reading might lead one to think that Nicole is mediaphobic, but she is not. Nor is she a passive viewer of media. She is one of the most active media-makers in the Clayoquot Project. Her exceptionally thin body is quite able to carry around a tripod and one of those old Panasonic camcorders in its heavy silver metal case.

For their Clayoquot project, she and her classmate Terri-Lynn decide to conduct a series of video interviews. Not only do they set up the camera in the classroom, they also run around their home town, Brentwood Bay, interviewing. In one day, they interview 25 people, including family members. When I ask how they did it, Nicole explains:

> **Nicole:** Well, everyone has to do a project on Clayoquot Sound. We're interviewing people about what they know about Clayoquot Sound. We ask: "Do you know where it is? Who do you side with and why? What do you think about the loggers and the environmentalists and the protesting—keeping in mind we have to live in the future? What do you think the future will look like if everything is cut down or nothing is cut down? How do you think the government is handling the situation? What do you think about clearcutting? What do you think about selective logging?" And then we're going to digitize the video onto a computer, and we can add titles and fade-aways and everything. [Our project] is just, like, opinions of what people think is going on.

Terri-Lynn, a bit more succinct than Nicole, explains their project like this:

---

172. See footnote 6 in the introduction.

> **Terri-Lynn**: We just thought up about 15 questions like: Do you know about Clayoquot Sound? Where is it? Or, what do you think should happen to Clayoquot Sound? And we are interviewing everyone in our class, and some people in our school, and then we went to Brentwood Bay and interviewed some just people.

Their goal is to get a picture of what people know and how they feel about the issues surrounding the Clayoquot conflict. Although Brentwood Bay is less than half an hour from Victoria and only a 4-hour drive from Clayoquot Sound, and the *Times Colonist*, the Victoria newspaper, runs a feature story on the controversy more than once a week, Nicole and Terri-Lynn are not even sure that everyone knows where it is. (In fact, in answering the question "Where is Clayoquot Sound?" one of their classmates answered that Clayoquot Sound was "a clacking sound in the air.") Some of the people they interview do not know that Clayoquot Sound is situated on the west coast of Vancouver Island.

> **Nicole**: We'd come up to someone who just looked like they had an opinion on something and we'd say, "We're doing a project for Bayside Middle School and can we ask you a few questions?" And they'd ask what for, and we'd say, "about Clayoquot Sound. And if you don't know the answers or anything, we'll be editing it, so it's not like you'll have all the bloopers or whatever."

Nicole is deeply concerned with what other people think. Watching the video in which she says, "and if you don't know the answers or anything, we'll be editing it," I smile. Nicole is aware of the delicate balance of power between filmmaker and those being filmed. She ethically announces that she will not embarrass anyone by making them seem ignorant or foolish. Her comment brings into play the issues of trust and truthfulness that are crucial to any form of reporting. She tries to convince those she is

   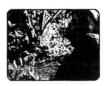

Annotation: This onerous task of editing out the "bloopers" is the same one that I face when editing. I am constantly confronted with how best to present, or represent, the young people, their teachers, and their parents. In the classroom, I spend months building a trusting and ethical relationship—a relationship in which I can remain honest about my interpretation of the events I have seen as they change and as my interpretation unfolds. In other words, I am interested in their opinions and in constantly reassessing my own. When editing, as I have mentioned in earlier chapters, the question is, do I select moments that "ring true" by virtue of their being representative of the whole of people's thinking, or do I select the golden moments where a person's voice is unique, expressing an idea that I might never hear again? Obviously there is no rule. The unique utterance often cuts through the more general theme, leading me to a clearer insight. In short, I select both, in different degrees and for different reasons.

interviewing that they can trust her not to make them appear foolish or, worse, ignorant.

In her seemingly naive comment, "and if you don't know the answers or anything, we'll be editing it," Nicole acknowledges her sensitivity to the process of both videotaping and editing documentary media. Technically, she speaks with ease about how to get analog signals onto the computer by digitizing them and adding titles and fadeaways. Theoretically, she addresses issues such as trust and truth in reporting. However, she not only is concerned with how the video stories will be presented; she also addresses the complexity of distinguishing between "opinions" and "facts." This is a critical issue in making media, especially in these times when our media culture is in transition—moving from analog broadcast signals (e.g., television and radio) to, as Nicholas Negroponte would say, digital atoms.[173] Being digital is not only about signals; it heralds an era of consciousness about our psychological parts, which can be reconstituted into new wholes, and a space where the boundaries between opinions and facts, or between advertising and content, may be blurred.

Nicole does not define digital media because reconstitutable media are as commonplace to her as are the telephone, radio, and television to those of us who are older. These are the tools she uses in her daily life. Her untangling of opinions from facts lays the foundation for an epistemological battle that she will probably deal with over and over again. Moreover, she will probably start the process at a much earlier age than we did because she has had hands-on experience in making documentary digital media. For example, when I ask her what we should do with the video and text data we have all been collecting on the Clayoquot Project, she

---

173. Nicholas Negroponte, *Being Digital* (New York: Alfred A. Knopf, 1995).

immediately addresses the issue of point of view. She explains how the media we collect and share can help shape the opinions of others, and how media representations enlarge our understanding of complex issues by enabling us to see them from others' points of viewing:

Nicole: Whatever we have on tapes, we can put it on email, and if Japan or somewhere wants to see what we're doing here, and if they're having trouble, they could view what opinions there are here. They might think we're a terrible country for cutting down all our trees, because they don't have any trees. And if they had trees, they would want to keep them. And if they saw what was really going on, they'd change their minds too.

Ricki: Why is it so important that we share our opinions with other people?

Nicole: People need to know all the facts before they can make a decision. Cause otherwise it wouldn't really be fair. So, like, we really need to gather up all the information before we can really make an important decision.

Ricki: So, it shouldn't be based on—

Annotation: Analog media uses a direct transfer of a group of signals from one place to another. With digital media, every atom can be reconstituted and dealt with as a separate entity. Anyone with the right tools and experience can massage that image, adding filters, effects and splicing techniques to alter what we have come to accept as documentary reality. Digital media blurs the lines between opinion and facts even more than regular analog video. It is relatively easy for a sophisticated digital cinematographer to "cut out" an image of a person or object from the (blue-light) background in which they have been filmed and to put this cut out into a place they have never been. As more of our "documentary" reality is affected by these media hacks (tricks), it will be harder for us all to know if what we have seen represents any version of reality, except for the one that lives in the mind of the media-maker and the reader of those media texts. And of course, to a greater or lesser degree, this has always been the case.

http://www.pointsofviewing.com/213

Nicole: —what you see or don't see.

Ricki: Are you saying it's a combination of the experience of something (like we had at Clayoquot Sound) with gathering and doing research? Is that what you're saying?

Nicole: Yeah!

Am I guiding her thoughts too much here? Nicole has already told me earlier in our interview how important it is for young people to go to the places they study.

Nicole: Kids right now, they're really rambunctious and they need their exercise.... If they go [to Clayoquot Sound], they will remember it for the rest of their life. Kids don't like to sit in desks; they like to be outside and stuff, like at lunch and stuff. So Clayoquot Sound was a really good idea, because we learned a lot more than we could have in the classroom.

Nicole is indeed trying to combine her hands-on experience of knowing a subject from the inside with her collection of other people's "facts" and opinions. Her interest in how people in Japan could learn from what we are doing by watching and reading what we have gathered demonstrates her deep concern with the importance of how others perceive us. This self-consciousness seems to be a relatively common experience for teenage girls, who are continually targeted (by the media and by adult culture in general) as the epitome of perfection because they are not fully developed, either physically or intellectually.[174] Living up to the expectations of others can become increasingly difficult for girls in their early teens.

---

174. James A. Doyle and Michele A. Paludi discussed a number of empirical studies conducted on print and television media as a socializing factor in "The Social Roles Perspective," in *Sex and Gender: The Human Experience* (Dubuque, IA: Wm. C. Brown, 1985), 122–149. Ingeborg Majer O'Sickey critiqued the values inherent in a culture that is both fascinated and disgusted with Barbie, the dolls and the magazine, in "Barbie Magazine and the Aesthetic Commodification of Girls' Bodies," in *On Fashion*, eds. S. Benstock and S. Feriss (New Brunswick, NJ: Rutgers University Press, 1994), 21–40. Mary Pipher in her best-selling book on teenage girls points out how women are depicted as "half-clad and half-witted, often awaiting rescue by quick thinking fully-clothed men," in *Reviving Ophelia: Saving the Selves of Adolescent Girls* (New York: Ballantine Books, 1994), 43. Her case studies of girls and their families emerged from her work as a therapist.

On a long walk around Tofino, one of the towns in Clayoquot Sound, Nicole and her classmates tell me how important it is to be "perfect." They recount how they wake up at 5:30, two hours before leaving the house for school, to wash and blow-dry their hair, put on make-up, and select clothing. The make-up has to make them look good, without it being apparent to anyone that they have it on. Only lipstick and a bit of eye color can show, they say. Their clothes have to make them look as thin as they can. And while they try to make their bodies look as streamlined as possible, they wonder why the boys want to wear big baggy pants. In a way, it is not surprising to hear how girls dream of attaining "perfection" in their looks. Watching television or reading newspapers or academic journals, we see examples of anorexia nervosa brought on by this learned desire to be perfect. Yet, hearing about this preening activity while walking down a dirt road in Tofino with a group of bright 13-year-old girls surprised me. I had thought these girls would let go of their "urban" sensibilities in a "natural" setting; I did not think that the girls (and some boys, too) would wake up at 5 or 6 to take showers and blow-dry their hair for a walk in a rainforest.

It is not surprising that Nicole and Terri-Lynn chose to show how others view what we are doing to the rainforests of Clayoquot Sound. Viewpoints are their thing, which is common at this age. Finding out about how others view what they do deeply interests them. Making connections between what is inside (how we see ourselves and how we see others) and what is outside (how others see us and how they see themselves) is one of the balancing acts teenage girls are learning. Epistemologically, this fits well with how we, as sentient beings, come to make sense of our worlds. As we explore various points of viewing by continually examining how others see what we see and comparing this to how we see what we see, we form complex knowledge structures. The conflict between how we see ourselves and how others see us is at the root of how we balance and negotiate meanings. Nicole's seeming preoccupation with how she looks in the eyes of others is not merely a result of media pressure, although the

http://www.pointsofviewing.com/215

broadcast and print media play a large part in influencing the way in which teenage girls work at solving this inner-outer conflict, and we know that the cultural exploitation of this conflict can lead to an addictive behavior focused on the desire for beauty at any cost.[175]

For many girls and some boys, the external is endowed with characteristics of the personal. There can be no knowledge of the other without knowledge of self. There can be no connecting points of viewing without first developing an identity, and that means knowing, or trying to know, who one is in the company of self and others. Balance comes with imbalance—the often embarrassing moments of showing more than we wanted to show and, worse, having feelings that we are not quite equipped to control. These are difficult times for children who are already experiencing the tingling sensations of puberty as they move into the world of adults. All the more difficult when they are still trying to learn from their pasts and the pasts of those who came before them.

Learning from Past Accomplishments and Mistakes

> **Brianne:** I don't understand. Why can't you just learn from someone else's mistakes? You know, like, I mean, Europe's really lucky because they, their growth is starting to come back and they're doing everything to preserve it and try to keep it the way it is.

When I see 14-year-old Brianne in the hallways of Bayside Middle School, she bounces in front of me, ready to give me a hug hello. Sadly, I can only mimic her bouncy excitement as a way of responding in kind to her response at seeing me. (Adults who are not their parents can no longer show affection to children, not physical affection, given the potential misuse of power.) Nevertheless, I know that Brianne knows I'm interested in her ideas and in her life at school.

Brianne wonders why people don't learn from other people's experiences, especially from others' mistakes. She has no trouble in reaching a decision about what should happen to the temperate rainforests of Vancouver Island. She is against clearcutting. Yet, she worries about loggers and their families and respects them more than she does the

---

175. See Naomi Wolf, *The Beauty Myth* (New York: Anchor Books, 1991).

protesters, whom she thinks might be "welfare bums," which is how they have been described in some newspaper articles. She says, "I feel sorry for the loggers because a lot of the protesters that are on the site now live on welfare. Lots of them. I'm not saying all of them do. Of course all of them don't, but a lot of them do. And they're the ones every day sitting down and protesting while the loggers are out trying to work and earn money."

A straitlaced young person, Brianne is concerned about the trees because she and her grandparents hike through the rainforests of Clayoquot Sound on summer vacations. When she finds that her trip to the Sound might be canceled due to protesters blocking the road, Brianne tells me that she "wouldn't be a person to go up and protest right now." When I ask her what she might do, she thoughtfully responds that she too would "like to go up and give [the loggers] a couple of words, but I wouldn't sit there, you know, and get dragged away by the police. I'm not that type of person." On another occasion, I ask her what she wants to do about the problem. We are sitting outside on a rock. Her unbleached, white-blonde hair is tied loosely behind her head; she is wearing a crisp white T-shirt; and she is sitting quite upright and poised. She is surprised when I ask her what she would do to solve the conflict, and says, "I don't really know yet. Like, I mean, hey, I'm only 14!"

Brianne uses poetry to help her form her ideas. For a language arts assignment she writes a poem called "Ancient Gardens":

> As I walk through an ancient garden
> I see the tall green trees
> Awaken, with little friends sitting upon their arms.
> I sometimes wonder what it would be like to live in such a peaceful place.
> But as I watch and hear the trees
> Severed from their soft moist beds,
> I know that the next time I walk in an ancient garden
> It will no longer be.

http://www.pointsofviewing.com/217

When I ask her about her poem, she tells me that when she is "really interested in something" she can "write and write and write. Cause if you just really have the feeling towards something, it just makes it so easy." I ask how she gets inspired. Brianne tells me that she sits down and thinks for a long time about what she wants to describe. And sometimes she uses pictures to spark her imagination. "You think about a tree, and what it would be like if you were a tree And that's where I got that [idea] from"— here we see anthropomorphizing, or attaching human qualities to nonhuman entities. Brianne first has to see herself as a tree, and then she can create her own representation of what an ancient garden might be. To explore biodiversity, she first has to put herself into the forest and imagine what it is like to have birds sitting on her arms. She connects to the broader issues by first reaching into her inner thoughts and feelings. From this core identification, she can talk about history, statistical reports of the percentage of rainforest in Clayoquot Sound to be preserved, and global concerns. She points to illustrations provided by British Columbia's provincial government.

> **Brianne:** When people first came to this island, it was covered in trees. It was all forest. Now look how much has been logged and what's supposed to be logged, and that's what we're supposed to have left. That tells me that our government isn't trying hard enough; they're just being very very stubborn in some ways. And the ancient temperate rainforest in Clayoquot Sound—you know, 4.4% is supposed to be saved.... Like, I mean, we had so much and we're coming down with so little. And the people in Europe regret every minute of logging now.

Brianne expects us to learn from countries that have devastated their forests. "You should always learn from someone else's mistakes," she restates. For Brianne, knowledge is constructed by others for our advancement. One could say that Brianne, like Nicole, is concerned with how people in other countries view us, but she is more concerned with what we learn from our viewing of them. For Brianne, knowledge is something that can be shared and transferred, learned.

Bringing the Science Curriculum "Home"

> **Terri-Lynn:** I really didn't like science until I came into this year's class and we did the Clayoquot Project. This kind of science I really do like.

In this chapter, I described the thinking of several teen girls' while they participated in a socioscientific project. I have drawn portraits of their attitudes about their thinking processes, using point of viewing as a focus. The idea that the learning process should relate to their lives is obviously a key component in their sense of empowerment. For example, Terri-Lynn, Nicole's partner, tells me that, in previous years, they had not done anything that was "as hands-on as what we're doing now. It was mostly book work and reading questions and stuff like that." Terri-Lynn began to like science as a result of studying it in relation to a social issue that was relevant to her life. She also became more interested when she knew that her work was not ending up in a pile of papers at the bottom of a drawer—an assignment that no one would see or read. She knew that her work with the Clayoquot Project was adding to a database of video and text that, through the Internet, would be available to young people in other places.

Terri-Lynn's forthright "pedagogical" attitude and her ability to take charge of her own learning led her to think about how doing something in which she was really interested made it easier for her to learn about science.

> **Ricki:** Which aspects of the project so far have you found the most interesting and which the most boring?
>
> **Terri-Lynn:** Well, like, on our field trip, I really like doing hands-on stuff and not just reading and writing; the trip was really fun. I really haven't done anything boring in the Clayoquot Project

because I'm doing digitizing, and then the video project, and then we went to Clayoquot Sound and there's really nothing boring about it.

Ricki: Does this project relate to your life, Terri-Lynn?

Terri-Lynn: Yeah, cause we have to live in the future, and what happens to Clayoquot Sound could really change the future. If more old-growth rainforests are cut down and whatever happens. Yeah, it really does relate to our real life!

Ricki: And does that make it easier or harder for you to study science?

Terri-Lynn: I think it's better, like it's easier, because you're more interested in it. Like, if it's only about frogs and you're really not that interested, it's really not that appealing. But, if it's something that you want to know about and want to research, it's better.

I am not proposing that we make science "easy" in order to get more girls and boys interested in it. I am proposing, however, that studying a socioscientific issue that is directly relevant to young people is a good way to introduce them to science because it helps them both to understand its complexity and their relationship to what is going on in the world around them. Natalie, who is in the same class as Nicole and Terri-Lynn, points out an interesting problem of conducting research on something about which you care deeply. Studying a subject that you care about can make learning difficult. "Well, in a sense," she says, "it makes it easier because you know what you're dealing with, and in a sense it makes it harder because you know what you're dealing with but you're not sure how that's going to affect you." It's easier to learn science when you know what you are dealing with, Natalie points out, but knowing what you are dealing with also makes it more difficult because what you learn affects your life in a way that demands action.

For decades, teachers and curriculum designers have struggled with how to make learning more relevant to students. They know that both the content and process of learning have to keep changing if, as a society, we want young people to better connect their experiences with their thinking. The emerging goal is not to make all learning fun and effortless. Learning can be difficult, even painful, because it forces us to think about things that we did not either want to think about or that, when we do think about, we can find no easy answers. Enabling young people to connect to issues that relate to their lives means letting them see themselves as part of a solution, as does Mia. Or to use new technologies to create representations of what is seen and heard, as do Nicole and Terri-Lynn. Or to learn from the experiences of others, as has Brianne. Increasingly, in a digital world of seemingly infinite choices, students will need these critical skills to sort, sift, and filter various ways of viewing complex issues. As Caroline says, with regard to selecting articles from the newspaper, "I mean I'm getting it second hand from the newspaper reporters. If you can get it first hand, you'll know exactly what they say and if parts are not omitted and things like that." Although I may not agree with Caroline that we can get the news firsthand, she does remind us that young people need to "get out there and see what's happening." They need to critique media sources while making media. Forming diverse points of viewing, they can break the stereotypes that hold them back from expanding their notions of the world around them.

> **Ricki:** What do you mean when you use the word "stereotyping"?
>
> **Caroline:** Well, stereotyping is when people say protesters always eat granola and the loggers want to kill the trees and the protesters are all on welfare. Some things may be true for some people but they're not true for all of them. That people just kind of make generalizations and such. And ownership is like who owns land; the government kind of owns the land but the government really represents people so the people really own the land. So it's kind of confusing.

Indeed it is, Caroline. But worth changing.

http://www.pointsofviewing.com/221

9 Science as Friend

I think that science, what it does is, teaches you about things. Like, say there's one main person and say they taught me about Sean and I got to know Sean and I'd be his friend and I'd respect him. But if I didn't know him, I might not say "hi" and notice him that much, and respect him. That's the kind of thing with science, it gets all the things that teaches you to be a friend; and friends you respect.

—*Ross*

Relational Boys

I stand transfixed in the sand at the 10-mile beach of Pacific National Park in Clayoquot Sound, watching the Bayside Middle School girls tease the water with their toes, their jeans rolled to their knees. Then, jumping in the low waves on a cool damp autumn day, they become ignited by the excitement of possible danger. The girls and, now, a few of the boys decide to enter more deeply into the low, rolling waves. I watch them challenging each other, each going just a little further than the next. Ross seems oblivious to the game. A 13-year-old boy with a far-away look in his eyes and a lean body, Ross is suddenly the furthest from the shoreline. He is immersed in the experience of cold, hypnotic waves. I stand on the beach terrified. What if something happens? Will he remember to come back to shore, to the safety of the school bus?

He and the others are not in any imminent danger. Two teachers are nearby; the school vice-principal watches over the girls and boys as if they are his own—one of them is, indeed, his daughter. Nevertheless, when I look back on that event today, almost two years since we began to immerse ourselves in the rainforest controversy, I recognize that this event is the one that holds the most meaning for me. Before that day, I hadn't really noticed Ross. I hadn't paid attention to his somber intensity and his will to take charge of his life. And I hadn't realized my full responsibility in initiating a project that had the power to immerse young people into the world of their senses and to dramatically connect their bodies and minds.

When I ask a group of boys what they liked best about our 4-day field trip to the Sound, they talk about the purple sunset over Kennedy Lake, the shivering walk through the rainforests in their wet saltwater clothes, and the interviews they conducted with people. They talk about the food we ate: they didn't like the food at one place that served whole wheat breads, but loved the bacon and eggs, the "healthy" breakfast, at another restaurant. They talk about "the drunk" they interviewed and the person who lectured without showing pictures or slides.

When I ask Ross, Brian, and Sean what they think about studying Clayoquot Sound as part of their science classes, Ross looks up to the left with an intense glow, saying, "It's changed me. If I didn't know anything about this, I think I wouldn't have as much respect for the environment and respect for anything else that we learn in science."

I sit quietly, my camera nestled on my lap, noticing how his head tilts gently as he softly speaks. I am primed to hear his explanation of why he uses the word "respect" when he talks about science.

"Science ... teaches you to be a friend, and friends you respect." The comment is interestingly complex. Learning more about how the world works enables one to relate to it so that it becomes one's friend. And the deeper the relationship, the more respect one has for it. Connecting friendship with learning about science seems to be something a girl would be more likely to do than would a boy. After all, the extensive research on

---

176. Ricki Goldman-Segall, "Genderflexing: A Theory of Gender and Socio-Scientific Thinking," *Proceedings for the International Conference on the Learning Sciences* (Evanston, IL: Association for the Advancement of Computers in Education, 1996), 99–106. An excerpt of this paper can be found at <http://www.merlin.ubc.ca/pubs>.

gender and science addresses ways of making boys more relational because girls are allegedly more interested in relationships. To hear a boy
speak with such emotion in the company of two other boys, his friends,
points us toward a larger understanding of gender, teaching, and learning—an understanding I have begun to call *genderflexing*.[176] It means that
both girls and boys can, and are willing to, try on different "gendered"
ways of thinking and acting; and, while they do so, they flex their thinking, reaching beyond boundaries.

Ross, Brian, and Sean are sitting in the shade of cypress trees at lunch
time. Ants are abundant. We laugh about them being a nuisance, recognizing that they are part of the ecosystem we have been investigating all
year. Brian tells me about helping his father gather information on Clayoquot
Sound. Brian is a member of the Clayoquot Nation, a subgroup within the
Nuu-Chah-Nulth linguistic division. Brian's family lives near Brentwood
Bay, where the school is situated. His family, especially his grandmother, a
Clayoquot elder, shows much pride in Brian's accomplishments both inside and outside his school. Brian, a young person of determination and
kindness of spirit, works with a youth committee gathering materials on
issues to do with trees, land, and fishing. He sits on a log, his black hair
falling in front of his deep brown eyes, telling me how each band is "working differently for the same thing." In other words, he and his family are
right in the center of current government negotiations over the future of
these forests.

> **Brian:** I have to learn about this stuff anyway for my dad, because
> he needs help with it. He has to learn about this stuff as well and
> they didn't teach it when he was a kid because it wasn't a problem
> back then; it was just, if you want this [land], you can't have it.
> And now we're learning how you go through the procedure of
> getting something and negotiations and stuff.

http://www.pointsofviewing.com/225

During the year, Brian completes a HyperCard-based portfolio on the Sound that not only shows his interest in describing the First Nations' point of view about aboriginal rights, but also visually conveys the look and feel of the layers of mountains that surround the Sound. His sensitive portrayal of the Sound does not surprise me. He has always shown sensitivity to others. On our field trip, he came down with a violent case of the flu. His face puffed up and he could barely move. Instead of pretending not to be sick as would a "macho man," he allowed everyone around him to be part of his healing. And they were.

When he talks about science, he tells me that he mostly enjoys "hands-on" learning, not only in the form of electronically making and designing an interface for his portfolio, but also in the form of going on field trips.

> **Brian:** I think there should be more hands-on stuff, because you learn more when you are actually there rather than copying stuff. Some people say you can learn more by reading books and studying over and over again. But if you go there once, you'll never forget it.
>
> **Ricki:** And then the reading will make sense?
>
> **Brian:** Yeah, then the reading will make sense.

Brian is also interested in reading and gathering data that will help his community negotiate their position. He is simply situating his knowledge in experience. Sean reinforces the same idea, explaining to me that there should be "more hands-on projects, more trips in science."

> **Sean:** It's a good thing we got this opportunity, because the other science teachers just write things up on the chalkboard and kids just write things down and then you have your test, but when we had our test on Clayoquot Sound, we knew a lot more than anyone who had just copied it out of books. That was a big advantage.

Although I am surprised to hear that one of the teachers gave them a test on Clayoquot Sound, I pursue the thread of Sean's idea that first-hand knowledge of a subject in science gives students an advantage by providing them with a feel for the subject. He tells me that "other science" doesn't get you "into the real world." But when you go to a place, "you get to learn more about the topic, and the issues that are surrounding the place—the environmental issues and logging." To make his point more clearly, he provides an example. "Let's say I'm learning about this tree in class and the teacher draws this picture on the board. You don't really get the full idea of what's happening; when you go out to see the actual thing, you get a better idea, like, a 100% idea of what it is like and how it works." Their teacher Jordan Tinney, who was once a logger, was able to point out how the different trees in an old-growth forest depend on each other for sustenance and support. He identified varieties of coniferous trees, and various kinds of plant and animal life that grow on and around them, and connected these trees to the larger implications for the ecosystem. His in situ lectures were, indeed, more impressive than what he could do on a flat board.

Sean recalls these experiences and others that he shared with his friends. The field trip was particularly important to him because his mom was one of the parents who joined us. These parents, camping out in the local school gym and sitting for hours on a school bus listening to the repetitive drone of students making up travel songs, built connections between their children's home and school lives. The simple things they talked about around the dinner table after the trip, like "What did you do in school today?" became an opportunity to discuss something that had significance for the whole family. More curious was the fact that even those parents who were not part of the field trip began to participate in this project with their children. Surely this linking of home and school activities is our goal when we talk about using networked technologies for conducting investigations within the curriculum. Think how powerful learning will become when layers of knowledge taken from various perspectives become the subject of what children and parents do together to solve common problems. Brian working with his dad on First Nations treaty negotiations is the beginning of a deeper relationship with learning.

http://www.pointsofviewing.com/227

Projects Linking Home and School

By visiting Clayoquot Sound and recording a range of events, this project touched the lives of the students at Bayside Middle School. Many of the them have direct or indirect connections to the place and to its resources. The families of some camp in the parks in the summer. Some have relatives who are economically connected with the place: two of the local towns in and around the Sound, Ucluelet and Port Alberni, are basically one-industry towns (and that industry is the forest industry). Mill towns are scattered all across Vancouver Island. For decades, the economic well-being of towns centered around the forest industry. On the other hand, some families are adversely affected by the logging. Jessie's father, for example, is a fisher who has fished the inlets around the Sound for years. Jessie, sitting comfortably in his chair, his pale face becoming animated with a pink glow, tells me that every year the fishing is worse. The clearcut has added silt to the streams, and salmon have trouble spawning.

> **Jessie:** My dad's a commercial fisherman and he knows a lot, right? Well, he fishes around Tofino and he says it gets worse every year because of the logging. Like, the salmon eat the little herring but the herring, I think, put their eggs in the kelp. And the mud [from clearcutting] collects in the kelp, and the mud goes on the herring eggs and the salmon don't like mud and wouldn't want to eat mud so they don't eat the fish eggs and I guess they starve and they die. So my father told me it's getting worse and stuff like that.

Jessie's dad works with him on his Clayoquot project. From his comments, I gather that Jessie's dad does not usually help him with class assignments. However, on this project, his dad "was excited. He liked working with me. It was fun." So one way to bring the personal lives of these students into their curricular activities is to find subjects that are also of interest to their families. Jessie's dad got involved on many levels. He not only took Jessie to the Sound to fish, but also gathered maps and collected information from a fisher's point of view. Jessie's experience of navigating the waters of Clayoquot Sound with his dad enabled him to talk about alternatives to a logging-based economy:

Jessie: Like, we, he had a whole bunch of maps ... oh, here's one of my maps. Oh, that's Clayoquot and Tofino. He told me about Port Hardy and stuff. And here is Meares Island, the big Indian reserve. And Tofino is right here and I bet if they log Meares Island, because Meares is right there, tourists will probably be turned off.

Ricki: So I guess the two issues you are most interested in are the fishing industry and tourism?

Jessie: Yeah, I like tourism.... There's a lot of things happening in Tofino right now, like whale-watching and stuff like that. And it's exciting to learn about that stuff. I feel bad about, like, I know the loggers can lose their jobs and all, but there's other ways to make money, other than logging. They can get another job at ... something else. They can be, they can work in, like, a whale-watching thing or something. Then you don't need to log to make money. Maybe that's what they think. Maybe that's a good way of making money. But you can make money some other way.

Not only does working on an issue that relates to his life and the life of his family expand his thinking about alternatives to logging, it also enables Jessie to think about his future, about what occupations he might pursue. Jessie wants to become a biologist and study birds, trees, and, of course, the ocean. "That's one of the reasons why I like to go fishing with my dad, cause I pass a lot of forests and there's a lot of clearcut. That's what I hate, but other than that it's really nice. Like trees and birds." When I ask him if studying Clayoquot Sound as a class project helped him define his career choice, he tells me: "I never knew much about Clayoquot until I finished this; all I really knew was Mike Harcourt is the premier of British Columbia!" Since beginning his project, he has started reading the papers regularly, looking for articles on Tofino. Now "it all makes sense. Like, I never understood much. Like, say the teacher was talking about something that they heard; I didn't understand it at all until I did this."

http://www.pointsofviewing.com/229

Ricki: What was important in helping you learn?

Jessie: Well, my dad. My dad was part of that; and just watching the news. You got to see people that were loggers, and in Ucluelet—you got to see people in Ucluelet and the people in Tofino talking about what they think about Clayoquot; and the Native people on Meares Island, what they think. It was really neat just to watch. And it was interesting just to watch all these people ... talk about what they think about Clayoquot Sound and stuff.

In other words, what Jessie found interesting was working with his dad and hearing many points of viewing. "This is probably the most interesting project of what I've done, cause I got to take it home and get opinions of my family, and it was interesting."

More Views from More Vantage Points

Ryan spends most of his waking time in a wheelchair. He has walker extensions that enable him to get around on his own two feet from time to time, but most of his school day is spent maneuvering his electric chair as he goes from class to class. A birth problem resulted in his being physically challenged both in speaking and in moving his body. But his will to partake in exciting adventures on land and at sea is stronger than his physical disadvantages. It was a special moment for me when I watched him on a public service announcement on television, sailing around Victoria's harbor and explaining how important it is to change our views about people with physical challenges. A spokesperson, Ryan has taken on an activist role at the age of 13.

Ryan sports a funky, cropped haircut and has soft blue eyes that search for contact. But, it's his smile that endears him to classmates and teachers. Whenever there is a class event, Ryan is in the center of it. Over the 2 years I spend observing this group of adolescents, I never once observe any anger or frustration directed toward Ryan. Everyone, especially the teachers, respects and encourages him. When there are games, Ryan participates—slowly. When teachers or visiting lecturers invite opinions from students, Ryan always speaks out and is listened to. And, in his carefully pronounced, monosyllabic speaking rhythm, Ryan clearly, albeit with a fair degree of difficulty, articulates what is on his mind. I remember speaking to his mom about whether I could feature Ryan on the CD-ROM, *The Global Forest*. (I spoke to the parents of all the girls and boys who "featured" in the program.) His mom said it was up to Ryan to decide, and he thought it was a great idea.

On our trip to Clayoquot Sound, Ryan seems particularly aglow. I can see his excitement as he and the others get ready for their "camp-out" in sleeping bags on the floors of the local gym in the Wickaninnish School at Tofino. On the lookout he holds the video camera videotaping the vast tumbling waves. Although his dexterity does not enable him to use the camera with ease, he is happy to videotape. He calls out to his classmates, reminding them that he has the camera and is videotaping them. And he giggles to himself for being a bit naughty.

Yes, there are parts of the trip in which Ryan cannot participate. The walk through the old-growth rainforest is not wheelchair accessible. And the inviting sandy beaches with their magical tidal pools at low tide remain a hidden treasure to a person in a wheelchair. But his joy at being in the company of his class is obvious to us all. His teacher Laurie Roche has given up her weekend for this class outing. With her intelligent explanations and questions, she continually pushes Ryan to think more deeply about what he is seeing, feeling, and thinking. As Ryan tells me in one

Annotation: Ryan's talking about eyes-together learning reminds me of Seymour Papert's comment that what young people need in their constructionist learning cultures is "heads-in" thinking about their constructions.

of our many conversations over the following year, "Actually going to Clayoquot was better than reading books and jotting down information." "How come?" I ask. "Because I would much rather like to be there and see what it's really like with my own eyes."

Once again, I hear about the importance of learning from one's own experiences—the need for what so many of these boys and girls call "hands-on" learning. The only difference for Ryan is that he is promoting "eyes-together" learning.

http://www.pointsofviewing.com/231

Cautiously, I ask him what he likes about studying science and social studies through the lens of forest issues. He says that he likes doing group projects. "Working with someone takes away some of the pressure. I mean … you have two people and it makes it go a lot quicker." Then he explains in a matter-of-fact manner that we need to take notes on "what we see" and "sharpen up our understanding of these issues." Ryan helps me understand that seeing into the anima of the objects and things we study within a robust community of inquiry provides us with "more views from more vantage points." Hearing these words, I repeat them:

> **Ricki:** "We'd have more views from more vantage points." Can you explain what you mean?
>
> **Ryan:** We'd see other opinions to things and we'd think about them and talk them over and see what other people's opinions are; and to me that's really interesting. To know what other people think about it.
>
> **Ricki:** Why is that? Why are you so interested in how other people think about these issues?
>
> **Ryan:** Cause, maybe, maybe we can take these thoughts into consideration and really learn from other people and maybe know what side you want to take.

I sit in my seat, rendered speechless by his idea that learning is a result of layering others' views with our own, and his broad understanding about how we make sense of the living world around and inside us.

Views from Experience and Research

For his project, Ryan chooses to study the history of logging practices in British Columbia. He examines how logging has changed since the advent of various logging technologies. "In the past, they have been using much more manpower." A year earlier, with the first group of students studying Clayoquot Sound, the logging practices of the forest companies was the subject which Aaron, a terribly shy teen with a serious streak, also chose to study. Aaron spoke of his research process with pride, but he thought his portfolio could have been better.

> **Aaron:** There's other people who've done better. Like, after seeing what I've seen, I feel that I could have done better.
>
> **Ricki:** After seeing what?
>
> **Aaron:** Carol's got a really good report. It's got all these pictures; the wording is mixed in with the pictures so that looks really good. She's got pictures of the animals in there, got hand-drawn pictures, she's got maps, she's got everything. And it's all really done up nicely in those plastic covers. So that looks really good.
>
> **Ricki:** So it's the presentation that is different? Maybe your content is just as good.
>
> **Aaron:** Well, yeah. The content should be just as good, but I feel that setting it up and organizing it could have been much better.
>
> **Ricki:** You thought deeply about the issues, didn't you?
>
> **Aaron:** Yeah, but I'm not a straight-A student.
>
> **Ricki:** You're *what?*
>
> **Aaron:** I'm not a straight-A student, so I don't think quite as deeply. Straight-A students think more about these things. They think bigger and better.
>
> **Ricki:** You don't think that you thought really deeply about the Clayoquot Sound dispute?
>
> **Aaron:** I don't think I thought as deep as I could. Which is about 30 feet.

http://www.pointsofviewing.com/233

Ending this conversation with some humor seems like a pretty smart thing to do. And looking back, I would say that Aaron thinks very deeply about the issues that are important to him, but hasn't developed the "tools" to put his ideas into a form that is accessible to others. He has conducted quite an extensive piece of research, exploring the government's role in forest management. He makes calls to local government officials. He goes to the public library to read and photocopy sections of articles. He copies maps and pie charts, and then cuts and pastes them into his text-based report. (The first year of the project, we gathered our data without the use of multimedia technologies.) He also visits the Ministry of Forestry in downtown Victoria and picks up "about 20 leaflets and brochures and stuff from there." His project shows "how much is to be logged and how much is to be saved. How the government and how the loggers felt about it." The focus of study is a comparison of different reports on Clayoquot Sound—each containing its own notion of the amount of forest to be logged. His teacher, Jordan Tinney, has already shown the class how each of the various interest groups uses graphs in ways that fudge statistical data (to their respective advantages, of course). Aaron's portfolio contains an introduction and various short sections describing the role of the government; actions by protesters; and the effects of logging practices on animals, the forest, fishing, and the rights of First Nations peoples. True, his project is not housed in a beautiful form; his data do not look inviting to the reader. However, Aaron is curious and serious about the issues. He is deeply concerned about the future of loggers and their families. He worries about the economy. And he tries to make sense of government policy by continually asking questions. The issues confuse him, and this confusion leads him to look at them in a step-by-step fashion. When I finally ask him what his views are, he uncomfortably answers:

> **Aaron:** I'm more towards the government's side. After what I heard. I phoned the government about 8 times; like, each time, there was a different person. And so I got all their opinions on it and they all told me exactly what the government was thinking. And so after what they told me, I found out that I was more towards their side. At first, I was on the protesters' side. Loggers shouldn't be logging as they are. They shouldn't be clearcut logging, cause that's really bad for the environment. And they shouldn't be logging as much as they are. The government is now

making sure that they don't have any landslides or anything near rivers, cause they were telling me that in the past the government has been going near rivers and the loggers logged out both sides, and a rainfall just washes the land straight down into the river. Yeah, so yeah, so I'm more on the government's side.

Aaron uses the video camera as his investigative and creative tool. He and I have our first lengthy conversation on the way to a logging site—a trip sponsored by a logging company and arranged by one of the teachers, Kathryn Godfrey. At the beginning of the trip, I notice Aaron sitting by himself at the front of the bus, while most of the teens are huddled together as close to the back of the bus as they can get, playing with their *Game Boys*. I am videotaping the logging company spokesperson, who is offering pro-logging views en route. Our spokesperson, yelling into a microphone to get the students' attention, gets a little frustrated about their seeming lack of concern. Only Aaron pays strict attention and asks numerous questions. He also asks me how I use the video camera. I explain how to shoot a sequence and edit in-camera, so that each shot follows the one in a contiguous flow. We talk about these technical and aesthetic issues as well as about interviewing techniques. And we listen to our spokesperson, of course.

Within an hour, Aaron is shooting his own video. When we arrive at the top of the mountain, the fine Pacific Northwest mist becomes a drenching rain. Aaron asks one of his classmates for her hot pink umbrella and uses it to shelter the camera from the rain as he interviews the logging foreman. He asks him how much money one full truck of logs brings the company. The foreman does not take his question very seriously; with a smile, he says that the logs might not be sold. Aaron persists, not responding to the possible sarcasm in the foreman's voice. Convinced by Aaron's persistence, the foreman tells Aaron about himself and his family. This vigorous man in his early 50s has been logging all his life. His father and grandfather were loggers, his sons are loggers. He tells Aaron to "stay in

school, get a good education and then take a job in the logging industry." Aaron has shot his first video story—the story of a man from Ladysmith, British Columbia, who has his roots in logging. But Aaron doesn't stop with only one story. He goes back on the bus to interview the bus driver, an outgoing sort of fellow with a love for the logging industry. He tells Aaron about how he got a job, "a good-paying job," without a high-school education. The logging companies paid him well for his tenure as a faller. It's a bittersweet interview—logging isn't what it used to be. I stand close by, videotaping Aaron while he videotapes the bus driver. Here is a teen who is able to move from scene to scene in a chameleon-like manner. Later, back at the school, when I ask him whether these videotaping experiences are an interesting way of learning, he says: "Yeah, instead of just sitting in the classroom listening and hearing what the teacher can say about it, I got to make something."

I wonder what does this shy person who does not "hang out" much with others thinks about working with other students in the class. "Did you have much interchange with other students during the project?" I ask.

> **Aaron:** Yeah, we were talking about the issues that we could put up on the board, when we were starting our reports. Yeah, yeah, a whole bunch of good [ideas] came up that I never thought of, so I used all those.

> **Ricki:** So people's ideas helped inform how you think about logging issues.

> **Aaron:** I had trouble thinking of five [issues]—which was how many that we had to [come up with in class], but we ... did a whole bunch more [as a group].

Once again I hear that, when students work with their peers, ideas grow. What did not happen to Aaron, at least in my observations, was a deep collaboration in which discussions led to new ways of thinking. It was fun to interview the loggers, he tells me. It was fun to go to the logging site. And he obviously found the videotaping of interviews a challenge. However, what really made the project special was being "allowed to phone and actually see what [government officials] have to say about it. So just sort of talking with somebody of importance made it fun." Whatever it was that drove Aaron to write 32 pages of detailed descriptions of Clayoquot Sound, he learned to layer different views on a controversial subject-—views that are critical to the life of his community. In the opening page of his end-of-year portfolio, he clearly lays out the controversy:

> Clayoquot Sound is a very important forest. It is located on the western side of Vancouver Island near Tofino and Ucluelet and that's over up by Port Alberni. It contains some of the oldest trees in Canada. Many of them are over 500 years old. Clayoquot Sound has been the center of British Columbia's attention for over half a year and will be the center of attention until the government changes its decision to log it or until Clayoquot Sound has been totally logged and been bared of life. There are many issues surrounding the topic of Clayoquot Sound. Many of the topics are important. Some of them sound like they have nothing to do with Clayoquot Sound. Some of those issues are related to logging and some of them are related to tourism and the job industry. Some of them are related to decisions that could change British Columbia forever. Three of the main topics are the ones that make up nearly all of the Clayoquot issue. These topics are the loggers, the protesters and mainly the government. They are the most important topics that make up Clayoquot Sound. The protesters think that the loggers and the government are wrong. The loggers think that the protesters are wrong and the government thinks that the protesters are wrong. Loggers have no choice but to do what they are told to do because it is their job. The government needs the money from logging to pay for imports and to help pay for all the things that come out of our tax money. The protesters think that Clayoquot Sound needs to be saved because of its natural importance here in British Columbia. They're all good reasons for pro-logging or for anti-logging and they're all around the same issue which is Clayoquot Sound.

http://www.pointsofviewing.com/237

From Scientist-as-Magician to Scientist-as-Friend

For many educators and parents, it seems a stretch to think that learning about science in schools can be like getting to know a friend. But the more you get to know science, the more you respect it. And it can teach you how to respect the world around you as well as the world inside you, as Ross tells us. These teenage boys from Bayside Middle School have shown that they want to learn about science in ways that connect them to each other and to the environment in which they live. They have deep concerns about the future of this planet. They want opportunities to learn from others' perspectives, because they know that their own views are still growing. They connect growth with finding out how others see what they see. They know that if they can come together, and, as Ryan tells us, "talk it over," better decisions can be made.

Immersion is a key concept for understanding how students think about their own knowledge. As Ross explains, he wants to know how something "looks and feels." A kinesthetic response is imperative for these teens as they move from childhood to adulthood. The world of touch and feel is often taboo; they are told not to experience sensuality in their daily lives, yet they continually bump into each other in the school playgrounds at recess and lunch or near their lockers. The first drops of sexuality fall from a faucet they can no longer turn off just by willing it so. They dream of immersion of self in others while wanting to be independent persons in their own right.

Early adolescence is the last chance for peace before the tumult of raging hormones, the anger of self-consciousness, and the loss of ability to express deep emotions. It is the last chance to connect to the more malleable and flexible parts of one's self. And it is our last chance, as educators or parents, to provide experiences that young people will never forget. As Brian says of Clayoquot Sound, "if you go there once, you'll never forget it." What Brian is talking about does not apply only to going to the Sound; "it" can be any new intellectual space, including cyberspace, that is to be discovered in the company of one's peers. Students need to feel that they are the ones going there, that they are the ones entrusted with the responsibility for their own learning.

> **Ross:** I think trust has a lot to do with the way we feel about this
> project. Like, normal teachers, they would say, like, if we asked,

"Can we go to Clayoquot?" "No, you're too young and stuff. You'd go crazy." But when you can be trusted by a teacher, like, when you're an adult, you feel more trusted. And you feel more grown up and privileged and something. But when you're being put down, like, from other teachers, saying that you're too young; I'd just like to show them, we aren't too young and we can do this.

You might be thinking, "Ricki, where's the science? What does this stuff about trust, respect, and friendship have to do with science?" True, we did not conduct scientific "experiments." And in fact, when I asked these young people what they would like to do next with regard to studying science, they spoke about conducting local experiments on the soil and air as well as waste disposal, the use of farmlands for housing, and other issues that connect to their lives in Brentwood Bay. Yet as a community of inquiry, we learned how to observe, how to interview, and how to gather reports from a variety of viewpoints. We meticulously examined and critiqued the statistical data that was being promulgated by various interest groups. Our goal was to explore issues surrounding a matter of grave social and scientific concern, and we used various media forms to build our understanding of it. We looked at it from the points of viewing of loggers, environmentalists, government officials, First Nations peoples, and local townspersons. Our goal was never to memorize facts; it was to explore an issue that would encourage students to connect with it in a personal and social way. Our purpose was to bridge students' home and school lives, using as many technologies as possible; it was to learn skills in collaboration, to build on each other's perspectives, and to investigate things from the basis of a community of inquiry.

Perhaps my biggest surprise was that the Bayside Middle School boys repeatedly told me how they needed a "hands-on" (or "eyes-together," as Ryan might say), connection to science, just as often as the girls did. These are the in-between years, when boys still talk sensitively in front of adults and their peers. They are willing to engage and immerse themselves. When

http://www.pointsofviewing.com/239

I ask Justin, a cool 13-year-old who has a role on a local television show, if the project relates to his life, he tells me how he lives three minutes from a forest. "If they were cutting that down I wouldn't have any place to go, cause I usually go there, like every single day. And it's this huge forest and there's a whole bunch of trails in it, so I always go there."

Justin and his buddies ride the bike trails after school. The forest is large enough for them to ride many different rock trails, constantly hunting out new ones. He tells me how he's done pretty well in science because "we never did any experiments; we've only done stuff on nature and stuff. So that's kind of cool." I ask him what he means by "we've only done stuff on nature."

> **Justin:** Like, for science I always thought it was kind of like being a chemist and putting some things together and like making different things. But it has to do with nature, big time.
>
> **Ricki:** Big time.

I joke with him, repeating the words, "big time," but then I realize that he, like many other young people, thinks that scientists wear white lab coats and mix solutions.[177] Magicians and chemists. Instead, Justin learns how to conduct a form of observational research that makes use of both text and computer data, as well as visits to the investigative site. "You get to go outside and actually do something; and you, like, don't even stay inside and make some stuff up but you're, like, actually studying nature and looking at different

Fieldnotes (April 1995): During the interview, one of the girls from the class walks into the room where we are talking. Immediately, he slouches down in his chair, spreading out the legs lost somewhere in his baggy pants. When she leaves the room, he sits up straight in his chair! How well I remember having to be cool in front of my friends and proper in front of adults.

things." Justin also uses the Internet for conducting all his searches. He and his buddy Chris surf the net, looking for articles on Clayoquot Sound. He uses it for his own assignment, which is "about the environment and trees and stuff." He enjoys this kind of searching for data because he likes "working with, like technology, cause it gives you

---

177. See Aaron Brandes, *Seeds of Science Practice: Parallels Between the Science Thinking and Activities of Sixth-Grade Children and Professional Scientists*, Ph.D. diss. (Massachusetts Institute of Technology, 1997).

more up-to-date stuff on, like issues and things." And, needless to say, a 13-year-old boy needs to be up to date on the latest "stuff."

To use Justin's words, "it was kinda cool" doing this study of students doing a study of a rainforest (using computers, video, the Internet, and, mostly, their eyes). Several boys told me that they never really thought that Jane Goodall (who observes chimpanzees) and Jim Darling (an internationally renowned ocean biologist who studies whales in Clayoquot Sound) were doing "science." And there are probably scientists and science educators who will say that the process of observation, recording, and looking for patterns in data is not "enough." But for middle school kids who are dropping out of science because they cannot see its connection to their lives, studying science in this concrete way is critical. They can reach beyond previous limitations and see themselves as observers, recorders, analysts, and makers of forms that may educate others. As Justin says, our technologies can provide up-to-date data that we, as observers, can add to as we conduct our own local investigations. These are indeed magical times; they are also critical times for becoming friends with the world around us.

10 Attitudes for Genderflexing

We must begin to think in terms of more encompassing categories—the individual's experiences, his frames of reference, his means of sense making, his overall world view.

—Howard Gardner
Frames of Mind: The Theory of Multiple Intelligences

Selecting Mindful Frames

Humbled by the breadth and scope of children's thinking, I resist putting my frame on what I have seen and heard at Hennigan Elementary School and Bayside Middle School. The creation of categories within which to place their thinking at first seems to be anathema to what I have repeatedly called for in this book—the inclusiveness of multiple points of viewing. However, recognizing that my viewing may provide readers with a sense of completion, I have decided not to exclude my final analyses. In other words, although I am concerned that putting my frame on other people's stories might be perceived as appropriation, I also recognize that this book is a story that needs the author's framing.[178]

---

178. See Ruth Behar and Deborah A. Gordon, *Women Writing Culture* (Berkeley: University of California Press, 1995).

Framing opens possibilities for seeing things differently. Frames can enable readers to grasp deeper meanings than those that are available from simply reading text portraits or viewing video. Frames offer opportunities for viewers to situate images within a broad spectrum. Moreover, frames can be changed in order to attain different effects. For instance, a heavy wooden frame around a garden scene constrains the garden; the frame becomes a separate window seemingly cut out from the wall on which the picture is hung. Replacing the wooden frame with a lighter encasement brings the garden into the room. Our points of viewing change as our framing changes. (Yes, they also change when we reposition ourselves or invite the positions of others to influence our viewing, as I have claimed throughout this book.) Thus, acknowledging the choices that lie before me, I tread slowly around these portraits, deciding which frames best suit them, at least for now, knowing full well that readers will choose frames of their own.

The students used technologies in ways that put them in touch with each other and with themselves. Most adults cannot fully grasp what students understand—even though adults have designed the tools they use for their explorations. Learning a language as a child is different from learning it as an adult. We adults always have the accent of our former language. In a similar fashion, those of us who are plugged into the emerging wired and wireless communications systems carry the accents of older technologies: television, radio, and telephone. Our fluency is based on the rules we learned when using the older technologies. Consequently, when I make my decision about how to frame the portraits I have woven together from multitudes of moments, I hear my own accent!

I select frames mindfully, as Gavriel Salomon *et al.* would ask us to do, in order to share what I learned and to invite readers and viewers into the interpretation phase of my analysis.[179] In the past, I framed my portraits by defining a set of epistemological styles: causal/empirical, social/relational, and narrative.[180] I have become less comfortable with the notion of

---

179. Gavriel Salomon, David N. Perkins, and Tamar Globerson, "Partners in Cognition: Extending Human Intelligence With Intelligent Technologies," *Educational Researcher 20*, no. 3 (1991): 2–9.

180. See Ricki Goldman-Segall, "Three Children, Three Styles: A Call for Opening the Curriculum," in *Constructionism*, eds. I. Harel and S. Papert (Norwood, NJ: Ablex Publishing Corp., 1991), 235–268.

styles, which is the term my colleagues Sherry Turkle, Seymour Papert, and others have asked us to consider over the last decade.[181] I now choose a different kind of framing—one that is conscious of the precariousness of any framing of others' lives.[182] The kind of frames I now choose open the possibility for both those who are being portrayed and those who view them to become partners in framing.

Why not style, you might ask. For me, style is a word that has always connoted distinct and particular characteristics, akin to "genre" in literature. "Style" suggests an approach that is somewhat fixed. I find myself interpreting the stories that children have shared with me as being more elastic and flexible. Postures performed in front of my camera. Positions held for a period of time. In other words, instead of concluding that there are three (or more) thinking styles, as I have done in previous works, I now make sense of portraits by exploring their epistemological *attitudes.*

I define attitudes, not as psychologists have used the word in any number of studies that start with the phrase "children's attitudes *toward* ...," but as indicator of a fluid state of mind. Attitude is a ballet pose in which the dancer, standing on one leg, places the other behind it, resting on the calf. Attitude, as a pose, leads into the next movement. Thus attitude is a more flexible notion than style, as it brings together both the positionality and the orientation of the dancer. Positionality and orientation are concepts that have occupied considerable bandwidth over the last decade of

---

181. See Sherry Turkle and Seymour Papert, "Epistemological Pluralism: Styles and Voices within the Computer Culture," in *Constructionist Learning*, eds. I. Harel and S. Papert (Cambridge, MA: MIT Media Laboratory, 1990); Sherry Turkle, "Computational Reticence: Why Women Fear the Intimate Machine," in *Technology and Women's Voices*, ed. C. Kramarae (New York: Routledge and Kegan Paul, 1988).

182. The word *frame* is particularly useful for the activities of a postmodern ethnographer. We place frames around a picture, and around doors and windows. Frames also surround the glass or plastic lenses in our eyeglasses, literally containing and limiting what we see and what we do not. The notion of "frames of reference" and "frames of mind" can also be included in this list—see Howard Gardner, *Frames of Mind: The Theory of Multiple Intelligences* (New York: Basic Books, 1985). Filmmaker Trihn T. Minh-Ha has used the term ironically to capture the notion that the person who is framing is, in some sense, being framed. See Trihn T. Minh-Ha, *Framer Framed.* For a historical understanding of the notion of frames in linguistics, psychology, and artificial intelligence, see Deborah Tannen, "What's in a Frame? Surface Evidence for Underlying Expectations," in *New Directions in Discourse Processing*, ed. R. Freedle (Norwood, NJ: Ablex Publishing Corp., 1979), 137–181.

postmodern feminist theorizing and critical theory.[183] But the most applicable use of the word is in the African-American phrase, "Girl, you got attitude." Attitude is something that you have, you own, you shape—something that you bring to the various contexts of your life. Consider the attitude of someone like Mindy.

> **Mindy:** Like, when you make a picture in Logo, you're not sure how it's gonna come out; you're not sure it's gonna come out like you want it to come out, and if it doesn't, you kinda like it. Yeah, and you sort of say—it's a new invention!

Four Epistemological Attitudes

I have chosen four attitudes to frame my portraits: metaphysical, historical, ethical, and pedagogical—realizing that overlaps occur as we move from attitude to attitude, or pose to pose. Needless to say, there are many other attitudes that could be described. But these four best encapsulate what I have observed in children's thinking over the past years.

Metaphysical attitudes address the question, "What's the story?" They explore how children address causality, intention, existence, and truth. In ancient Rome, "meta" referred to the columns that acted as turning points in races. The racer retraced the linear track, moving in the other direction to complete the race. The more common use of "meta," of course, is as a prefix meaning "with," "along with," "beyond," or "after." The metaphysical attitudes in adolescence are rooted in the physical situatedness of their interactions with the people, plants, animals, and places that surround them. They are turning points.

Historical attitudes are not about the study of history, at least as it is traditionally taught in school, but about the search for understanding how

---

183. See bell hooks, *Yearning: Race, Gender, and Cultural Politics* (Boston, MA: South End Press, 1990); Michelle Fine and Pat Macpherson, "Over Dinner: Feminism and Adolescent Female Bodies;" and Mary Bryson and Suzanne de Castell, "En/gendering Equity: On Some Paradoxical Consequences of Institutionalized Programs of Emancipation," *Educational Theory 43*, no. 3 (1993): 341–355; Mary Bryson and Suzanne de Castell, "So We've Got a Chip on Our Shoulder! Sexing the Texts of Educational Technology," in *Gender In/forms Curriculum: From Enrichment to Transformation*, eds. J. Gaskell and J. Willinsky (New York: Teachers College Press, 1995).

things began. They are about how we learn from our past and make sense of it; how we situate ourselves within our past and think about our future. For example, Brian's concern with First Nations issues and how they relate to Clayoquot Sound addresses a historical attitude, as does Brianne's fear that if we do not learn from the mistakes of the past, then we will not have a forest in the future.

Ethical attitudes confront the eternal struggle between inner and outer selves. Governing and controlling our actions in relation to expectations and rules is a critical part of developing an ethical attitude. Balancing right and wrong is particularly challenging, as rules tend to be made in the "interests" of those with power—of parents and teachers if you are a child, of Whites if you are a person of color, of males if you are female, and of heterosexuals if you are gay or lesbian. An ethical attitude is one that looks at the delicate balance between how others see us and how we see others. It addresses such questions as: "Who really cares? How do we value different points of view?"

To a great extent, pedagogical (or activist) attitudes overlap with ethical attitudes. I have separated them because many students mention their ethical concerns without believing that they can do anything about them. Mia is a good example of a young person who is concerned with doing something about what she thinks is wrong. "If you believe in something and even if you just do a little thing towards it," she says, "you feel better about yourself. Like, even if you recycle paper or even little things ... One of the things you can do is learn more about it and if you learn more about it, you can inform others about it and share your opinions with others, and maybe they'll feel the same way and all together as a group you can go and try to save something." Pedagogical attitudes are concerned with such questions as "What can we do? How do we change?"

Instead of assigning one attitude to each girl and boy in my portraits, I "invite" different girls and boys into each attitudinal frame. From my own perspective, I discuss how their theories suggest a flexible notion of gender within computational learning environments.

Gender is a more pliant, flexible structure than we once thought it to be. Neither boys nor girls seem to be limited to being either "soft" or "hard" programmers.[184] My portraits do not indicate a gender-specific division with

---

184. Sherry Turkle and Seymour Papert, "Epistemological Pluralism: Styles and Voices Within the Computer Culture."

regard to "risk-takers" as opposed to tactile, artistic users.[185] Although it was once considered helpful to conceptualize girls as relational, soft learners needing warm fuzzy experiences, I think now it is time for a reconceptualization, a paradigm shift. Adolescent and pre-adolescent boys and girls are more willing and able to try on roles that were once thought to be "sissy" or "tomboy." Blurring the boundaries by making things "unisex" was commonplace in the 1960s; this generation of young people is extending gender boundaries, not merely crossing over from time to time to see what's on the other side.[186] Earrings and other metal objects pierce the skin of both genders; tattoos and hair color are also without gender preference. And thinking attitudes have definitely become more malleable and fluid—even elastic. As mentioned earlier , I call this tendency to extend gender boundaries *genderflexing*.[187] To better explain this notion of genderflexing, I describe the four attitudes that frame my portraits.

The Metaphysical Attitude:
What's the story? How do we make sense of what we experience?

The first thinking attitude is a concern for the inner condition of knowing, a metaphysical attitude toward life that is expressed in unique ways by different young people. Early adolescence is a time in which people reflect on ideas that are still difficult to articulate. This concern with metaphysics is not what we expect from youth, who seem to be more interested in bouncing around the Internet than in serious reflection. Yet, the glow of early adolescence shines on: What is knowing? Where is it located? What is its nature? These questions emerge as young people become deeply engaged with working on issues that are important to them. For Josh, for example, moving objects are worth contemplating. Through an almost obsessive concentration on moving objects, whether they are on his computer screen or in a toy store, Josh is fascinated by how one action can cause another action in a different object. The flow of energy. He is also

---

185. Sherry Turkle, "Computational Reticence: Why Women Fear the Intimate Machine," 50.
186. See Henri Giroux, *Border Crossings* (Norwood, NJ: Ablex Publishing Corp., 1991).
187. For a comprehensive discussion of genderflexing see Ricki Goldman-Segall, "Genderflexing: A Theory of Gender and Socio-Scientific Thinking," *Proceedings of the International Conference on the Learning Sciences* (Evanston, IL: Association for the Advancement of Computers in Education, 1996): 99–106.

interested in how people "dream up" new things. Josh's notion of how we make sense of experiences at first seems rather empirical: we invent new things by looking at what exists in the world and then putting these things together in new ways. The inspiration for how he constructs ideas comes from external objects. Yet his theory is not so neat and tidy. Josh is also convinced that there are "geniuses" who can put new things together by just thinking deeply about the nature of moving things—*le Penseur*.

His friends Thomas and Mindy express their metaphysical attitude with an approach that is more negotiational than Josh's. Thomas and Mindy think best, not when planning, but when conversing. Thomas's humorous and quizzical approach to making games, for example, keeps him active in figuring out the best strategic next move—whether it be how to get even with the school bully, Chester, or how to engage Josh in yet another round of interesting arguments about the design of their computer game. I have alluded to Thomas as the "fox" who surveys the perimeter of the computer pod looking for the next space to approach.[188] His fast thinking and quick responses are the stuff of conversational and interactional intelligence. And as I have said, he is as relational as Mindy in her metaphysical attitude. Mindy's theory of invention has to do with things happening serendipitously. You put things together and something occurs that you don't expect, and "you say, it's a new invention." Mindy spends most of her school hours thinking about "making girls." Her metaphysical attitude is the contemplation of the inventive process. Mindy's "making girls" are objects-to-think-with, as Papert would say. As Deborah Chetcuti and Kate Maistre have found, adolescent girls often "look for approval from others and describe themselves only in terms of a relationship as wife or mother."[189] Mindy, on the other hand, sets new rules for how she is going to be treated by means of projecting herself into her possible future role as wife and mother. She changes herself by taking charge of her future, since this is the only real power she has in her present circumstances.

Nicole, 2 years older than Mindy, Josh, and Thomas, is a much more self-conscious thinker than are they. Being a preteen, she worries about how others view her. Others determine how she feels about her knowledge. Facts live

---

188. See chapter 6 for a discussion of the hedgehog and the fox.
189. Deborah Chetcuti and Kate Maistre, "Adolescent Girls' Culture and its Impact on their Science Interests," *Textual Studies in Canada 7*, no. 1 (1995) : 123.

"out there" and opinions are made through our interpreting those facts, she tells me. Her theory is similar to Josh's notion that the world of knowledge exists out there and that it is the learner's responsibility to get the stuff inside and do something with it; yet it is slightly different, because Josh doesn't worry about how others view him. Nicole worries about how others will view us as people if we cut down our forests. Brianne, striking a slightly different metaphysical pose, believes people should learn from others' mistakes. Knowledge is constructed by others, but we should make sure we acquire it so that "we don't make the same mistakes." Brianne's notion of learning is interactional, as is Ross's. He wants to build an emotional connection to the natural world through learning about it. In this way, he hopes, science will become his friend. For Ross, knowledge occurs when you interact with your subject matter over a long period of time, long enough so that what you are studying becomes your friend. "And friends, you respect."

Historical Attitudes:
How did it start? How do we learn from our past?

Historical attitudes encourage students to respect the world around them. Brian's roots, for example, are deeply entrenched in the Clayoquot conflict. Whether he studies the issue at school, goes to the beaches of the Sound, or works with his dad on gathering material for treaty talks, Brian is immersed in this work. His identity as an active member of the Clayoquot tribe provides him with a spiritual connection to the place that goes back thousands of years. However, his historical attitude is also intertwined with a physical connection to the Sound, a hands-on kind of learning. As he says: "Let's say I'm learning about this tree in class and the teacher draws this picture on the board. You don't really get the full idea of what's happening; when you go out to see the actual thing, you get a better idea, like a 100% idea of what it is like and how it works." Terri-Lynn repeats the same idea but is less situated in the chronology of the past. She likes hands-on learning because it brings her present life and her thoughts about the future right into the curriculum. Her historical attitude consists of situating herself in the present but looking into the future. "What happens to Clayoquot Sound could really change the future," she tells me. She and Mia show a historical attitude toward their learning when they project themselves into the future and then look back to the present. What are we doing to provide clean air for future generations? How can we rethink logging practices? Mia is constantly looking at history through this lens. In fact, she wonders about the "history" of trees. "How come we only study our human history and not the history of the living things around us?" she once asked me. Can you imagine a course in school that explored science through the historical presence and rights of nonhuman partners? Quite an idea! Thus, a historical attitude is an attitude of deep concern with the sources of problems. This could be as global as being concerned with rainforests or it could be as local as trying to make sense of one's family. The questions asked by students who have this attitude include: How did it start? Where did it all come from? What's the source of this? Josh, asking how words pop up on a computer screen when we are key-boarding shows not only a metaphysical attitude, but also a historical one. Mindy's concern with making girls can also be seen as a historical atti-tude. At 12 years old, she is on the verge of womanhood and is being confronted by bodily changes. "Where does life come from?" is probably the question that pushes many adolescent girls and boys into trying to find out how to balance what came before, what is, and what will be.

Ethical Attitudes:
Who really cares? How do we value different points of view?

When we think of an ethical attitude, we think of choosing right over wrong. Yet we know that life is not so clean and crisp. Distinguishing between good and bad is often extremely difficult, especially when one is still young. For example, in an Israeli newspaper, *Maariv*, an article ap-peared in the September 30, 1996 weekend edition about tourists visiting the Beit Jamal Monastery near Beit Shemesh. A young girl writes the fol-lowing comment in a book that is addressed to God: "To God, I am still young and I don't always know the difference between what is good and what is bad. I want you to know that the things I might do that aren't good, I don't do them on purpose." Ethical attitudes, as we learn them, can become positions we take to balance the many differing possibilities we see in front of us. For example, Ryan takes a range of views into consider-ation by including how others see things from their vantage points. We would see "more views from more vantage points," he says. When I ask him to explain this idea, he tells me that "we'd see other opinions to things and we'd think about them and talk them over and see what other people's opinions are." Ryan is not only talking about how to manage the forests of Clayoquot Sound. He is talking about his own delicate balance. As a person who spends a great deal of his time in a wheelchair, Ryan has learned how to achieve his independence by involving others in his life. No, he cannot get around as easily as the other young people in the school. Nor can he speak as quickly. So the people around him have learned how to be patient. And Ryan encourages their patience by his show of interest in the things around him. He has no desire to compete with others; he looks at what he can offer and then makes sure his voice is heard.

Nicole deals with ethical considerations differently. She feels it is her responsibility to ensure that the video she produces will not make those she interviewed look or sound silly. She states quite clearly that she will edit out the "bloopers." It is not surprising that someone as concerned with the opinion of others is also concerned with appearing to be ethical. Her image of herself as aiming for perfection does not only mean that she is interested in being perfect physically. She also wants to be regarded well, ethically, and intellectually. Her classmate Terri-Lynn's ethical concerns are about being fair. When she and her editing team (Kori and Lindy) sit down to digitize the video they are preparing for presentation, they are mostly concerned with how best to represent the whole class. One of the boys has put a little pressure on them to make sure he is in many of the shots, but they kindly resist his influence, explaining that their editorial decision is to be fair to everyone.

Fair is the word I heard the most from young people at Bayside and Hennigan. Josh and Annie spend hours in sibling fights over what is fair. Is it fair that Annie gets to go to Europe and Josh does not? What does Josh get that is not given to Annie? Is it fair that Josh can't watch television for a month because, after not doing his French homework, he spoke back to his French teacher? Josh tells me, "It's not fair." His mom thinks it is. And what about Thomas and Josh? An example of how Thomas decides what is ethical is Thomas telling Josh there is no homework—just to get Josh into trouble. What "wrong" is he balancing (with payback) in his mind? How is he coming to terms with his limits and what is fair treatment? Young people work out ethical issues as they negotiate the day-to-day pecking order and the group/gang consciousness occurring in every school and in every generation.

One such incident occurs at Bayside. In the first year of my study, a group of girls thinks that Shannon gets "special treatment" because she is the daughter of one of the staff persons. She has more access to the school; she can visit her parent whenever she needs to. I notice how Shannon responds to these comments. She becomes somewhat aloof, finding success in her studies and in extracurricular events. (In fact, she has become extremely successful in high school.) The following year, with the second class I get to know, I pay more attention to the cliques that emerge. Now I am more sensitive to who is "in" and who is left "out." At first I notice how the class seems to work as one group. Gradually, over the course of the year, things change. Some young people choose to opt "out" for good reasons. They find ways to succeed that do not depend upon playing up to a leader.

Yes, young teens struggle to find an inner and outer balance. One that will enable them to grow as individuals and to make the world a fair place for themselves and others. They start off with what is fair for them, but they expand this view to examine what is fair and just for others. When Kelli tells me that she and Joanne cannot get access to the more powerful computers because they are only working with video and the boys are doing "the hard stuff," the programming, I question what is happening. I ask myself if we can afford not to pay attention to how teens weigh right and wrong in order to determine their ethical positions. And I ask how we, as adults in their midst, can find ways to help them strengthen and flex their ethical attitudes so as to provide a more equitable platform for all.

Pedagogical Attitudes:
What can we do? How can we make changes?

Mia stands out in my mind as a young person concerned with teaching herself and others how to make changes. She says, "just do it"—don't sit and talk about it! Most of the young people, although they might not be as committed to this issue as Mia is, express their concern about informing others about the research they have conducted. When I ask the Bayside students what we should do with the video, projects, and newspaper articles we are collecting, they tell me that we should put all the stuff together so that other kids can learn from what we did. They realize that their research can be "shipped off to Japan in a video or a CD-ROM," or made available on a website to other kids in schools. Hilary tells me that we should make a "big big big video and a lots of like projects and, like, type them on a computer and send them away to other places." When I ask her if other people would be interested, she tells me she would want to watch it "because I would get to, like, see different people and, like, see what they did and, like, what they're learning about and stuff like that." Hilary is obviously a learner who believes she learns best from others who are experiencing similar circumstances. Tiffany tells me something quite similar: "Some kids, they don't like adults or they get mad at adults; they can learn best from what we've done because it's fun and we've already done it." Tiffany's message is that kids learn best when "the information comes from … kids to other kids." And Terri-Lynn, always the educator and innovator, says that "it could be of a lot of use for other people, so, like put it all onto one documentary or whatever and people can like just use it. People in the schools, or we could send it out to other schools." Children learning from other children through their projects, through their constructions, is more than an apprenticeship model of learning. High-tech tools enable a kind of learning that was common in the days before institutionalized schooling, a time when children passed their understanding of the world to each other through their games, their songs and their stories.

The young people also think that if adults who are in charge of curriculum learn about what we are doing, they will change things in schools. Natalie thinks that we should "show it to the school board. They might change their attitudes and do something about it and make school a little bit harder or a little bit easier, depending on what people think." Terri-Lynn, Meagan, and Nicole want adults in the Ministry of Education to know more about this project so that there will be more hands-on, outdoor projects that connect young people to their senses. As Nicole reminds us, "boys are rambunctious at this age and they need their exercise!" In fact, many of the young people at Bayside think it is important for adults to see how responsible they are in conducting a research project. Ross comments on how teachers might not understand that young people can be responsible for their own learning. When students are trusted, they feel grown up, he points out. And "when they feel more grown up, they feel privileged." And they feel they can make changes that affect their learning.

Young people are ready to learn from each other and see themselves as educators, and the Internet and video technology are the tools to out their activities. Many are reading each other's projects online, and finding out about various school cultures by having email chats with kids from around the world. For Ryan, the purpose of learning is to share one's knowledge. In this way, everyone has "more views from more vantage points." Through talking and sharing our opinions with others, we make life more interesting. More than that, as members of communities of inquiry we can "take these thoughts into consideration and really learn from other people and maybe know what side you want to take." Ryan's theory of knowledge is not just that there is stuff out there to be poured back into the minds of children through the funnel called a teacher. Ryan believes that knowledge is constructed through sharing our views and taking each other's views into consideration. What better pedagogical attitude could an educator have?

Thinking Attitudes and Genderflexing

In my early days at Bayside, the girls surround me, curious about my camera and about why I am recording them with this little machine. The boys seem much less interested in my role as video ethnographer and more interested in the hardware itself. The girls love to sit around the tables and interview each other, taking on roles and pretending to be reporters. When we use cameras to explore the world around us, the girls are excited about videotaping each other and the objects within their view. They personalize the external, bringing it into their spectrum of relationships. Through extending from personal to less personal, they broaden and reach as they learn, spiraling outwards. Ross and his friends seem to move from the outside to the intimate. Ross walks out into the waves, lost in the experience, and returns to the shore slightly changed. As he says, "It's changed me." The boys are more interested in covering the basics without having to engage in much personal reflection, at first. But as soon as they reflect on what certain actions mean, they move toward the intimate—as long as there isn't another peer around whom they feel they have to impress. When Nicole walks into the room during an interview between Justin and myself, Justin immediately slouches into his "cool" position.

I am neither romanticizing the learning process nor saying that these modes are gender-specific. What I see is a range of gender that can flex beyond sexed differences. Both boys and girls need to have the opportunity to attain intimacy and breadth, and not remain fixed in a gender style at the early phases of their learning process. In other words, it is important for girls not to get stuck in the personal ease that their gender "disposition" (dare I use the word?) encourages, and boys not to remain hung up in their fascination with how things work while denying the personal. When the full curve is explored, both girls and boys learn to flex beyond their roles, meeting and contributing to each other's explorations.

Framing Representations of Representations

In this milieu of competing positions and definitions, we face the dilemma of representation. In my portraits, I have encouraged the participation of readers, viewers, and users of digital media. I have also argued for constructing texts to include the participation of those who have a stake in the issues—students, teachers, administrative and custodial staff, parents, and the community at large. When selecting frames to view the portraits, I invite participation. It may seem ironic that I sit in my office at home framing these stories to involve readers I have not met. After all, I sit here alone. A solitary author placing her "word" on what she has experienced. Yet am I really alone?

I sit surrounded by books and articles, videotapes, videodisks, and CD-ROMs. My computer desktop has windows with digital video opened in Adobe Premiere and text windows with transcripts opened in Microsoft Word. Constellations, the data analysis tool I described in chapter 5, is also running as an application on my computer, so that I can build groupings, and annotate and analyze video conversations. The Internet browser called Netscape lets me easily jump to millions of computers sitting in offices, homes, and research labs around the world. And I am in constant "multilog" on email, on the phone, and in person with colleagues and close friends. Not to mention chatty conversations with people—conversations that quite often provide moments of reflection and insight. My community also includes the teachers and students at the schools, who have been the focus of my interest these past years. And over the coming years, these layers will expand to welcome readers and viewers who will become part of new constellations, all meeting and discussing these ideas as well as their own.

To conclude, representations can no longer be thought of as individually constructed works by solitary authors. Nor are they limited to our final products. We can frame what we see for others to annotate, comment on, and use within their own frames of reference. We frame and thus represent whenever we are in the process of creating. The process of making a representation is itself a representation. And several kinds of representations emerge until we finally decide to put closure to a work, theory, or investigation and move on to another.

Thus every phase in the process of conducting a study or making an artistic work is a representation of what came before. The video I shoot is a representation of the kids working with computers and new media. The video *star chunks* are a different kind of representation. The clustering of *stars* into *constellations* is yet another. And the text portraits still another. So are the CD-ROM clusters, the computer programs for analyzing and organizing digital video, this book, and the website for collaborative video data analysis. As Geertz once told us:

> There is an Indian story—at least I heard it as an Indian story— about an Englishman who, having been told that the world rested on a platform which rested on the back of an elephant which rested in turn on the back of a turtle, asked (perhaps he was an ethnographer; it is the way they behave), what did the turtle rest on? Another turtle. And that turtle? "Ah, Sahib, after that it is turtles all the way down."[190]

Geertz uses this story to explain the incomplete nature of any form of cultural analysis. This applies equally well to how we make meanings from the digital stories we collect. Each form is derivative of another form until it reaches down to the action we thought we were describing; that is, until we realize that this turtle rests on the back of yet another turtle.

---

190. Clifford Geertz, *The Interpretation of Cultures* (New York: Basic Books, 1973), 28.

conclusion
configurations, confusions, and contentment

A postmodern anthropologist is interviewing her informant. "Finally the informant says: 'Okay, that's enough about you; now, let's talk about me.'"

—Ester Newton,
"My Best Informant's Dress:
The Erotic Equation in Fieldwork"

Building Platforms of Diverse Voices

I have repeatedly asked how we can enter into a partnership, not only with our technological tools, but also with those we study. Even though we know that we can never know the "other," and that trying to study the "other" is fraught with the possible misuse of power, I cannot believe that we want to take the position that only those who are being oppressed can write about or discuss their oppression. Surely there is a role for witnesses and reporters. I do not claim to know what it was like to be a child in the Holocaust, but I have spent a lifetime trying to figure out what I could have done if I had been sent to a concentration camp. And I remember as a child walking around my house at night with a stocking tied over my eyes to try to understand what my dear zaida, my grandfather, experienced when he lost his sight.

Similarly, I cannot claim to be able to feel what it is like to be an African-American girl in an inner-city school in Boston. Or to know the difficulties she faces every day, both as a young woman and as an African-American. But I have spent many years trying to connect with her world. And I will continue to find ways to get to know those who are not like me and help bring their stories to the forefront of our conversations, because it is not enough to report to others what we have seen and heard when we conduct research. We need to act on our knowledge. And as a researcher listening to Mia, Brianne, and the other young people at Bayside Middle School who want to make things better for the next generation, I hope I have provided a platform for them to make their issues clear, by building a bridge between their worlds and yours.

When multiple voices are heard on an electronic platform, we are still stuck with the problem of validating what is being said. Whose interpretation do we trust? Who has the final word, the authority, to decide on action? How do we validate and authenticate an electronic story or interpretation of a group of stories in light of the elasticity of the medium? Do we have to change our definition of validity and authenticity when even an article in a scholarly journal is a hoax?[191]

---

191. A case in point is Alan Sokolov's "A Physicist Experiments with Cultural Studies," published in the journal *Lingua Franca* in May of 1996, which revealed how he deliberately wrote a fake article called "Transgressing Boundaries: Toward a Hermeneutic of Quantum Gravity" in the journal *Social Context*. This scholarly prank set off a flurry of debates

Configurational Validity

Imagine using digital or analog video to construct portraits. Video is a medium that can easily be reshaped, as Nicole from the Bayside Middle School reminds us when she tells prospective interviewees not to worry because she will "edit out their bloopers." When writing about events, most writers and readers have given up the notion that one true or even one best interpretation exists. They accept that the most they can do is try to be as fair and as forthright as possible; they accept the fact that others also have important perspectives to offer, depending on where they are situated—that is, on their standpoints.[192] So how do we come to believe our interpretations have strength?

A configuration is a group of stars in a constellation or of constellations in a solar system. However, it is also a grouping of parts that have neither a definite center nor finite relationships. A range of perspectives and points of view build the whole.

Configurational validity is a theory for making meaning in a digital world—a world in which different authors use images stored in digital video to layer and reconstitute original documentation. Configurations are combinations or arrangements of disparate views that can be assembled and reassembled in any number of patterns. As described in

---

in the academy. Postmodern theorists called the hoax unethical, whereas empirical purists praised Sokolov for exposing the "emperor's new clothes."

192. Feminist theorists call this the *standpoint theory*. They maintain that we can only see the world from our own position, our own standpoint, in terms of race, culture, and gender. They also maintain that we can only view the world and be viewed from that static lens. However, in my opinion, the lens needs to be a moving lens, one that can change positions by bringing together different viewpoints—viewpoints that are reflexive and sometimes transparent. Most importantly, I look at the positioning rather than the positioned. The difference is reflected in the history of the visual image. Once we took pictures with standing cameras of people seated, posing for the camera. People were positioned in time and space, captive in their clothing and fake settings. A video camera can now provide moving images to the videographer. Those who are being filmed are in some sense directing the filmmaker through their movements. The camera follows the movements. Backgrounds change. Positions change. The camera is passed around and those who were being filmed can film. Positions change when we have opportunities to see and understand other positions. For more on this subject, see Leslie Roman, who insightfully challenges standpoint theory in her article, "White is a Color! White Defensiveness, Postmodernism, and Anti-Racist Pedagogy," in *Race, Identity, and Representation in Education*, eds. C. McCarthy and W. Crinchlow (New York: Routledge, 1993), 71–89.

previous chapters, the views of multiple "authors" can be layered in clusters or constellations so that larger, more representative theories may begin to unfold. In other words, when different constellations are gathered, layered, and analyzed, new patterns emerge. For example, let's say I build a constellation of video segments about students' views on logging practices in Clayoquot Sound. Once these segments have been coded, I can search the database of coded images for "logging practices" (assuming that I have chosen "logging practices" as one of my codes). Viewing the various segments, I can choose which ones to put into my constellation. Now here's the leap: Let us suppose I want to have a broader view of the issues surrounding the dispute. I know that Jason did a constellation on fishing and that Larry did one on the views of First Nations peoples. With digital media tools, I can bring together different constellations in order to view not only what students think about logging practices, but also how they see other aspects of the controversy: fishing, tourism, local people's views, global implications, the legal rights of First Nations peoples, and so on. I might not be able to determine the true meaning of a specific event (as Geertz suggests one might do through the process of thick description), but I will be able to see the larger patterns, tensions, and connections that emerge from this collaborative venture. When we acknowledge others' perspectives, changes can occur. Together we can begin to understand how children think about their future—what they think about the possibility of living in a world lacking abundant natural resources, for example. Building constellations can take on dramatic permutations when combined with others' points of viewing.

One does not really need multimedia tools to understand configurational validity. If five people sat down to talk about a controversial issue, such as the Clayoquot Sound dispute, and asked themselves "What patterns emerge from our various perspectives?" perhaps they would come to a deeper understanding of the dispute than if they simply tried to figure out the meaning of the controversy. Instead of trying to find the best interpretation, they could look for ways to layer and combine their various points of viewing so that a more general understanding could emerge. The goal would not be to convince others that one voice is the best voice; it would be to hear the various voices that make up the configuration and to base one's action on finding ways of making sense of various points of viewing so that the actions taken represent more than one person's perspective.

The Roots of Configurational Validity: Partners in Theory

Configurational validity is related to the work of many poststructural theorists. However, few have taken up the current postmodern "crisis" of representation in the context of educational research and emerging technologies. In my own bringing together of validity, educational research methods, and technology, I have interwoven storyreading (gathering and organizing video and text data), storymaking (creating digital tools to help us organize our data), and storytelling (representing our artifacts as we interact with technologies) to show how video data are elastic, mutable forms, continually being shaped by "authors." In digital media environments, these video segments can be shared even before they have been molded by the expert hands of the researcher.

An obvious dilemma in sharing data is that the process of creating representations may become even more difficult to manage than before. As previously mentioned, Elliot Eisner describes qualitative research as a messy process, akin to sculpting, writing a novel, or painting; but he also maintains that the final products of research should show the same connoisseurship as do works of art.[193] I have tried to expand his theory by noting that, in order to learn the art and science of research, we must create works that show the messy process of evolving from novice to connoisseur. In doing so we must always realize, of course, that there is yet another version to create—the more you know about something, the more there is to know. However, I maintain that the validity of research that uses media tools is felt not only through perfectly sculpted representations, but also through giving voice to the less sculpted and often silenced voices of those we study. Validity can be constructed through bringing together new configurations emerging from broad-based communities of inquiry. And it can reposition those who feel locked into one standpoint by providing them with more flexible boundaries. In short, works of art are welcome, but they are not the only possible qualitative outcomes of research. Valid accounts do not necessarily need to be works of art.[194]

---

193. Elliot Eisner, *The Enlightened Eye: Qualitative Inquiry and the Enhancement of Educational Practice* (New York: Macmillan, 1992).

194. Eisner is not implying that the only valid representation in educational inquiry is a work of art. However, Eisner has endeavored to bring works of art and other media representations into the educational arena.

Validity, in the sense of the strength of an argument, emerges through layering the various points of viewing of multiple readers—readers who have become authors. And these portraits, descriptions, case studies, or whatever we want to call them can both "be about" and "be with" those we study. To "be with" is not just a Geertzian twist; it is a way of conducting research that encourages the "researched" to become members of the community, and vice versa—to create communities together. Several poststructuralist researchers—Patti Lather, for example—work collaboratively with those they study.[195] She claims that a *transformative agenda* aimed at advancing emancipatory theory-building empowers the researched while "protecting our work from our own passions."[196] Does Lather mean that she still places herself apart from her emotional relationships with her subjects when she partakes in her scholarly reporting, or is she simply trying to placate those who worry that the personal views of the researcher infuse the work with passion rather than reason? Digital ethnography could advance what Lather terms *catalytic validity*—a form of validity that changes both those who are being researched and those who are doing the research. Digital media are obvious tools with which to give voice to those whose voices are not usually heard and thereby to bring about catalytic changes to their lives. An electronic platform (equipped for sharing perspectives, methods, and data sources) with which to re/view analyses and build stories upon stories is part of a catalytic praxis.

Harriet Bjerrun Nielsen argues that all texts are seductions.[197] Validity rests in the ability of the author to convince and persuade, to cause us "to lose our senses," as it were.[198] She also posits that the validity of a story should not be a final verdict; interpretations need to be open-ended. A reader struggles with a text, finding different meanings, while being seduced by it. While proposing the need to lose our senses, Nielsen also looks for a safe "breathing space." Nielsen "marks off the field" with two opposing teams.[199] The first team includes those who think

---

195. Patti Lather, "The Validity of Angels: Interpretive and Textual Strategies in Researching the Lives of Women with HIV/AIDS," *Qualitative Inquiry 1* (1995): 1–39.

196. Patti Lather, "Issues of Validity," *Interchange 17*, no. 4 (1981): 78.

197. Harriet Bjerrun Nielsen, "Seductive Texts With Serious Intentions," *Educational Researcher 24*, no. 1 (1995): 4–12.

198. Ibid.: 4.

199. Ibid.: 6.

qualitative researchers should tone down the narrative and descriptive nature of their texts, reducing it to language matrices and linguistic quantities (e.g., Miles and Huberman's continual recommendations to make qualitative research more quantitative).[200] The second team includes those who believe that the use of literary tropes is all-important (e.g., Clifford Geertz, Jerome Bruner, James Clifford, and George Marcus).[201] At first, Nielsen seems to be rooting for both sides. Then she throws the final pitch: "If the text does not have serious intentions, the seduction does not tempt us." Is this a curve ball, a way to avoid taking sides? Serious for whom? Under what conditions? Would one say that if a documentary film or a novel does not have serious intentions, then its attempt at seduction will not tempt us? Isn't part of the excitement of seduction to be found in the fear that the seducer's intentions may not be serious? My own point of view is that a good story, whether its mode of representation be one of words, video, film, music, or multimedia, is often less about seduction and more about involvement in learning about self and other.

A most compelling analysis of validity is found in Lous Heshusius's "Freeing Ourselves from Objectivity." Heshusius bridges the gap between knower and known, subject and object, insider and outsider.[202] She proposes a collaborative model for building validity that dovetails with configurational validity—a telling of events that emerges from a "participatory mode of consciousness."[203] She examines the role of the ethnographer as someone engaged in "being with" someone or something. She points out that ethnographic texts emerge from writing about a subjective knowing of the other. "Reality is no longer understood as truth to be interpreted, but as mutually evolving."[204] Heshusius is concerned with a methodology of participation that entails merging with the other, being with the other, and telling the stories of the other. A difficult task, but one that

---

200. Matthew B. Miles and A. Michael Huberman, *Qualitative Data Analysis: A Sourcebook of New Methods* (Beverly Hills, CA: Sage, 1994).

201. Jerome Bruner, *Actual Minds, Possible Worlds* (Cambridge, MA: Harvard University Press, 1986); James Clifford and George Marcus, eds., *Writing Culture: The Poetics and the Politics of Ethnography* (Berkeley: University of California Press, 1986).

202. Lous Heshusius, "Freeing Ourselves from Objectivity: Managing Subjectivity or Turning Toward a Participatory Mode of Consciousness?," *Educational Researcher 23*, no. 3 (1994): 15–22.

203. Ibid.: 15.

204. Ibid.: 18.

we are sometimes lucky enough to experience when making sense of the stories we have gathered from living among others.

What We Learn from our Digital Portraits

What do we learn from constructing portraits using digital media as our cultural partners? By portraits, I mean narrative structures that are put together using words, images, and sounds. One may begin addressing this question by pointing out that there is never a single approach to using media forms, even when conducting research. Each person, whether teacher, parent, student, or researcher, can find ways to honor the potential of any given media form and to push it beyond its boundaries. Or they can choose to use it as a hammer, a simple tool that may help them get their jobs done. Each digital author brings her particular background and training to the making of media forms. The author is artisan and explorer, creating artifacts for others to share, change, and exchange. She creates an environment in which readers may form new meanings based on their interpretations of what she presents. However, because digital media stories are fluid, we need to ask what we can learn from these narratives that we might not have learned from more traditional, more linear works.

One of the things we learn in using digital media is that a flexible relationship can emerge when a "participating author" observes "others" and constructs "texts" that can then be reconstituted by "readers." Electronic media are closing the gaps that have traditionally separated these disparate roles. And with this shared research comes a greater opportunity for those who are being studied to become part of the process of making meaning. Imagine Margaret Mead asking the Samoans to help her build stories about them, or sharing her data with her fellow anthropologists while building her theory about childrearing practices.[205] Even though she and Gregory Bateson shot innumerable photographs and films of those they

---

205. Mead went so far as to name people who, according to her, had no name. From her fieldnotes, as cited by Clifford, she writes, "We are just completing a culture of a mountain group here in the lower Torres Chelles. They have no name and we haven't decided what to call them yet.... They are very difficult to work, living all the place with a half dozen garden houses and never staying put for a week at a time." See James Clifford, *The Predicament of Culture: Twentieth Century Ethnography, Literature, and Art* (Cambridge, MA: Harvard University Press, 1988), 230.

studied, they did not set up an international forum for data analysis that included Samoans or their colleagues. The products made available to colleagues were books containing photographs, long after the events took place and without access to those people or places.

Two summers ago, Avraham Biran, a noted Israeli archeologist and a dear friend, would not, on video, share the details of his latest findings with me until they were published in his book and in a scientific journal.[206] I wanted to interview him in order to be able to capture those first moments of his excitement. I wanted to give the video to him and his family as a gift. I thought he would enjoy looking back at the videotaped recording of himself talking about his discovery. After all, it is not every day that a scientist in his 80s makes his most significant contribution to his chosen field. For me, sharing the details of my research in an electronic form is commonplace. Most of my energy is currently devoted to building a website for annotating video data. For Biran, it was important both to ensure respect for ownership and to have his discovery acknowledged within the academy. However, I have to question what "discovering" an ancient artifact from biblical times means. What ownership can any of us have over what we "discover?" Surely our western civilization, like any other, is built on finding things that were already part of someone else's life and livelihood; walking through the British Museum, or any museum for that matter, is all it takes to make my point clear. How do we own "findings?" James Clifford writes that "the history of collections (not limited to museums) is central to an understanding of how those social groups that invented anthropology and modern art have appropriated exotic things, facts, and meanings."[207]

---

206. Avraham Biran, *Biblical Dan* (Jerusalem: The Israel Exploration Society, Hebrew Union College–Jewish Institute of Religion, 1994), 275–278.

207. See James Clifford, *The Predicament of Culture: Twentieth Century Ethnography, Literature, and Art*, 220–221, for a description of the history of collecting both art and culture. Clifford saw both kinds of collection as being intimately intertwined. In a schema on page 224, he placed art and culture opposite non-art and non-culture. The diamond that encompasses these four is held together by our ascribing values of authenticity and inauthenticity to collected objects. Inventions and fakes are not culture, but history and folklore are; tourist art is not art but connoisseurship and the art market are. He also made the point that the *object systems* of art and anthropology are not fixed (229). Categories change according to tastes and fetishes. However, what remains is the collection of that which is different from ourselves. This form of "othering" is also described by

However, Biran does own his particular way of framing and contextualizing this object. After all, as Josh from the Hennigan School has told me, an invention is a new way of arranging things that exist (or are experienced) in the world. In short, perhaps the most precious thing we own is our points of viewing with regard to what we understand—our ability to construct new possibilities from a diversity of experiences of and with others. And Biran has certainly contributed to our understanding of antiquity in his mindful framing of cultural artifacts.

Electronic media, especially the Web, will not only blur the existing boundaries between author, reader, and the persons or ideas under discussion, but will also create a more elastic relationship for all.[208] When using digital media, we build a *digital commons*, a more collaborative form of ownership, combining how we make sense of our world with how others make sense of their worlds. The digital commons is not just a public meeting place, it is a common space for taking action, as Mia from the Bayside Middle School would tell us. As a teacher and professor, I have always known that my main contribution to students had to do with the way I put ideas together in order to make them clear and challenging, thus enabling students to create their own points of viewing, their own groupings or configurations. I see the next generation of ethnographers and digital artists as voyagers exploring and creating digital cultures on the Internet and sharing their configurations with others. We can now form more permeable partnerships both with those we study and with our readers, creating a digital commons. In this culture, ethnography becomes a process of mediation and artistry rather than simply a matter of disclosing scientific findings. And the tools to which we now have access can become our cultural partners. They are not just tools used by our culture; they are tools used for making culture. They are partners that have their own

---

other scholars. Clifford cites Donna Haraway's study of the American Museum of National History and American manhood. She studied the ways in which gender historically defines how we display the exotic. See Donna Haraway, "Teddy Bear Patriarchy: Taxidermy in the Garden of Eden, New York City, 1908–1936," *Social Text 11* (Winter, 1985): 20–64. He also cites Walter Benjamin's essay "Unpacking My Library" in *Illuminations*, ed. H. Arendt (New York: Schoken Books, 1969), 59–68. Here, Benjamin articulated the passion (fetish?) of the collector of books who creates order from chaos and feels a loss of identity without these collections.

208. See Glorianna Davenport and Hans Peter Brondmo, "Creating and Viewing the Elastic Charles Hypermedia Journal," *Hypertext: State of the ART 5* (1989): 43–51; and Glorianna Davenport, "Smarter Tools for Storytelling: Are They Just Around the Corner?" *IEEE Multimedia 3*, no. 1 (1996): 10–14.

contribution to make with regard to how we build a cultural understanding of the world around us.[209]

In this digital commons, the use of electronic partners may enable us to learn noncolonialist strategies for engaging with those we study. The students at Bayside Middle School view my video of them, read my notes in my portable computer, and not only comment on themselves, but also add their comments about me. They can do their own study of me, or of themselves, or of any subject they choose; and they have at their fingertips a publishing platform that has a global readership. As members of a community, we build video and text stories that convey messages to and between readers. Readers, who are also electronically connected on the Internet (and on whatever other future communication devices that emerge down the road) can also contribute their own interpretations to these messages, thus changing the story. Readers of our socially constructed texts can either be silent lurkers or decide to make their presence known to us. Layers build, patterns emerge, friendships or enmities grow, and digital inquiry becomes a reflexive practice—with an emphasis on flexing, stretching, and strengthening our inquiry.

Thus, with digital media, young people can learn how to produce and publish their own ideas. Educational researchers are no longer the only ones reporting on the lives of children and teachers; those operating within the walls of classrooms have begun producing their own stories to share with others. After all, some kind of camera or camcorder is available to children in most schools and in many homes. (For less than 10 dollars one can buy a disposable still camera with film). Children and teachers in schools with advanced technologies can learn about places they have never been to in order to find out what Bayside Middle School students, for example, have to say about Clayoquot Sound. They can do so by browsing the Web and then establishing direct links with the students. Moreover, software environments, such as the one we developed, *The Global Forest*, become a stage upon which many players may learn collaboratively and share their studies with each other. This process of layering and adding new interpretations promises a constant shifting in focus as topics change and grow.

A common fear, of course, is that changes will become so seamless that we will not be able to see the "original" documentation. But this is true of any

---

209. Donna Haraway, "Situated Knowledges: The Science Question in Feminism and the Privilege of Partial Perspective," *Feminist Studies 14*, no. 3 (1988): 575–599.

published manuscript. How many editors work on a print document until the product is finished? This is also true in the making of movies. Next time the credits roll, think about the degree of social construction that has taken place in front of your eyes. Although we might focus our attention on a particular actor or director, the product we see is a highly collaborative construction. What is new in our digital culture, however, is the fact that those with access to the Internet and other media can now take part in the process of publishing their cultural artifacts without having been "part of the original crew!"

Thus the theory of configurational validity is both a point of closure and a point of departure for the ideas articulated in this book. I use this theory to conclude the tale of my sojourn in two schools and to acknowledge the innumerable scholarly works that have influenced my thinking. My effort to get annotation and research tools up and running smoothly is, as always, in process. Yet I leave the writing of this book with a newly designed tool called Web Constellations on the Web waiting for readers, for you, to annotate "my" data and make it "yours." I leave this book knowing that this job is not *my* job but *our* job. As a community, we will shape digital tools into our cultural partners. Some of us will do the designing; some will do the theorizing; and some will make the technical connections. Some of us will do a bit of all three. In the end, new ways of conducting ethnography and learning about learning will emerge that, in our nonwired past, we could only "point at around the corner."[210]

Postscript: Closing Viewpoints

To propose where we might go in the future, I revisit viewpoints presented throughout this book. I see these viewpoints as guides or signposts, not as fixed locations. I see them as phases in my own past and future learning.

Viewpoint 1: Building Platforms for Writers and Readers

One of the first places on my journey as a digital ethnographer was to build an interface to include the voices of writers and readers. It was a

---

210. Margaret Atwood, CBC television interview conducted by June Callwood (1995).

platform that enabled writers and readers to view together. As I described in my early observations of children, we need to explore the blurring of relationships among and between readers and writers that occurs in electronic formats. When I started this adventure in multimedia ethnography in 1985, I thought that I could understand the lives of others by working with them and analyzing their actions using tools that would enable me to constantly review those actions. (As I became more knowledgeable about ethnography, I became less convinced that I could fully understand their motives and intentions but more convinced that I could create my story about them with better acuity.) In my first ethnography, I did not wonder whether penetrating their lives with my eyes and the lens of my camera was ethically correct. I did not ask myself as I do now, how my role as a stranger who enters their world to tell others about it affected their stories. However, from the moment I started collecting video, it became clear to me that I wanted to build a platform for letting readers and readers/viewers share what I had seen in these schools. I was opening school doors to those who would never otherwise have access to them. My main goal in the mid-1980s was to construct a description that would give others a sense of "being there." Using Learning Constellations, I could cut, paste, and layer video streams into segments.[211] Readers and viewers could view my data and add their annotations or layers. Fleeting moments rich in gestural meaning, such as when Josh slaps his thigh and speaks about inventions, were viewed and annotated by others. I could watch patterns emerge as I tried to make sense of these moments. I was building my first platform for enabling readers to become writers and authors in a collaborative, hyperlinked text media environment.

Viewpoint 2: Convincing My Readers that I Was There

Layering video data did not fully address the complexity of webbing these interpretations together. I never deluded myself into thinking that my readership was able to "know" Josh or Mindy or any of the other children as I knew them or as they knew themselves. (But I did want them to get closer than they could with text.) What viewers saw was still my "cut,"

---

211. See chapter 5 for descriptions of Learning Constellations, Constellations, and Web Constellations.

my selection, my window into the culture of children using computers in school settings. Because I saw myself as the children's friend and even their spokesperson, a translator from their culture to the adult culture, I not only wanted to tell their story, but also wanted educators to think again about inequality, especially gender inequalities. Teachers would recognize that the girls and boys in their classes needed a curriculum that promoted diversity with regard to how children think about important issues. Researchers would stop putting boys in one box and girls in another. And the general educational community would recognize that inequality is still a major problem in our schools today. In short, my actions were not without intention. I was the author trying to convince my readers that I was there and, therefore, could be believed.

> The ability of anthropologists to get us to take what they say seriously has less to do with either a factual look or an air of conceptual elegance than it has with their capacity to convince us that what they say is a result of their having penetrated (or, if you prefer, been penetrated by) another form of life, of having, one way or another, truly "been there."[212]

Viewpoint 3: Building Platforms for Extending Our Boundaries

My current interest is in encouraging those we study to explore electronic communities of discourse in order to build their own portraits. It will take time before enough children have the expertise to be able to create their own portraits and points of viewing. However, throughout the world, pockets of adolescents are designing their own electronic portraits using sophisticated software packages, such as Adobe Photoshop, Adobe Premier, HyperCard, or Macromedia Director. Home pages are a forum for viewing young people's artifacts. Students are reaching beyond their school walls to find their own audiences and sources of information. Students and their teachers are no longer afraid to peer beyond the fences that once separated them from other worlds. In this new era of social reconfiguration, a theory such as configurational validity can support the ways in which we make sense of and understand what we see, using a model of global

---

212. Clifford Geertz, *Works and Lives: Anthropologist as Author*, 37.

social construction. Verisimilitude becomes a goal for researchers, teachers, and parents as we reach beyond the old boundaries that once kept children and teenagers and their guardians inside school walls.

The Confusion

Throughout this book, I have presented a way of thinking about multiple-voiced media texts as a platform for multiloguing. But how do we begin to sift through the vastness of the digital terrain to create both personal and social meaning? The answer may be less complicated than it seems. When we think about a digital culture, we need to envision a large platform. Instead of seeing two people engaged in a dialog, imagine a virtual community on a 3-dimensional platform engaged in multiloguing. At any point, different people may choose to enter the conversation or to listen. Some lurk at a safe distance. This description naturally fits an electronic chat group, or a MUD, a multi-user domain. Not only are there different conversations going on in different corners of the electronic room, there are different conversations in different knowledge domains. We need to accept that our filter will be unlike anyone else's filter, yet the result of our filtering through the terrain will be linked, deeply, with others.

The learner of the future is a constructor of knowledge, a meaning-maker; the digital culture has made us more aware of our being meaning-makers. We are not only beholders and readers, we are creators. We create our truths, our meanings, through our points of viewing; and we do this while making new meanings both for ourselves and for others. However, we cannot make meaning from the plethora of choices we are offered each moment in an electronic environment if we are passive about exploring our own and others' points of viewing. The purpose of making our perspective clear is to invite others to explore how we see the world. In other words, our goal is to create a platform encouraging full participation in this wondrous exploration. We do not end our search by understanding our own perspectives; that is where we begin our journey. We build out from the center to fringes that may, in turn, become new centers. And we continue learning by looking for new perspectives that deepen and broaden our ways of looking at the world around us.

We are at a critical time and place in our understanding of who we are as learners and researchers: We can now choose to become partners in building a convivial and equitable place for many voices. We can no longer expect the permanence and stability of fixed theories; new interpretations will emerge as we view ever-changing representations and creations. Within the emerging digital commons, readers and viewers will become full partners in the creation of multiple media documents. Those we study will study us; they will place our views in theirs as we will place theirs in ours, in the constant search for conviviality. Yes, we can, like the postmodern ethnographer in the joke quoted in the beginning of this chapter, just talk to and about ourselves. Or, we can invite new audiences of readers and viewers to share what they see from their points of viewing. Maybe together, as a community, we can create a time and a place of understanding.

The Contentment

As daylight leaves the skies at the close of Yom Kippur, a benediction for entering the gates of life is chanted by the congregation:

> Do not remain standing at the outer gate.
> The gates are made to be entered.
> The sun is low, the hour is late.
> Let us enter the gates at last.[213]

I leave this phase of my work knowing that adventures lie around the corner, waiting. In years to come I will look back at the stories I have written with different points of viewing and whisper to myself: Why didn't I think about this then? But that will be another story, and, by then, I will have opened a new gate.

---

213. Rabbi Jules Harlow, ed., *Mahzor for Rosh Hashana and Yom Kippur: A Prayer Book for the Days of Awe* (New York: The Rabbinical Assembly, 1975), 699.

People and Topics

Bennington, G. 2
Benstock, S. 214
Bereiter, C. 50
Berge, Z. L. 74
Berlin, I. 170
bias 3–4, 9, 10, 22–24
Biklin, S. K. 180
Biran, A. 267
Blumenfeld, P. 50
Boas, F. 11, 32
Brade, K. 50
Brand, S. 117
Brandes, A. 240
Bransford, J. D. 49, 50, 141
Britzman, D. 180
Brondmo, H. P. 119, 121, 268
Brooks, K. 120
Brown, A. 141
Brown, J. S. 27, 49
Bruckman, A. S. 172
Bruner, J. 15, 265
Brunner, C. 49
Bryson, M. 246
Buckingham, D. 9, 10
Burnett, R. 3
Burson, N. 127
Buxton, B. 127

C
camera. *See also* video
   technique 25, 107
   still 32
Carbol, B. 44
Carling, R. 127
catalytic validity. *See* validity
Chaika, M. 186
Chetcuti, D. 249
Chipman, S. S. 50
Chopra, J. 96
chunks. *See* video: chunking
cinema
   narrative 106
   observational 99
   vérité 92–99
Clayoquot Sound 12, 62, 73, 104, 223
   and First Nations 144
   and media 210–211
   CD-ROM. *See Global Forest*
Clayoquot Sound Project 71–72, 135–139,
   202–211, 226–233
Clements, P. 49
Clifford, J. 11, 17, 31, 95, 265–267
cognition 49–51. *See also* learning

and apprenticeship 27, 140
and flexibility 27
Cognitive Technology Group 26
Cohen, D. 136
Cohen, M. 107
collaboration. *See* learning: collaborative
Collins, A. 27, 49, 141
Collins, J. L. 93, 106
Collins, M. P. 74
computer
   agents 5, 6, 120, 172
   and cognitive apprenticeship 49
   and collaboration 130.
      See also learning: collaborative
   and connections 207–208
   and constructionism. *See* constructionism
   and constructivism. *See* constructivism
   and gender 75, 185–186, 202, 224–245, 204
      See also gender
   and hypertext 119, 122
   and instructionism. *See* learning: instructionist
   and making meaning 27–28
   and making things 78, 182, 185, 185–186
   and moving objects 164–177, 188, 248
   and project-based learning
      See learning: project-based
   and schools 45–46, 76, 102–104
   and situated learning 140–142
   and the Internet 59, 68, 140, 204, 254–255
   and videodisks 124–126
   as partners 4–8, 51–52, 256–257, 269
   as prosthesis 4, 33
   cultures 48–52, 74, 81, 93–94, 245, 248
   games 76, 202, 249
      and designers 76
      LEGOLogo. *See* computer: tools
      MUDS 74, 273
      Obstacle Mania 164–167
      playing 76, 168–173. *See also* playing
   microworlds 51
   mindfulness 52
   programming 50, 79–81, 165, 174–175, 253
   tools. *See also* analysis tools
      Boxer 50
      CSILE 50
      LEGOLogo 75–77, 162–164
configurational validity
   See validity: configurational
Constellations. *See* analysis tools
constellations 4, 6, 80, 124, 144, 138, 262
constructionism 51, 53, 70, 76–78, 88, 119, 140,
   159–160, 169, 199
constructivism 51, 52

Flinn, S. 131
Forman, G. 48, 50, 51
Fountain, R. 26
Fox Keller, E. 202
frames 243–257
    and AI 245
    and filmmakers 38, 98
Francis, I. 202
Frank, A. 180, 181
Freedle, R. 245
Freud, A. 180, 181
Freud, S. 31

G
games. *See* computer: games
Gardner, H. 245
Gaskell, J. 202, 246
Gaskell, P. J. 26, 202
Gay, G. 143
gazes, photographic 106
Geertz, C. 17, 25–34, 172, 257, 272
gender
    and bodies 192
    and design 49
    and display of exotic 268
    and games 186. *See also* computer: games
    and learning 256, 190
    and multicultural education 180
    and playgrounds 56–57
    and race 93, 181–182, 187, 194, 246
    and science 202, 225. *See also* science: gender
    and technology. *See* computer: and gender
    differences 202
    equity 246–248, 272
    flexibility 224–240
    identities 3–4, 181
    performance 109
    preferences 186
genderflexing 243, 247, 248–257
    and socioscience 224
    and thinking 255–256
gestures 28, 28–30, 127
Gilligan, C. 47
Giroux, H. 55, 248
Glazer, R. 50
Global Forest 12, 134–135, 138–140
Globerson, T. 52, 244
Godfrey, K. 235
Goffman, E. 106
Goldman-Segall, R. 31, 35, 87, 102, 129, 132,
    224, 244, 248
Gomez, L. M. 49, 204
Gordin, D. N. 204

Gordon, D. A. 243
Granott, N. 162–163
Greeno, J. G. 141
Greschler, D. 124
Grewal, J. 12, 59, 69, 71, 102, 208
Groppe, L. 186
Grumet, M. 69
Guzdial, M. 50

H
Halff, L. 40, 129, 131–133, 135, 144
Hall, W. 120
Hann, B. J. 118
Haraway, D. 268–269
Harel, I. 52, 76, 160, 244
Harlow, J. 274
Harper, D. 97
Harrison, B. 127
Hartley, J. 10
Hasselbring, T. 50
Hawkins, J. 49
Healey, D. 143
Heath, C. 127
Henderson, A. 130
Hennigan School
    description 60–61
    lunchtime at 63–64
    playground 56
    teachers 39, 76–78, 79–81, 155–156
    visit to 46–47
Heshusius, L. 265
Higginson, W. 47
Hill, A. 2
Hockings, P. 24, 32, 92, 96, 97, 107
Hoebel, M. 44
Hohmann, L. 50
Honey, M. 49
hooks, b. 194, 246
Horney, M. A. 143
Huberman, M. K. 265
Hunter, W. 58
Husband, V. 136
Hymes, D. 37
hypermedia 27, 50–51, 122
    See also digital: media
hypertext 27, 118

I
Illich, I. 76, 141
Inkpen, K. 202
Innis, H. A. 9, 10